T0294816

ACTUARIAL PRINCIPLES

ACTUARIAL PRINCIPLES

Lifetables and Mortality Models

ANDREW LEUNG

ACADEMIC PRESS

An imprint of Elsevier

Academic Press is an imprint of Elsevier
125 London Wall, London EC2Y 5AS, United Kingdom
525 B Street, Suite 1650, San Diego, CA 92101, United States
50 Hampshire Street, 5th Floor, Cambridge, MA 02139, United States
The Boulevard, Langford Lane, Kidlington, Oxford OX5 1GB, United Kingdom

Notices

Knowledge and best practice in this field are constantly changing. As new research and experience
broaden our understanding, changes in research methods, professional practices, or medical
treatment may become necessary.

Practitioners and researchers must always rely on their own experience and knowledge in
evaluating and using any information, methods, compounds, or experiments described herein. In
using such information or methods they should be mindful of their own safety and the safety of
others, including parties for whom they have a professional responsibility.

To the fullest extent of the law, neither the Publisher nor the authors, contributors, or editors,
assume any liability for any injury and/or damage to persons or property as a matter of products
liability, negligence or otherwise, or from any use or operation of any methods, products,
instructions, or ideas contained in the material herein.

Library of Congress Cataloging-in-Publication Data
A catalog record for this book is available from the Library of Congress

British Library Cataloguing-in-Publication Data
A catalogue record for this book is available from the British Library

ISBN: 978-0-323-90172-7

For information on all Academic Press publications
visit our website at https://www.elsevier.com/books-and-journals

Publisher: Katey Birtcher
Editorial Project Manager: Sara Valentino
Project Manager: Rukmani Krishnan/Janish Aswin
Designer: Renee Duenow

Typeset by VTeX

Printed in the United States of America

Last digit is the print number:
9 8 7 6 5 4 3 2 1

Working together
to grow libraries in
developing countries

www.elsevier.com • www.bookaid.org

Contents

1. **Lifetables and their applications**   **1**
   1.1. Introduction   1

2. **Lifetables and the principle of equivalence**   **3**
   2.1. Modelling mortality   3
   2.2. Lifetables   3
   2.3. Uncertainty in benefits   4

3. **Modelling mortality**   **5**
   3.1. The Australian life tables 2005–2007   5
   3.2. Mortality rates   6
   3.3. The curtate lifespan   6
   3.4. Types of lifetable   7

4. **Basic types of benefit (CT5: §1, §2, §3.4, §4)**   **9**
   4.1. The value of a lifetime insurance   9
   4.2. The value of a lifetime annuity   10
   4.3. Other types of benefits   12
   4.4. The value of an endowment insurance   12
   4.5. The value of an annuity with finite term   13
   4.6. The value of a pure endowment   14
   4.7. Value of deferred benefits   14
   4.8. Variances of insurances and annuities   16
   4.9. Increasing insurances and annuities (CT5: §6.1–6.3)   16
   4.10. An increasing annuity certain   17
   4.11. Annuities payable frequently   18
   Appendix 4.A Supplementary material   19

5. **Annuities payable frequently – a simpler approach**   **21**
   Appendix 5.A Supplementary material   22

6. **Benefits in continuous time (CT5: §1.8, 2.8)**   **23**
   6.1. Insurances payable continuously   24
   6.2. The value of a continuous lifetime insurance   24
   6.3. The value of a continuous lifetime annuity   25

7. **Select mortality (CT5: §3.6)**   **29**
   7.1. How selection operates in practice   29

8. Benefits involving multiple lives (CT5: §8, §9)   **33**
  8.1.   The joint life table   33
  8.2.   The curtate joint lifespan   33
  8.3.   A joint lifetime insurance   34
  8.4.   A joint lifetime annuity   34

9. The last survivor status   **37**
  9.1.   Relationship between curtate lifespans   37
  9.2.   Last survivor insurances and annuities   37

10. Pricing and reserving in theory (CT5: §5)   **43**
  10.1. Introduction   43
  10.2. Pricing   43
  10.3. Premium for an endowment insurance   43
  10.4. The insurer's risk   44
  10.5. Reserving   44
  10.6. Prospective reserves   45
  10.7. Retrospective reserves   45
  10.8. Equality of prospective and retrospective reserves   47
  10.9. Mortality profit/loss   47
  10.10. Death strain at risk   49
  10.11. Thiele's equation   49

11. Pricing in practice (CT5: §6, §7)   **55**
  11.1. How an insurance company works   55
  11.2. Practical issues   55
  11.3. Types of expense   55
  11.4. Expense recovery   56
  11.5. Premium assessment   56
  11.6. Bonus loadings   57
  11.7. The with-profit gross premium   57

12. Multiple decrement models (CT5: §10.2, §13)   **61**
  12.1. Multiple decrement tables   61
  12.2. Dependent and independent rates of decrement   61

13. Defined benefit superannuation (CT5: §14)   **67**
  13.1. Trusts   67
  13.2. Defined benefits   68
  13.3. The salary scale   68
  13.4. Benefit rules   68
  13.5. An example of defined benefits   68
  13.6. Accrued defined benefits   69

13.7. The value of accrued defined benefits   70
13.8. Future contributions   71
13.9. Value of future service benefits   71
13.10. Future contributions   72
13.11. A more complex defined benefit fund   72
13.12. Final average salary   73
13.13. Accrued benefits   73
13.14. Value of accrued benefits   73
13.15. Value of future service benefits   74

14. Life insurance modelling (CT5: §10; §11)   **75**
14.1. Profit testing   75
14.2. A model of an insurer   75
14.3. The profit vector   75
14.4. The profit signature   76

15. Profit signature   **77**
15.1. Profit signature   77
15.2. The return on transfers   77
15.3. Unit linked insurances   78
15.4. Testing unit linked insurances   80
15.5. Reserves under profit testing   80
15.6. Zeroisation   80

16. Multiple decrements and multiple states (CT5: §10)   **85**
16.1. Multiple decrements and multiple states in continuous time   85
16.2. Multiple states   85
16.3. Transition intensities   86
16.4. Kolmogorov forward equations   86
16.5. A sickness example   88
16.6. A sickness example with no recovery   89
16.7. Using transition probabilities   90

17. More complex benefits on multiple lives (CT5: §9)   **95**
17.1. More complex contingent insurances   95
17.2. Contingent insurances as double summations   96
17.3. Contingent insurances dependent on term   97
17.4. Even more complex contingent insurances   97
17.5. Contingent annuities   98

18. Risk factors in mortality   **103**
18.1. Life tables   103
18.2. Mortality factors   103

18.3. Selection   104
18.4. How selection operates in practice   105

19. Types of life tables   **107**
19.1. Life table construction   107
19.2. Construction of a life table   107
19.3. Exposures to death   108
19.4. Assessing mortality rates in practice   108
19.5. Mortality comparisons   109
19.6. Comparing mortality of two different populations   109
19.7. Indirect standardisation   110

20. Constructing a life table   **115**
20.1. Lifetime distribution   115
20.2. Censoring   115
20.3. Censoring examples   115
20.4. Information from censoring   116
20.5. Censoring and truncation   116

21. Maximum likelihood estimation   **117**
21.1. Background   117
21.2. Likelihood function   119
21.3. Maximising the log likelihood   119
21.4. Second-order conditions   120
21.5. Conditions for a local maximum   121
21.6. General conditions for a local maximum   121
21.7. Properties of ML estimators   122

22. Binomial and Poisson models (CT4: §10)   **123**
22.1. Estimating q 123
22.2. The MLE for q 124
22.3. Different observation periods   124
22.4. Likelihood function   125
22.5. The Balducci assumption   125
22.6. The Balducci estimator   126
22.7. Initial and central risk exposures   127

23. The Poisson model   **129**
23.1. Properties of the Poisson model   129
23.2. The MLE for the Poisson model   129
23.3. Choosing between the binomial and Poisson models   130

24. The Kaplan–Meier estimator (CT4: §8)   **131**
24.1. Mortality investigation with censoring   131

24.2. Notation for the investigation 131
24.3. The likelihood function 131
24.4. Kaplan–Meier estimator 134
24.5. Application of the KM method 136
24.6. Nelson–Aalen estimator 137

25. The Cox regression model (CT4: §9) **141**
25.1. The Cox model 141
25.2. Proportional hazards 141
25.3. Partial likelihood 142
25.4. Example of Cox model 143
25.5. Breslow's approximation 144
25.6. Example of Breslow's approximation 145
25.7. Applying the Cox model 145

26. Graduation **149**
26.1. Some issues with raw estimates 149
26.2. Definition of 'graduation' 150
26.3. Aim of the graduation process 150
26.4. Do mortality rates progress smoothly? 150

27. Graduation techniques (CT4: §12) **153**
27.1. Pros and cons of graphical techniques 153
27.2. Mathematical graduation methods 154
27.3. Makeham and Gompertz 154
27.4. Example for estimating the Gompertz curve 155
27.5. Perk's curve 156
27.6. Barnett's formula 156
27.7. Heligman–Pollard 157

28. Methods of estimation of the parameters **159**
28.1. Maximum likelihood (MLE) 159
28.2. Least squares (OLS/WLS) 160
28.3. Minimum chi-square method (MCSM) 161
28.4. Which estimation method to use? 161
28.5. Pros and cons of the mathematical approach 161
28.6. Standard table graduation 161
28.7. Variations of the standard table approach 162
28.8. Summary of the standard table approach 162

29. Assessing a graduation (CT4: §13) **165**
29.1. Testing for smoothness 165
29.2. Testing for fidelity 165

29.3. Standardised mortality differences z_x 166
29.4. The χ^2 test for goodness-of-fit   166
29.5. The χ^2 test for normality   167
29.6. The sign test for overall bias   167
29.7. Example of χ^2 test and sign tests   168
29.8. The cumulative test for goodness-of-fit   168
29.9. Tests based on ordering   169
29.10. The grouped signs test   169
29.11. Example of the grouped signs test   170
29.12. The serial correlation test   170

30. Summary: estimation and graduation   **171**
30.1. Modelling   171
30.2. Graduation   171

31. Experience rating and Markov processes   **175**
31.1. The risk premium   175
31.2. Exposures   175
31.3. Exposures and asymmetry in information   176
31.4. Experience rating   176
31.5. NCB schemes   176
31.6. Modelling NCB schemes   177
31.7. Equilibrium distribution   177
31.8. Equilibrium distribution   178
31.9. Exercises   178

A. International actuarial notation   **183**
Discrete time   183
Continuous time   184
AMC00 – life table and benefit values   185

B. Useful mathematical techniques   **187**
B.1.   Eigenvalues and eigenvectors   188
B.2.   Diagonalisation   188
B.3.   The benefits of diagonalisation   189
B.4.   Nondiagonisable matrices   190

C. Exercises for Section 1.9 – defined benefits   **193**
C.1.   Assignment   193
C.2.   Assignment   194
C.3.   Assignment   196
C.4.   Assignment   198
C.5.   Supplementary material   199

D. Sample exams **201**

    D.1. Sample Exam 1   201

    D.2. Sample Exam 2   215

    D.3. Sample Exam 3   227

    D.4. Sample Exam 4   236

Bibliography *245*

Index *247*

CHAPTER ONE

Lifetables and their applications

1.1. Introduction

The core of actuarial science is the study of mortality and other risks, and especially their applications. All the actuarial associations have their own versions of what is to be covered, particularly the Society of Actuaries in the United States and the Institute and Faculty of Actuaries in the UK. This book is based primarily on the CT1, CT2, CT4, CT5 and CT6 courses of the UK, but it also delves into and extrapolates material from other subjects which would bring a more detailed picture of the subject.

There are, of course, many textbooks and courses available (O'Neill, 1977; Dickson et al., 2009). Some of these are heavily mathematical and theoretical in nature (Promislow, 2015). This book attempts to steer a middle course, and offers some history of the subject; the reason why actuarial notation has become universal, and how the theory can be applied to many situations. Above all, it provides numerous exercises (and their solutions), along with complete self-contained real-life assignments where the mathematics is but a tool to assessing practical situations (such as in pensions).

This book adheres to one final principle. It is in the philosophy of discrete versus continuous time. Many theoretical tracts favour the latter, as it produces elegance in the way that actuarial functions can be expressed, but there is a cost in doing so. For whilst one may imagine living in continuous time, we can compute only in discrete time, notwithstanding that modern computers can do so at great speed, and with arbitrarily small, but finite, time intervals.

This leads to the debate between determinism and the concept of natural chaos. The great mathematician, Laplace, whose name is closely associated with the former, once remarked that given the position and momentum of every particle in the universe, it should be possible to plot its future (and its past) with confidence. Of course the concept is flawed, as quantum mechanics most recently demonstrates. First, we do not (and perhaps cannot) know all the laws of nature. Second, even if we had the data, our limitations in computing mean that the tiniest errors in computation may have drastic consequences for our predictions. The saying of chaos theory is that the fluttering of a butterfly may result in a hurricane.

Actuarial Principles
https://doi.org/10.1016/B978-0-32-390172-7.00005-1

Thus this book is devoted to computable examples, even in subjects that are often expressed continuously (such as in multiple lives). These examples are drawn mainly from actual UK exams. However, assignments (often with subjective solutions) and sample exams are included. These are original in content. The exams are structured to test concept, not arithmetic, which is the focus of the assignments.

The content of this book was based on a course delivered by the author at Monash University during 2009-2012. As such, some of the material has an Australian bias, but most of this is confined to the data.

The exercises, sample exams and assignments come complete with solutions, some of which are in Excel format. In the PDF version of this book, the solutions may be hidden by suppressing the 'solution' layer, which is available in most PDF readers.

CHAPTER TWO

Lifetables and the principle of equivalence

2.1. Modelling mortality

In the mid 1800s, the University of Göttingen were concerned about the viability of their widows and orphans' fund. Previous assessments had little scientific basis, so they turned to one of their esteemed professors, Carl Friedrich Gauss, for his opinion (Vajda, 1984). He was in no doubt that extensive data on mortality was required. This, and the development of life insurance in the UK in the 17th century, was the impetus to discover the laws governing mortality.

The traditional way of modelling mortality is with the *life table*. This is a table of the number of survivors starting from a given age, often from birth. There are several ways in which life tables can be constructed, but we start with the most common form, the *population* life table.

2.2. Lifetables

The universal principle in pricing is that

$$\text{Value of premiums} = \text{Value of benefits.}$$

Here, 'value' means expected present value:

$$\text{Value of benefit} = \text{Discount factor} \times \text{ probability} \times \text{amount of benefit}$$
$$= v^t \cdot p \cdot B$$

where:
- the benefit of amount B is payable at time t hence, with probability p.
- $v = \frac{1}{1+i}$ is a discount factor for interest at rate i,
- in this unit, we take the interest rate i generally as known and certain. So we assume everyone can invest or borrow at rate i.

Example 2.1. *Suppose you promised a friend to pay her $1 in 12 months' time if she throws 'heads' on a coin. Suppose also you can invest at 5% pa. How much money would you have to hold now to honour your promise?*

Actuarial Principles
https://doi.org/10.1016/B978-0-32-390172-7.00006-3
3

Answer:

Value of benefit = *Discount factor* × *probability* × *amount of benefit*

$$= \frac{1}{1.05} \cdot \frac{1}{2} \cdot 1$$

$$= \$0.476.$$

However, the benefits (i.e. payments) B may be far from certain. Though 'present value' is a simple concept,
- there may be many types of benefit,
- there may be many factors which affect the probability of paying a benefit.

2.3. Uncertainty in benefits

Here are some of the factors that affect the benefits we study in this unit:
- mortality – benefits may depend on the death or on the survival of an individual
- sickness – benefits may depend on whether an individual is sick and on the type of sickness
- employment – benefits may depend on when an individual leaves the service of his employer, and whether that is by retirement, resignation, death or disability

Here are some examples:
- lifetime insurance contract – an insurer promises to pay $1 at the end of the year in which an individual dies
- temporary (term) insurance – an insurer promises to pay $1 at the end of the year in which an individual dies, provided death occurs within 5 years
- lifetime pension – the government promises to pay an amount of $200 per week whilst an individual is alive
- sickness insurance – an insurer promises to pay 60% of an individual's salary for up to 2 years whilst he cannot work because of sickness or injury.

Note: The term 'life insurance' is traditionally used in the UK and other Commonwealth countries to distinguish it from general insurance (hence the symbol A). However, 'life insurance' is used in the United States, and increasingly used in other countries. We adopt the US expression in this book.

CHAPTER THREE

Modelling mortality

The traditional way of modelling mortality is with the *life table*. This is a table of the number of survivors starting from a given age, often from birth. There are several ways in which life tables can be constructed, but we start with the most common form, the *population* life table.

3.1. The Australian life tables 2005–2007

ALT2005-07 was constructed from Australian census data. Here is a chart showing the number of survivors to any given age, starting with 100,000 people born at age 0. Males and females are shown separately.

We denote the number of survivors to age x as ℓ_x. It is customary to use x as a male age and y as a female age.

Here are some implications:

- The ratio $\frac{\ell_x}{\ell_0}$ is the probability of survival from birth to age x.
- The difference $\ell_x - \ell_{x+1}$ is the number of deaths between ages x and $x + 1$, out of the ℓ_0 born.
- Hence the probability for a newborn of death between ages x and $x + 1$ is $\frac{\ell_x - \ell_{x+1}}{\ell_0}$.
- If K denotes a random variable representing the age just before death (the *curtate lifespan*), then

$$\mathbf{prob}\,(K = x) = \frac{\ell_x - \ell_{x+1}}{\ell_0}.$$

More generally, think of an individual (or a group of such individuals) who are already aged x (i.e. they have managed to survive to this age). Then:

- the ratio $\frac{\ell_{x+t}}{\ell_x}$ is the probability of survival of a male aged x for t years
- in particular, $\frac{\ell_{x+1}}{\ell_x}$ is the probability of surviving for 1 year, so $q_x = 1 - \frac{\ell_{x+1}}{\ell_x}$ is the probability of dying within the next year (the mortality rate for age x).

Actuarial Principles
https://doi.org/10.1016/B978-0-32-390172-7.00007-5

If K_x denotes a random variable for the year just before death (the *curtate lifespan*), for someone already aged x, then

$$\textbf{prob}\,(K_x = t) = \frac{\ell_{x+t} - \ell_{x+t+1}}{\ell_x}$$

$$= \frac{\ell_{x+t}}{\ell_x}\frac{\ell_{x+t} - \ell_{x+t+1}}{\ell_{x+t}}$$

$$= q_{x+t}\frac{\ell_{x+t}}{\ell_x}.$$

The ratio $\frac{\ell_{x+t}}{\ell_x}$ is usually written as ${}_tp_x$, the probability of the survival of x for t years. The probability of survival for just one year ${}_1p_x$ is usually written simply as p_x, so that $p_x + q_x = 1$.

3.2. Mortality rates

Here is a chart of mortality rates q_x for various ages with a logarithmic scale.

It looks like males between the ages of 16 and 30 experience a sudden rise in mortality. Can you guess why?

3.3. The curtate lifespan

The curtate lifespan K_x for an individual aged x is a very useful concept in valuing benefits based upon mortality. It is a random variable, with a known distribution as shown below.

As a random variable, K_x has a mean derived in the usual way:

$$\textbf{E}\,(K_x) = \sum_{t=0}^{\infty} t \cdot \textbf{prob}\,(K_x = t)$$

$$= \sum_{t=0}^{\infty} t\frac{\ell_{x+t} - \ell_{x+t+1}}{\ell_x}$$

$$= \sum_{t=0}^{\infty} t\frac{\ell_{x+t}}{\ell_x} - \sum_{t=0}^{\infty} t\frac{\ell_{x+t+1}}{\ell_x}$$

$$= \sum_{t=0}^{\infty} t\frac{\ell_{x+t}}{\ell_x} - \sum_{t=1}^{\infty} (t-1)\frac{\ell_{x+t}}{\ell_x}$$

$$= \sum_{t=1}^{\infty} \frac{\ell_{x+t}}{\ell_x}.$$

This is given a special symbol, the curtate expectation of life e_x. The variance of K_x can also be computed from

$$\mathbf{var}\,(K_x) = \mathbf{E}\left(K_x^2\right) - \mathbf{E}\,(K_x)^2$$

and

$$\mathbf{E}\left(K_x^2\right) = \sum_{t=0}^{\infty} t^2 \frac{\ell_{x+t} - \ell_{x+t+1}}{\ell_x}$$

$$= \sum_{t=0}^{\infty} t^2 \frac{\ell_{x+t}}{\ell_x} - \sum_{t=1}^{\infty} (t-1)^2 \frac{\ell_{x+t}}{\ell_x}$$

$$= 2 \sum_{t=1}^{\infty} t \frac{\ell_{x+t}}{\ell_x} - \sum_{t=1}^{\infty} \frac{\ell_{x+t}}{\ell_x}.$$

3.4. Types of lifetable

As a result of these different risk factors, it is appropriate that different lifetables be used for different purposes. These might cover:

- the population at large (e.g. ALT2005-07)
- insured lives for endowment insurances (AMC00)
- insured lives for temporary insurances (TMC00)
- annuitants (IML00, those who buy an annuity from a life insurer – rare in Australia)
- retired pensioners (RMC00)
- disability pensioners.

CHAPTER FOUR

Basic types of benefit (CT5: §1, §2, §3.4, §4)

Using the random variable K_x, benefits can be expressed generally as follows:
- If the curtate lifespan is K_x, a benefit of amount $B(K_x)$ is payable at time $F(K_x)$.
- The value of the benefit is then a random variable $B(K_x)\,v^{F(K_x)}$.

Note: the term 'life assurance' is traditionally used in the UK and other Commonwealth countries to distinguish it from general insurance (hence the symbol A). However, 'life insurance' is used in the United States, and increasingly used in other countries. We adopt the US expression in this book.

Very often the amount of the benefit is 1, as will be seen in the examples below.

4.1. The value of a lifetime insurance

Using K_x, it becomes possible to value the simplest type of benefit:
- this is the *lifetime insurance* (or whole of life insurance)
- when a benefit of $1 is payable at the end of the year in which death occurs.

A lifetime insurance can be valued like this:
- the discounted value if the curtate lifespan is $K_x = t$ is

$$v^{t+1} = v^{K_x+1}$$

- its expectation is

$$A_x = \mathbf{E}\left(v^{K_x+1}\right) = \sum_{t=0}^{\infty} v^{t+1} \cdot \mathbf{prob}\left(K_x = t\right)$$

$$= \sum_{t=0}^{\infty} v^{t+1} \frac{\ell_{x+t} - \ell_{x+t+1}}{\ell_x}$$

$$= \sum_{t=0}^{\infty} v^{t+1} \frac{\ell_{x+t}}{\ell_x} - \sum_{t=0}^{\infty} v^{t+1} \frac{\ell_{x+t+1}}{\ell_x}$$

Actuarial Principles
https://doi.org/10.1016/B978-0-32-390172-7.00008-7

$$= \sum_{t=0}^{\infty} v^{t+1} \frac{\ell_{x+t}}{\ell_x} - \sum_{t=1}^{\infty} v^t \frac{\ell_{x+t}}{\ell_x}$$

$$= v - (1-v) \sum_{t=1}^{\infty} v^t \frac{\ell_{x+t}}{\ell_x}.$$

This can be readily computed from the life table provided. It is given a special symbol: A_x.

4.2. The value of a lifetime annuity

Lifetime annuities are similar to life insurances, but they are payable whilst the insured is alive, rather than dead. In this case:

- we consider an annuity due of \$1 pa, that it is payable *immediately* and at the *start* of every year whilst the insured is alive
- its value is denoted $\ddot{a}_x$
- the probability of survival of x to time t is by definition $_t p_x$.

So the simplest way of deriving its value is to use expected values directly:

$$\ddot{a}_x = \sum_{t=0}^{\infty} v^t \cdot {}_t p_x$$

$$= \sum_{t=0}^{\infty} v^t \frac{\ell_{x+t}}{\ell_x}.$$

This can also be computed directly from the life table. But notice that this term appears in the expression for A_x as well. Is there a connection between $\ddot{a}_x$ and A_x? There is

$$A_x = v - (1-v) \sum_{t=1}^{\infty} v^t \frac{\ell_{x+t}}{\ell_x}$$

$$= v - (1-v)\left(\ddot{a}_x - 1\right)$$

$$= 1 - d\ddot{a}_x$$

where $d = 1 - v = \frac{i}{1+i}$ is standard notation.

The usual annuity is defined as one which is payable at the *end* of every year whilst the insured is alive, so the first possible payment is in one year's time. Its value is denoted a_x (without the two dots), and it is obvious that $a_x = \ddot{a}_x - 1$.

Example 4.1. *The lifetime annuity may be defined alternatively in terms of the curtate lifespan K_x as follows:*

- *for a given value of K_x, we have the annuity certain $a_{\overline{K_x}|}$*
- *then define $a_x = \mathbf{E}\left(a_{\overline{K_x}|}\right)$*

  Show that the two definitions of a_x are equivalent.

This also means that $\ddot{a}_x = a_x + 1 = \mathbf{E}\left(a_{\overline{K_x}|} + 1\right) = \mathbf{E}\left(\ddot{a}_{\overline{K_x+1}|}\right)$.

Example 4.2. *The relationship $A_x = 1 - d\ddot{a}_x$ is one of the most fundamental in life contingency valuation, and similar relationships hold between other types of insurance and annuity functions. By considering the interpretation of $d\ddot{a}_{\overline{K_x}|}$, prove this relationship from first principles:*

Hint: $d\ddot{a}_{\overline{K_x}|} + v^{K_x+1} = 1$.

4.2.1 Exercises

Refer to the spreadsheet ALT2005-07.xls for the Australian population life tables.

In terms of these life tables, complete the following exercises:

1. Calculate the probability that a male aged 65 survives another year (i.e. p_{65}).
2. Calculate the probability that 20-year-old male survives to age 65.
3. Calculate the probability that a married couple, with a 65-year-old male and a 60-year-old female, both survive for 10 years. Assume independence of male and female mortality.
4. Verify that the curtate expectation of life for a 20-year-old female is $\mathbf{E}(K_{20}) = e_{20} = 63.7$ years.
5. The complete expectation of life is defined as the expected period to the moment of death (rather than to the birthday preceding death). This is denoted $\overset{\circ}{e}_{20}$. Approximate this value.
6. Chart the distribution of K_{20} for a 20-year-old female.
7. Calculate $\mathbf{var}(K_{20})$.
8. For an interest rate of 3% pa., calculate A_{20}.
9. From the result in (8), derive the value of a_{20}.
10. Verify that the result in (9) is the same as $\mathbf{E}\left(a_{\overline{K_{20}}|}\right)$.
11. Calculate $a_{20:\overline{15}|}$
12. Calculate $A_{20:\overline{15}|}^{\,1}$
13. Calculate $A_{20:\overline{15}|}^{1}$
14. From (12) and (13), derive $A_{20:\overline{15}|}$ and confirm that $A_{20:\overline{15}|} = 1 - d\ddot{a}_{20:\overline{15}|}$.

15. Value a lifetime assurance growing at 1% pa.
Solution See E1.xls.

4.3. Other types of benefits

Lifetime insurances and annuities are the basic types of benefits. But there are many others. Here are some common types:
- those with limited term
- deferral of payments
- where payments are not constant over time.

4.4. The value of an endowment insurance

Notice that the benefit under a lifetime insurance is certain to be paid eventually, because the insured is certain to die eventually.
- An endowment insurance is similar, except that once the insured survives a certain period, say n years, it becomes immediately payable.
- Thus if the insured has a curtate lifespan of K_x, the benefit is payable at time $\min(K_x + 1, n)$.

Its value is

$$A_{x:\overline{n}|} = \mathbf{E}\left[v^{\min(K_x+1,n)}\right]$$

$$= \sum_{t=0}^{n-1} v^{t+1} \cdot \mathbf{prob}\,(K_x = t) + v^n \cdot \mathbf{prob}\,(K_x \geq n)$$

$$= \sum_{t=0}^{n-1} v^{t+1} \frac{\ell_{x+t} - \ell_{x+t+1}}{\ell_x} + v^n \frac{\ell_{x+n}}{\ell_x}$$

$$= \sum_{t=0}^{n-1} v^{t+1} \frac{\ell_{x+t}}{\ell_x} - \sum_{t=1}^{n} v^t \frac{\ell_{x+t}}{\ell_x} + v^n \frac{\ell_{x+n}}{\ell_x}$$

$$= v - (1 - v) \sum_{t=1}^{n-1} v^t \frac{\ell_{x+t}}{\ell_x}.$$

Note the following:
- The value is written $A_{x:\overline{n}|}$ because the status $x:\overline{n}|$ is a combination of two statuses: the life x and the period certain $\overline{n}|$. The insurance is payable if *either* status fails.
- The expression for $A_{x:\overline{n}|}$ is quite similar to that for A_x, except that the summation is to $n-1$, not ∞.

- In general, $A_{x:\overline{n}|} > A_x$, because the benefit in $A_{x:\overline{n}|}$ is paid sooner.

4.5. The value of an annuity with finite term

The question arises: Does the relationship $A_x = 1 - d\ddot{a}_x$ also hold for endowment insurances? The answer is: yes.

- An annuity due with a finite term is the same as a lifetime annuity, except it is payable for at most n years, whilst the annuitant is alive.
- The value of such an annuity can be found in the same way as for a lifetime annuity:

$$\ddot{a}_{x:\overline{n}|} = \sum_{t=0}^{n-1} v^t \cdot {}_t p_x$$

$$= \sum_{t=0}^{n-1} v^t \frac{\ell_{x+t}}{\ell_x}.$$

It can then be shown in the same way that

$$A_{x:\overline{n}|} = 1 - d\ddot{a}_{x:\overline{n}|}.$$

This provides a convenient way of calculating $\ddot{a}_{x:\overline{n}|}$ or $A_{x:\overline{n}|}$ from the other. Just as annuities can have a finite term, so can insurances:

- These differ from endowment insurances in that no payment is made if the insured survives the term.
- Thus if the insured has a curtate lifespan of K_x, a benefit is payable only if $K_x < n$.
- The benefit payable is thus χ_{n-K_x}, where χ_z is the indicator function, equal to 1 only if $z > 0$ and 0 otherwise.

The value of such a benefit is

$$A^1_{x:\overline{n}|} = \mathbf{E}\left[v^{K_x+1} \chi_{n-K_x}\right]$$

$$= \sum_{t=0}^{n-1} v^{t+1} \cdot \mathbf{prob}\,(K_x = t)$$

$$= \sum_{t=0}^{n-1} v^{t+1} \frac{\ell_{x+t} - \ell_{x+t+1}}{\ell_x}$$

$$= \sum_{t=0}^{n-1} v^{t+1} \frac{\ell_{x+t}}{\ell_x} - \sum_{t=1}^{n} v^t \frac{\ell_{x+t}}{\ell_x}$$

$$= v - (1 - v) \sum_{t=1}^{n-1} v^t \frac{\ell_{x+t}}{\ell_x} - v^n \frac{\ell_{x+n}}{\ell_x}.$$

Notice that:

- the value is denoted $A^1_{x:\overline{n}|}$, with a '1' above the x. This means that the insurance is payable if the combined status $x : \overline{n}|$ fails, but the status x has to fail first, before $\overline{n}|$.
- The expression is very similar to that for $A_{x:\overline{n}|}$, except for the term $v^n \frac{\ell_{x+n}}{\ell_x}$. What does this represent?

4.6. The value of a pure endowment

A pure endowment is simply a benefit payable on a certain date, say n years; hence, even if the recipient is then alive. It is therefore a degenerate case of an annuity (and is not common in practice). Its value is

$$A_{x:\overline{n}|}{}^{1} = \mathbf{E} \left[v^{\min[K_x+1,n]} \chi_{K_x-n} \right]$$
$$= v^n \cdot \mathbf{prob}\,(K_x \geq n)$$
$$= v^n \frac{\ell_{x+n}}{\ell_x}.$$

This is the odd term in $A^1_{x:\overline{n}|}$. Hence

$$A_{x:\overline{n}|} = A^1_{x:\overline{n}|} + A_{x:\overline{n}|}{}^{1}$$

which, in words, says that:

- an endowment insurance has a component which is pure insurance;
- and another component that is a pure endowment.

4.7. Value of deferred benefits

All the benefits discussed so far are potentially payable immediately.

- What happens if they are deferred into sometime in the future?
- A simple technique allows us to make a general adjustment for deferral of benefits for, say, m years.

Let $F(K_{x+m})$ be the time of the benefit payable once the deferred period is complete, when the insured is aged $x + m$.

- The value of the deferred benefit at that time is $v^{F(K_{x+m})}$.

- Note that the distribution of the random variable $K_{x+m} = \mathbf{E}(K_x | K_x \geq m)$ is the conditional expectation of K_x, given survival for m years.
- Thus

$$\mathbf{prob}\,(K_{x+m} = t) = \frac{\ell_{x+m+t}}{\ell_{x+m}} q_{x+m+t}.$$

- Then the value of the deferred benefit can be expressed at the present time as $v^m v^{F(K_x-m)} \chi_{K_x \geq m}$ when $K_x \geq m$.
- This has the expectation

$$\mathbf{E}\left[v^m v^{F(K_x-m)} \chi_{K_x \geq m}\right] = v^m \sum_{t=m}^{\infty} v^{F(t-m)} \cdot \mathbf{prob}\,(K_x = t)$$

$$= v^m \sum_{t=m}^{\infty} v^{F(t-m)} \frac{\ell_{x+t} - \ell_{x+t+1}}{\ell_x} q_{x+t}$$

$$= v^m \frac{\ell_{x+m}}{\ell_x} \sum_{t=0}^{\infty} v^{F(t)} \frac{\ell_{x+m+t} - \ell_{x+m+t+1}}{\ell_{x+m}} q_{x+m+t}$$

$$= v^m \frac{\ell_{x+m}}{\ell_x} \sum_{t=0}^{\infty} v^{F(t)} \cdot \mathbf{prob}\,(K_{x+m} = t)$$

$$= v^m \frac{\ell_{x+m}}{\ell_x} \mathbf{E}\left[v^{F(K_{x+m})}\right].$$

Whilst this computation seems complex, the result is very simple:
- The deferred benefit can be valued $\mathbf{E}\left[v^{F(K_{x+m})}\right]$ at the time that deferral is complete,
- and then further discounted to the present time using a factor of

$$v^m \frac{\ell_{x+m}}{\ell_x}.$$

- This allows for both an interest discount for a period of m years as well as the probability of survival of the deferral period of $\frac{\ell_{x+m}}{\ell_x}$.
There are two simple applications of this deferral procedure:
- $_m|a_x = v^m \frac{\ell_{x+m}}{\ell_x} a_{x+m}$ is the value of a lifetime annuity deferred for m years.
- $_m|A_x = v^m \frac{\ell_{x+m}}{\ell_x} A_{x+m}$ is the value of a lifetime insurance deferred for m years.
Similarly, for $_m|\ddot{a}_{x:\overline{n}|}$ and $_m|A_{x:\overline{n}|}$.

4.8. Variances of insurances and annuities

Each of the basic types of benefit has been valued as an expectation involving the curtate lifespan K_x.

However, their variances may also be computed in the same way.

An example is given of the variance in value of the endowment insurance $v^{\min(K_x+1,n)}$:

$$\mathbf{var}\left[v^{\min(K_x+1,n)}\right] = \mathbf{E}\left[v^{2\min(K_x+1,n)}\right] - \left(A_{x:\overline{n}|}\right)^2$$
$$= {}^2A_{x:\overline{n}|} - \left(A_{x:\overline{n}|}\right)^2.$$

Notice that:

- the expectation $\mathbf{E}\left[v^{2\min(K_x+1,n)}\right]$ has the same form as that for $A_{x:\overline{n}|}$, but with v^2 replacing v.
- The symbol ${}^2A_{x:\overline{n}|}$ is used to suggest that this insurance is valued at an interest rate j such that $1+j=(1+i)^2$.

The variance of an annuity is similar:

$$\mathbf{var}\left[a_{\overline{K_x}|}\right] = \mathbf{var}\left[\ddot{a}_{\overline{K_x+1}|}\right]$$
$$= \mathbf{var}\left[\frac{1-v^{K_x+1}}{d}\right]$$
$$= \frac{1}{d^2}\left[{}^2A_x - (A_x)^2\right].$$

Calculation of the variances of other types of benefit is similar, and will be given as exercises.

A word of caution:

- The variances arising in this way result from treating K_x as a random variable.
- In practice, this is not how most people would measure uncertainty in the value of benefits.
- They would probably think of uncertainty in the construction of life tables (i.e., mortality rates q_x), or even in discount rates i.

4.9. Increasing insurances and annuities (CT5: §6.1–6.3)

So far, benefits have been assumed to be constant over an individual's lifetime. What happens when benefits are increasing or reducing? Here are some simple examples.

The general case is where a benefit of $B(K_x)$ is payable at time $K_x + 1$ for a curtate lifespan K_x. Its present value is $\mathbf{E}\left[B(K_x)v^{K_x+1}\right]$.

- In the case $B(K_x) = (1+g)^{K_x}$, the benefit grows exponentially with age at death, at rate g.
- Its value is

where $w = (1+g)v$, and the insurance function A_x^j is calculated at an interest rate j such that $w = \frac{1}{1+j}$.

Similarly, we can value an exponentially increasing annuity where $B(K_x) = a_{\overline{K_x}|}$, where the annuity is growing. In the case $B(K_x) = 1 + K_x$, we have benefits growing by a constant amount of 1 with age at death. Its value is given by

$$IA_x = \mathbf{E}\left[(1 + K_x)v^{K_x+1}\right]$$

$$= \sum_{t=0}^{\infty}(1+t)v^{t+1}\frac{\ell_{x+t} - \ell_{x+t+1}}{\ell_x}$$

$$= \sum_{t=0}^{\infty}(1+t)v^{t+1}\frac{\ell_{x+t}}{\ell_x} - \sum_{t=1}^{\infty}tv^t\frac{\ell_{x+t}}{\ell_x}$$

$$= v + a_x - (1-v)\sum_{t=1}^{\infty}(1+t)v^t\frac{\ell_{x+t}}{\ell_x}.$$

4.10. An increasing annuity certain

An increasing annuity certain is one where the payments at time $t = 1, 2 \ldots n$ are $1, 2 \ldots n$. The value is given the symbol $Ia_{\overline{n}|}$. We can evaluate this as follows:

- $\ddot{a}_{\overline{n+1}|} = 1 + v + v^2 + \ldots + v^n = \frac{1-v^{n+1}}{1-v}$
- differentiate with respect to v:

$$Ia_{\overline{n}|} = v + 2v^2 + \ldots + nv^n$$

$$= v\frac{d}{dv}\left(\frac{1-v^{n+1}}{1-v}\right)$$

$$= v\frac{1-v^{n+1}}{(1-v)^2} - v\frac{(n+1)v^n}{1-v}$$

$$= v\frac{1-v^n}{(1-v)^2} - v\frac{nv^n}{1-v}$$

$$= \frac{\ddot{a}_{\overline{n}|} - nv^n}{i}.$$

An immediate increasing annuity certain is one where the payments at time $t = 0, 1 \ldots n-1$ are $1, 2 \ldots n$. The value is given the symbol $I\ddot{a}_{\overline{n}|}$.

Clearly, we have

$$Ia_{\overline{n}|} = v.I\ddot{a}_{\overline{n}|}.$$

Similarly, with increasing lifetime annuities,

$$I\ddot{a}_x = \mathbf{E}\left(I\ddot{a}_{\overline{K_x+1}|}\right)$$

$$= \sum_{t=0}^{\infty} (1+t)\, v^t \frac{\ell_{x+t}}{\ell_x}$$

so that we get the relationship:

$$IA_x = v + a_x - (1-v)\left(I\ddot{a}_x - 1\right)$$
$$= \ddot{a}_x - d \cdot I\ddot{a}_x.$$

4.11. Annuities payable frequently

So far, it has also been assumed that benefits are paid only according to the year of death, and not the precise time of death. What happens when benefits are paid m times per year? A common situation is an annuity payable monthly, provided that the annuitant is alive at each monthly payment.

There are two approaches possible:
- Replace the concept of a 'year' with a period of $\frac{1}{m}$ of a year, so that the life table has to be constructed for non-integral ages $x + \frac{k}{m}$, $0 \le k < m$.
- Interpolate the life table linearly by using

$$\ell_{x+\frac{k}{m}} \simeq \left(1 - \frac{k}{m}\right)\ell_x + \frac{k}{m}\ell_{x+1}.$$

- With this approximation, an annuity payable m times per year has value:

$$\ddot{a}_x^{(m)} \simeq \frac{1}{m}\sum_{s=0}^{\infty} v^{\frac{s}{m}} \frac{\ell_{x+\frac{s}{m}}}{\ell_x}$$

$$= \frac{1}{m}\sum_{t=0}^{\infty}\sum_{k=0}^{m-1} \frac{v^{t+\frac{k}{m}}}{\ell_x}\left[\left(1 - \frac{k}{m}\right)\ell_{x+t} + \frac{k}{m}\ell_{x+t+1}\right]$$

$$= \frac{1}{m} \sum_{k=0}^{m-1} v^{\frac{k}{m}} \sum_{t=0}^{\infty} \left[\left(1 - \frac{k}{m} \right) v^t \frac{\ell_{x+t}}{\ell_x} + \frac{k}{m} v^t \frac{\ell_{x+t+1}}{\ell_x} \right]$$

$$= \frac{\ddot{a}_x}{m} \sum_{k=0}^{m-1} v^{\frac{k}{m}} \left(1 - \frac{k}{m} \right) + \frac{a_x}{mv} \sum_{k=0}^{m-1} v^{\frac{k}{m}} \frac{k}{m}$$

$$= \frac{a_x}{m} \left[\sum_{k=0}^{m-1} v^{\frac{k}{m}} \left(1 - \frac{k}{m} + \frac{k}{mv} \right) \right] + \frac{1}{m} \sum_{k=0}^{m-1} v^{\frac{k}{m}} \left(1 - \frac{k}{m} \right).$$

We now make a further approximation: $v \simeq 1$, which is reasonable to use for periods less than a year.

The expression above then simplifies to

$$\ddot{a}_x^{(m)} \simeq a_x + 1 - \frac{m(m-1)}{2m^2}$$

$$= a_x + \frac{m+1}{2m}$$

$$= \ddot{a}_x - \frac{m-1}{2m}.$$

Since $\ddot{a}_x^{(m)} = \frac{1}{m} + a_x^{(m)}$, this can also be written as

$$a_x^{(m)} = a_x + \frac{m-1}{2m}.$$

This is an important result! You don't need to remember the proof, just the assumptions behind it.

Appendix 4.A. Supplementary material

Supplementary material related to this chapter can be found online at https://doi.org/10.1016/B978-0-32-390172-7.00008-7.

Annuities payable frequently – a simpler approach

For an immediate annuity payable m times per year, a typical year's payment would be like this:

The average time of payment is $\frac{m-1}{2m}$. For those dying within the year, they will lose a payment of $\frac{m-1}{2m}$, so that

$$\ddot{a}_x^{(m)} \simeq \ddot{a}_x - \frac{m-1}{2m}.$$

Alternatively, the $m-1$ payments during the year could be replaced by payments of $\frac{m-1}{2m}$ at both the start and end of year.

- The total payment at time 0 would then be $\frac{1}{m} + \frac{m-1}{2m} = \frac{m+1}{2m}$.
- At any point of time, the payment for the previous year, plus the payment for the following year, would sum to 1.
- The only exception is commencement of the annuity, where the payment is $\frac{m+1}{2m}$.
- Hence, compared with an immediate annuity, the frequent payment has reduced its value by $\frac{m-1}{2m}$.

The result for frequent payment of an annuity can be extended to annuities with limited term.

- We use the result $\ddot{a}_{x:\overline{n}|} = \ddot{a}_x - v^n \frac{\ell_{x+n}}{\ell_x} \ddot{a}_{x+n}$.
- Similarly, $\ddot{a}_{x:\overline{n}|}^{(m)} = \ddot{a}_x^{(m)} - v^n \frac{\ell_{x+n}}{\ell_x} \ddot{a}_{x+n}^{(m)}$.
- Thus:

$$\ddot{a}_{x:\overline{n}|}^{(m)} = \ddot{a}_x - \frac{m-1}{2m} - v^n \frac{\ell_{x+n}}{\ell_x} \left[\ddot{a}_{x+n} - \frac{m-1}{2m} \right]$$

$$= \ddot{a}_{x:\overline{n}|} - \frac{m-1}{2m} \left(1 - v^n \frac{\ell_{x+n}}{\ell_x} \right).$$

Exercises

Refer to the spreadsheet ALT2005–07.xls for the Australian population life tables. Take this life table for questions 1–9.

Complete the following exercises for a male aged 40, and interest at 3% pa:

Actuarial Principles
https://doi.org/10.1016/B978-0-32-390172-7.00009-9
21

1. Calculate the distribution of K_{40} (remember that all persons must die eventually).

2. Calculate the value of the deferred annuity $_{10|}a_{40:\overline{30|}}$.

3. Calculate the value of the increasing assurance $IA_{40:\overline{20|}}$.

4. Calculate the value of the increasing annuity $I\ddot{a}_{40:\overline{20|}}$.

5. Verify that $IA_{40:\overline{20|}} = \ddot{a}_{40:\overline{20|}} - d \cdot I\ddot{a}_{40:\overline{20|}}$.

6. Calculate the standard deviation of the increasing assurance IA_{40}.

7. Calculate $a_{40}^{(12)}$.

8. Calculate $a_{40:\overline{20|}}^{(12)}$.

9. [UK CT5 exam, September 2007] An annuity makes monthly payments in arrears to a life aged 40 exact where each payment is $(\frac{1.03}{1.01})^{\frac{1}{12}} = 1.001636$ times greater than the one immediately preceding. The first monthly amount is \$1000. Calculate its value.

10. [UK CT5 exam, April 2009] For $\ell_x = 110 - x$, where $x \leq 110$, calculate $A_{40:\overline{20|}}^1$.

11. As in (10), calculate $A_{40:\overline{20|}}$

Solution

See E2.xls.

Appendix 5.A. Supplementary material

Supplementary material related to this chapter can be found online at https://doi.org/10.1016/B978-0-32-390172-7.00009-9.

CHAPTER SIX

Benefits in continuous time (CT5: §1.8, 2.8)

It makes no sense in practice to have insurances payable at a frequency of m times per year. But it does make sense to have them payable *continuously*, or immediately upon death (rather than at the end of the year of death). To model continuous mortality, we need a life table with continuous ages, that is a continuous life *function* $\ell(x)$. Here are some analogues of the life function $\ell(x)$, compared with the life table ℓ_x based on discrete ages:

- The ratio $\frac{\ell(x)}{\ell(0)}$ is the probability of survival from birth to age x.
- The difference $\ell(x) - \ell(x + \Delta x)$ is the number of deaths between ages x and $x + \Delta x$, out of the $\ell(0)$ born.
- Hence the probability for a newborn of death between ages x and $x + \Delta x$ is $\frac{\ell(x) - \ell(x+\Delta x)}{\ell(0)} \simeq -\frac{\Delta x}{\ell(0)} \frac{d\ell}{dx}$.
- If T denotes a random variable representing the age at death (the *complete lifespan*), then

$$\mathbf{prob}\,(T \geq t) = \frac{\ell(t)}{\ell(0)}.$$

More generally, think of an individual (or a group of such individuals) who are already aged x (i.e. they have managed to survive to this age). Then:

- The ratio $\frac{\ell(x+t)}{\ell(x)}$ is the probability of survival of a male aged x for t years.
- If T_x denotes a random variable for the time of death (the *complete lifespan*), for someone already aged x, then

$$\mathbf{prob}\,(T_x \geq t) = \frac{\ell(x + t)}{\ell(x)}$$

so that the probability density of T_x is $-\frac{1}{\ell(x)} \frac{d\ell(x+t)}{dt}\Big|_{t=T_x}$.

- The probability of death in a period within a period Δt for someone aged x is

$$\frac{\ell(x) - \ell(x + \Delta t)}{\ell(x)} \simeq -\frac{\Delta t}{\ell(x)} \frac{d\ell}{dx}.$$

- The quantity $\mu(x) = -\frac{1}{\ell(x)} \frac{d\ell}{dx}$ is defined as the *instantaneous mortality* rate (or force of mortality) at age x.

Actuarial Principles
https://doi.org/10.1016/B978-0-32-390172-7.00010-5

- The probability density of T_x can then be written simply as $\mu(x+t)\frac{\ell(x+t)}{\ell(x)}$.

6.1. Insurances payable continuously

Here is a comparison of the mortality models in discrete and continuous time:

Feature	Discrete	Continuous
lifespan	curtate	complete
symbol	K_x	T_x
mortality rate	$q_x = -\frac{\ell_{x+1}-\ell_x}{\ell_x}$	$\mu(x) = -\frac{1}{\ell(x)}\frac{d\ell}{dx}$
distribution/pdf	$q_{x+t}\frac{\ell_{x+t}}{\ell_x}$	$\mu(x+t)\frac{\ell(x+t)}{\ell(x)}$

Example 6.1. *A famous mortality law, due to Gompertz, has the life function*

$$\ell(x) = e^{-m(c^x-1)}$$

where $c, m > 0$ are constants and $\ell(0) = 1$. The mortality rate is therefore

$$\mu(x) = -\frac{1}{\ell(x)}\frac{d\ell}{dx}$$
$$= e^{m(c^x-1)} \cdot e^{-m(c^x-1)} \cdot m\ln(c)\,c^x,$$
$$= Bc^x$$

which increases exponentially with age.

6.2. The value of a continuous lifetime insurance

Using T_x, it becomes possible to value the continuous *lifetime insurance*, when a benefit of $1 is payable immediately on death. It works like this:

- the discounted value if the complete lifespan is $T_x = t$ is

$$v^t = v^{T_x}$$

- its expectation is $\overline{A}_x$ where

$$\overline{A}_x = \mathbf{E}\left(v^{T_x}\right) = \int_0^\infty v^t \mu(x+t)\frac{\ell(x+t)}{\ell(x)}\,dt$$

$$= -\int_0^\infty v^t \frac{1}{\ell(x)} \frac{d\ell(x+t)}{dt} dt$$

$$= -\left. v^t \frac{\ell(x+t)}{\ell(x)} \right|_0^\infty + \int_0^\infty v^t \ln(v) \frac{\ell(x+t)}{\ell(x)} dt$$

$$= 1 - \delta \int_0^\infty v^t \frac{\ell(x+t)}{\ell(x)} dt.$$

This can be readily computed from the life function provided. Just like in the discrete case, a continuous lifetime annuity can be defined with value:

$$a_x = \int_0^\infty v^t \frac{\ell(x+t)}{\ell(x)} dt$$

and there is also the relationship with continuous insurances

$$\overline{A}_x = 1 - \delta \overline{a}_x.$$

Similarly, we can define continuous insurances and annuities $\overline{A}_{x:\overline{n}|}$, $\overline{a}_{x:\overline{n}|}$, $\overline{A}^1_{x:\overline{n}|}$, etc.

6.3. The value of a continuous lifetime annuity

Example 6.2. *The lifetime annuity may be defined alternatively in terms of the complete lifespan T_x as follows:*
- *For a given value of T_x, we have the annuity certain $\overline{a}_{\overline{K_x}|}$.*
- *Then define $\overline{a}_x = \mathbf{E}\left(\overline{a}_{\overline{T_x}|}\right)$.*
  Show that the two definitions of a_x are equivalent.

6.3.1 Exercises

Q2 and Q4 are based on the AMC00 life table, which is provided in a spreadsheet.

1. In Q14 of Section 1, we calculated that $A_{20:\overline{15}|} = 0.643$ and $\ddot{a}_{20:\overline{15}|} = 12.272$ for a female under ALT2005–07 at 3% pa interest. Approximate the corresponding values of $\overline{a}_{20:\overline{15}|}$ and $\overline{A}_{20:\overline{15}|}$ using the relationship $\overline{A}_{20:\overline{15}|} = 1 - \delta \overline{a}_{20:\overline{15}|}$.
   How does this value of $\overline{A}_{20:\overline{15}|}$ compare with that from the approximation $\overline{A}^1_{20:\overline{15}|} = (1+i)^{\frac{1}{2}} A^1_{20:\overline{15}|}$?

Solution

We have the approximation

$$\ddot{a}_{x:\overline{n}|}^{(m)} \simeq \ddot{a}_{x:\overline{n}|} - \frac{m-1}{2m}\left(1 - v^n\frac{\ell_{x+n}}{\ell_x}\right).$$

Hence as $m \to \infty$:

$$\overline{a}_{20:\overline{15}|} \simeq \ddot{a}_{20:\overline{15}|} - \frac{1}{2}\left(1 - v^{15}\frac{\ell_{35}}{\ell_{20}}\right)$$
$$= 12.091$$

and thus

$$\overline{A}_{20:\overline{15}|} = 1 - \delta\overline{a}_{20:\overline{15}|}$$
$$= 1 - \ln(1.03)\cdot 12.091$$
$$= 0.643.$$

This compares with the approximation

$$\overline{A}_{20:\overline{15}|} \simeq (1+i)^{\frac{1}{2}}A^1_{20:\overline{15}|} + A^{\ 1}_{20:\overline{15}|}$$
$$= 1.03^{\frac{1}{2}}\cdot 0.004 + 0.639$$
$$= 0.643.$$

2. The AMC00 life table, with a 2-year select period, was based on the 1999–2002 experience of male insured persons in the UK. Calculate at 3% pa the value of $\overline{a}_{[20]:\overline{15}|}$ and $\overline{A}_{[20]:\overline{15}|}$.

Solution

The values are $\overline{a}_{[20]:\overline{15}|} = 12.079$ and $\overline{A}_{20:\overline{15}|} = 1 - \delta\overline{a}_{20:\overline{15}|} = 1 - \ln(1.03)\cdot 12.079 = 0.643$.

3. [UK CT5 exam, Sept 2008] Calculate the variance of the present value of benefits under an annuity payable to a life aged 35 exact. The annuity has payments of 1 per annum payable continuously for life.
   Basis: mortality $\mu = 0.02$ throughout; interest 5% pa.

Solution

For constant mortality, $\ell_x = e^{-0.02x}$. Hence the pdf of T_{35} at $T_{35} = t$ is
$0.02 \frac{\ell_{x+t}}{\ell_x} = 0.02 e^{-0.02t}$.

The value of the benefit for $T_{35} = t$ is $\bar{a}_{\overline{t}|} = \frac{1-1.05^{-t}}{\ln(1.05)}$, so its variance is

$$\mathbf{var}\left(\bar{a}_{\overline{T_{35}}|}\right)$$

$$= \frac{1}{\ln(1.05)^2} \mathbf{var}\left(1.05^{-T_{35}}\right)$$

$$= \frac{1}{\ln(1.05)^2}\left[0.02 \int_0^\infty e^{-0.02t} 1.05^{-2t} dt - \left(0.02 \int_0^\infty e^{-0.02t} 1.05^{-t} dt\right)^2\right]$$

$$= \frac{1}{\ln(1.05)^2}\left[\frac{0.02}{0.02 + 2\ln(1.05)} - \frac{0.02^2}{(0.02 + \ln(1.05))^2}\right]$$

$$= 35.945.$$

4. [UK CT5 exam, Apr 2008] The symbol $_tq_x$ denotes the probability of death of x within a time of t, just as $_tp_x$ denotes the probability of survival.

    Show that $_{t-s}q_{x+s} = \frac{(t-s)q_x}{1-sq_x}$ for $0 \le s < t \le 1$ using an assumption of a uniform distribution of deaths (i.e. ℓ_x is linearly interpolated between integral ages).

    Then calculate the value of $_{0.5}q_{62.25}$ using assumptions of:

    a. a uniform distribution of deaths

    b. a constant force of mortality $\mu = -\frac{1}{\ell(x)}\frac{d\ell(x)}{dx}$

    Basis: Mortality AMC000.

Solution

For a uniform distribution of deaths, $\ell_{x+t} = (1-t)\ell_x + t\ell_{x+1}$ for $0 \le t \le 1$. Thus

$$\ell_{x+t} = (1-t)\ell_x + t(1-q_x)\ell_x$$
$$= \ell_x[1 - tq_x].$$

Thus the number of deaths between ages $x+s$ and $x+t$ are $\ell_{x+t} - \ell_{x+s} = (t-s)\ell_x q_x$, and

$$_{t-s}q_{x+s} = \frac{\ell_{x+t} - \ell_{x+s}}{\ell_{x+s}} = \frac{(t-s)\,q_x}{1 - sq_x}.$$

For $_{0.5}q_{62.25}$, we have $x = 62$, $s = 0.25$, $t = 0.75$ and $q_{62} = 0.007662$:

$$_{0.5}q_{62.25} = \frac{0.5q_{62}}{1 - 0.25q_{62}} = 0.003838.$$

For a constant force of mortality, and taking $\ell_{62} = 1$ and $\ell_{63} = 1 - q_{62} = 0.992338$, we have $\ell_{62+t} = 0.992338^t$. Hence

$$_{t-s}q_{x+s} = \frac{\ell_{x+t} - \ell_{x+s}}{\ell_{x+s}} = 1 - \frac{0.992338^{0.75}}{0.992338^{0.25}} = 0.003838.$$

CHAPTER SEVEN

Select mortality (CT5: §3.6)

Lastly in this section, we consider a life table parametrised by a variable in addition to age (or sex). What can this variable be? Here are some examples:

- occupation
- a result of genetic testing
- exposure to some temporary risk factor – surgery
- passing a medical examination.

Selection is the term used to describe how one group of people may have different mortality characteristics from others.

Where a group of insureds have undergone an underwriting process (and are therefore expected to be healthier than those who have not). This is known as *temporary initial selection.*

Other forms of selection are:

- *class* selection – where there are *permanent* risk factors, such as sex, education, genetics (or even race).
- *time* selection – people in the 14th century experienced much higher mortality than today. More generally, medical advances mean people are living longer (though not necessarily better).
- *adverse* selection – the ability of people to act against an insurer by exploiting information not available to the insurer. A classic example is for an insurer who does not discriminate against smokers. It is likely it will end up insuring mostly smokers.
- *spurious* selection – this is not really a form of selection at all, but refers to mortality factors, which are suspected incorrectly. An example is using geography as a risk factor, when it is only a proxy for occupation and income.

7.1. How selection operates in practice

In life insurance, the *underwriting process* is the key to mortality experience. This mitigates adverse selection, and can take account of:

- occupation
- sex and other class characteristics
- individual characteristics such as genetics, risky activities (e.g. paragliding, rock climbing)

- the results of a medical screening (i.e. questionnaire and examination).

The last of these is the most common for insurance purposes:

- The medical exam (as part of the *underwriting* process) weeds out the bad risks, with the result that those who pass the test are healthier than the population at large.
- Those who pass the test have been 'selected'.
- However this effect is temporary—the insured will revert to normal mortality after a certain period.

This feature is modelled by having mortality dependent on age *and* on the period since the medical exam was passed:

- In practice the life table is written as $\ell_{[x]+t}$ where x is the age at which the medical was passed, and t is the time since then.
- The period t is restricted to a *select period*—typically 2 to 5 years—during which the selection effect persists.
- Applying the select life table is exactly the same as applying the normal life table.
- Thus in calculating $A_{[x]}$, we apply the life table $\ell_{[x]+t}$ for periods $t \geq 0$.

Example 7.1. *Suppose the life table based on normal (also called 'ultimate') mortality is denoted ℓ_x. Suppose also:*

- *We have analysed the statistics for people who have undergone medicals.*
- *For a select period of 2 years, we have select mortality as 50% of the ultimate mortality in the 1st year after the medical exam,*
- *and 75% in the 2nd.*

How would you determine the select lifetable $\ell_{[x]+t}$?

This can be approached as follows.

Example 7.2. *Consider a person who undergoes a medical at age x.*

- *At age $x+1$, his mortality rate is $q_{[x]+1} = 1 - \frac{\ell_{x+2}}{\ell_{[x]+1}} = 75\% \left(1 - \frac{\ell_{x+2}}{\ell_{x+1}} \right).$*
- *Therefore $\ell_{[x]+1} = \frac{\ell_{x+2}}{1 - 75\% \left(1 - \frac{\ell_{x+2}}{\ell_{x+1}} \right)} = \frac{\ell_{x+1}}{0.25 * \frac{\ell_{x+1}}{\ell_{x+2}} + 0.75} < \ell_{x+1}.$*
- *Similarly, at age x, $q_{[x]} = 1 - \frac{\ell_{[x]+1}}{\ell_{[x]}} = 50\% \left(1 - \frac{\ell_{x+1}}{\ell_x} \right).$*
- *Then $\ell_{[x]} = \frac{\ell_{[x]+1}}{1 - 50\% \left(1 - \frac{\ell_{x+1}}{\ell_x} \right)} = \frac{\ell_x}{0.5 \frac{\ell_x}{\ell_{[x]+1}} + 0.5 \frac{\ell_{x+1}}{\ell_{[x]+1}}} < \ell_x.$*

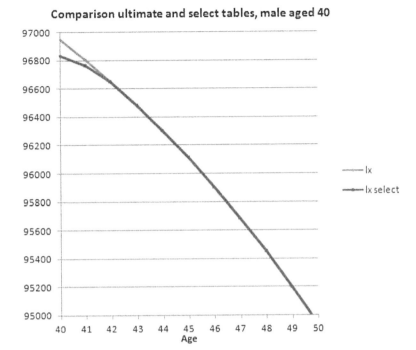

Comparison ultimate and select tables, male aged 40

7.1.1 Exercises

1. The AMC00 life table, with a 2-year select period, was based on the 1999–2002 experience of male insured persons in the UK. Calculate at 3% pa the value of $\bar{a}_{[20]:\overline{15|}}$ and $\overline{A}_{[20]:\overline{15|}}$.

Solution
The values are $\bar{a}_{[20]:\overline{15|}} = 12.079$ and $\overline{A}_{20:\overline{15|}} = 1 - \delta\bar{a}_{20:\overline{15|}} = 1 - \ln(1.03) \cdot 12.079 = 0.643$.

CHAPTER EIGHT

Benefits involving multiple lives (CT5: §8, §9)

So far the benefits valued in these lectures have involved a single life only. But the model can be extended naturally to more than one life. This is useful in several situations:

- It is common for retirement and superannuation funds to provide *reversionary* benefits, for example where the spouse of a pensioner receives a reduced lifetime pension after the death of the pensioner.
- Assurances are paid on the last death of a married couple, which reduces their cost whilst providing protection for children.

   This can obviously be extended to several lives, but looking at just two lives should illustrate what is possible.

8.1. The joint life table

Just like a single life table ℓ_x, it is possible to construct a joint life table ℓ_{xy} representing the number of surviving pairs xy starting from ℓ_{00} at birth.

- Here, x is usually taken to be a male life, and y a female, but that isn't necessary.
- ℓ_{xy} can be constructed from the single life tables ℓ_x and ℓ_y by making a simplifying assumption.
- The mortality of lives x and y is independent, so that

$$\ell_{xy} = \ell_x \ell_y.$$

This is only a convenient assumption—it doesn't mean that in reality married couples don't affect each other's health!

8.2. The curtate joint lifespan

Just as we introduced the curtate lifespan K_x for the random variable indicating the year just before death, we also have the curtate joint lifespan K_{xy}, the year just before the *first* death of x and y. Just as we had

$$\mathbf{prob}\,(K_x = t) = q_{x+t}\frac{\ell_{x+t}}{\ell_x} = \frac{\ell_{x+t} - \ell_{x+t+1}}{\ell_x},$$

we have also

$$\mathbf{prob}\left(K_{xy}=t\right)=\frac{\ell_{x+t,y+t}-\ell_{x+t+1,y+t+1}}{\ell_{xy}}$$

$$=q_{x+t,y+t}\frac{\ell_{x+t}}{\ell_x}\frac{\ell_{y+t}}{\ell_y}$$

$$=q_{x+t,y+t}\cdot{}_tp_{xy}.$$

Here, $q_{x+t,y+t}$ is the probability of *at least* one death in the year beginning time t, that is

$$q_{xy}=\frac{\ell_x\ell_y-\ell_{x+1}\ell_{y+1}}{\ell_x\ell_y}.$$

8.3. A joint lifetime insurance

In exactly the same way as for a single lifetime insurance, a joint lifetime insurance can be defined as payable on the failure of the joint status xy, that is whenever one of the lives dies. Its expectation is

$$A_{xy}=\mathbf{E}\left(v^{K_{xy}+1}\right)=\sum_{t=0}^{\infty}v^{t+1}\cdot\mathbf{prob}\left(K_{xy}=t\right)$$

$$=\sum_{t=0}^{\infty}v^{t+1}\frac{\ell_{x+t}\ell_{y+t}-\ell_{x+t+1}\ell_{y+t+1}}{\ell_x\ell_y}$$

$$=\sum_{t=0}^{\infty}v^{t+1}\frac{\ell_{x+t}\ell_{y+t}}{\ell_x\ell_y}-\sum_{t=0}^{\infty}v^{t+1}\frac{\ell_{x+t+1}\ell_{y+t+1}}{\ell_x\ell_y}$$

$$=\sum_{t=0}^{\infty}v^{t+1}\frac{\ell_{x+t}\ell_{y+t}}{\ell_x\ell_y}-\sum_{t=1}^{\infty}v^{t}\frac{\ell_{x+t}\ell_{y+t}}{\ell_x\ell_y}$$

$$=v-(1-v)\sum_{t=1}^{\infty}v^{t}\frac{\ell_{x+t}\ell_{y+t}}{\ell_x\ell_y}.$$

8.4. A joint lifetime annuity

In exactly the same way for an annuity payable whilst *both* x and y are alive,

$$\ddot{a}_{xy}=\sum_{t=0}^{\infty}v^{t}\cdot{}_tp_{xy}$$

$$= \sum_{t=0}^{\infty} v^t \frac{\ell_{x+t}\ell_{y+t}}{\ell_x \ell_y}$$

and we again have the familiar relationship

$$A_{xy} = 1 - d\ddot{a}_{xy}.$$

CHAPTER NINE

The last survivor status

So far the valuation of multiple life benefits is precisely analogous to single life benefits because the joint status xy can be treated like a single life.

However, things can rapidly become complicated when we consider benefits payable on the death of the *last* life:

- The status $\overline{xy}$ denotes the situation where *either* x or y is alive.
- Thus $\overline{xy}$ fails only when both are dead.
- The curtate last survivor lifespan $K_{\overline{xy}}$ is the year just before the last death, so that

$$K_{\overline{xy}} = \max\left(K_x, K_y\right).$$

- What is the relationship between $K_{\overline{xy}}$ and K_{xy}?

9.1. Relationship between curtate lifespans

There is an important relationship that we haven't noticed yet:

$$K_{xy} = \min\left(K_x, K_y\right).$$

Now we must have $\min\left(K_x, K_y\right) + \max\left(K_x, K_y\right) = K_x + K_y$, so that

$$K_{\overline{xy}} + K_{xy} = K_x + K_y$$

or

$$K_{\overline{xy}} = K_x + K_y - K_{xy}.$$

9.2. Last survivor insurances and annuities

This makes it easy to compute the distribution of $K_{\overline{xy}}$ when we know those for K_x, K_y and K_{xy}:

-

$$\mathbf{prob}\left(K_{\overline{xy}} = t\right) = \mathbf{prob}\left(K_x < K_y = t\right) + \mathbf{prob}\left(K_y \le K_x = t\right)$$
$$= \frac{\ell_{y+t} - \ell_{y+t+1}}{\ell_y}\left(1 - \frac{\ell_{x+t}}{\ell_x}\right) + \frac{\ell_{x+t} - \ell_{x+t+1}}{\ell_x}\left(1 - \frac{\ell_{y+t+1}}{\ell_y}\right)$$

Actuarial Principles
https://doi.org/10.1016/B978-0-32-390172-7.00013-0
37

$$= \frac{\ell_{y+t} - \ell_{y+t+1}}{\ell_y} + \frac{\ell_{x+t} - \ell_{x+t+1}}{\ell_x}$$

$$- \frac{\ell_{x+t}\ell_{y+t} - \ell_{x+t}\ell_{y+t+1} + \ell_{x+t}\ell_{y+t+1} - \ell_{x+t+1}\ell_{y+t+1}}{\ell_x\ell_y}$$

$$= \frac{\ell_{y+t} - \ell_{y+t+1}}{\ell_y} + \frac{\ell_{x+t} - \ell_{x+t+1}}{\ell_x} - q_{x+t,y+t}\frac{\ell_{x+t}}{\ell_x}\frac{\ell_{y+t}}{\ell_y}$$

$$= \mathbf{prob}\,(K_x = t) + \mathbf{prob}\,(K_y = t) - \mathbf{prob}\,(K_{xy} = t).$$

We have now the possible statuses, x, y, xy and $\overline{xy}$. Letting the symbol u denote any one of them, it is now clear that an insurance can *generally* be defined as

$$A_u = \mathbf{E}\left(v^{K_u+1}\right)$$

and similarly,

$$a_u = \mathbf{E}\left(a_{\overline{K_u}}\right)$$

or

$$\ddot{a}_u = \mathbf{E}\left(\ddot{a}_{\overline{K_u+1}}\right).$$

For any status u, we can also derive the variances:

$$\mathbf{var}\left(v^{K_u+1}\right) = \mathbf{E}\left(v^{2K_u+2}\right) - (A_u)^2$$

and similarly,

$$\mathbf{var}\left(a_{\overline{K_u}}\right) = \mathbf{var}\left(\ddot{a}_{\overline{K_u+1}}\right)$$

$$= \mathbf{var}\left(\frac{1 - v^{K_u+1}}{d}\right)$$

$$= \frac{1}{d^2}\mathbf{var}\left(v^{K_u+1}\right).$$

Using the relationship,

$$\mathbf{prob}\,(K_{\overline{xy}} = t) = \mathbf{prob}\,(K_x = t) + \mathbf{prob}\,(K_y = t) - \mathbf{prob}\,(K_{xy} = t)$$

and by multiplying by v^{t+1}, and then summing over t, it is easy to show that

$$A_{\overline{xy}} = A_x + A_y - A_{xy}$$

and similarly by multiplying by $\ddot{a}_{\overline{t+1}}$ and summing over t,

$$\ddot{a}_{\overline{xy}} = \ddot{a}_x + \ddot{a}_y - \ddot{a}_{xy}.$$

This can also be shown from first principles. Again using the relationship,

$$\mathbf{prob}\left(K_{\overline{xy}}=t\right)=\mathbf{prob}\left(K_x=t\right)+\mathbf{prob}\left(K_y=t\right)-\mathbf{prob}\left(K_{xy}=t\right)$$

it is also possible to multiply by $v^{\min(t+1,n)}$, and then summing, we get

$$A_{\overline{xy}:\overline{n}|}=A_{x:\overline{n}|}+A_{y:\overline{n}|}-A_{xy:\overline{n}|}$$

or multiply by $\ddot{a}_{\overline{\min(t+1,n)|}}$ to get

$$\ddot{a}_{\overline{xy}:\overline{n}|}=\ddot{a}_{x:\overline{n}|}+\ddot{a}_{y:\overline{n}|}-\ddot{a}_{xy:\overline{n}|}.$$

9.2.1 Exercises

1. Calculate $\overline{a}_{40:35:\overline{15}|}$ and $\overline{a}_{\overline{40:35}:\overline{15}|}$ on the basis of ALT2005–07 at 3% pa.

Solution
From the approximation $\overline{a}_{u:\overline{n}|}\simeq\ddot{a}_{u:\overline{n}|}-\frac{1}{2}\left(1-v^n\frac{\ell_{u+n}}{\ell_u}\right)$, where u is any status, we can calculate

u	$x:\overline{n}|$	$y:\overline{n}|$	$xy:\overline{n}|$
$\ddot{a}_u$	12.139	12.235	12.079
$\overline{a}_u$	11.948	12.051	11.883

From this, it can be calculated that $\overline{a}_{\overline{40:35}:\overline{15}|}=\overline{a}_{40:\overline{15}|}+\overline{a}_{35:\overline{15}|}-\overline{a}_{40:35:\overline{15}|}=$ 12.116.

2. [A reversionary annuity] Prove algebraically that the value of an annuity of \$1 commencing at the end of year of death of x and continuing for the lifetime of y is $a_{x|y}=a_y-a_{xy}$. Can this be derived without algebra?

Solution
The annuity is payable when x is dead and whilst y is alive:

$$a_{x|y}=\sum_{t=1}^{\infty}v^t\frac{\ell_{y+t}}{\ell_y}\left(1-\frac{\ell_{x+t}}{\ell_x}\right)$$

$$= \sum_{t=1}^{\infty} v^t \frac{\ell_{y+t}}{\ell_y} - \sum_{t=1}^{\infty} v^t \frac{\ell_{y+t}}{\ell_y} \frac{\ell_{x+t}}{\ell_x}$$

$$= a_y - a_{xy}.$$

This is clearly the value of a lifetime annuity payable to y, with a deduction of the annuity payable whilst both are alive.

3. [UK CT5 exam, Apr 2008] A parent who has just died left a bond in their will that provides a single payment of $15,000 in 10 years' time. The payment of $15,000 will be shared equally between the local cats' home and such of the parent's two sons (currently aged 25 and 30 exact) who are then still alive. Give a formula for the expected present value of the share due to the cats' home.

Solution

There are four possibilities:

- the son aged 25 survives and aged 30 dies, with probability $\frac{\ell_{35}}{\ell_{25}}\left(1 - \frac{\ell_{40}}{\ell_{30}}\right)$, in which case the cats' home gets $\frac{1}{2}$.
- the son aged 30 survives and aged 25 dies, with probability $\frac{\ell_{40}}{\ell_{30}}\left(1 - \frac{\ell_{35}}{\ell_{25}}\right)$, in which case the cats' home gets $\frac{1}{2}$.
- both sons survive with probability $\frac{\ell_{35}}{\ell_{25}}\frac{\ell_{40}}{\ell_{30}}$, in which case the cats' home gets $\frac{1}{3}$.
- neither son survives with probability $\left(1 - \frac{\ell_{40}}{\ell_{30}}\right)\left(1 - \frac{\ell_{35}}{\ell_{25}}\right)$, in which case the cats' home gets all.

The cats' home therefore has an interest with present value

$$15,000v^{10}\left[\frac{1}{2}\frac{\ell_{35}}{\ell_{25}}\left(1 - \frac{\ell_{40}}{\ell_{30}}\right) + \frac{1}{2}\frac{\ell_{40}}{\ell_{30}}\left(1 - \frac{\ell_{35}}{\ell_{25}}\right) + \frac{1}{3}\frac{\ell_{35}}{\ell_{25}}\frac{\ell_{40}}{\ell_{30}}\right.$$
$$\left. + \left(1 - \frac{\ell_{40}}{\ell_{30}}\right)\left(1 - \frac{\ell_{35}}{\ell_{25}}\right)\right].$$

4. [UK CT5 exam, Sept 2006] T_x and T_y are the complete future lifetimes of two lives aged x and y, respectively. Let the random variable $g(T_x, T_y)$ take the following values: ·

$$g(T_x, T_y) = \overline{a}_{\overline{\min(T_x, T_y)}}.$$

a. Describe the benefit, which has present value equal to $g(T_x, T_y)$.

b. Express $\mathbf{E}\left[g(T_x, T_y)\right]$ as an integral.

c. Write down an expression for the variance of $g(T_x, T_y)$ using assurance functions.

Solution

The annuity is payable to the earlier death, and thus has expectation $\bar{a}_{xy}$. Each payment during a time interval of length dt must be discounted for the probability of survival of both lives:

$$\bar{a}_{xy} = \int_0^\infty e^{-\delta t} \frac{l(x+t)}{l(x)} \frac{l(y+t)}{l(y)} \, dt.$$

If we define $T_{xy} = \min\left(T_x, T_y\right)$, then the variance of $g(T_x, T_y)$ is given by

$$\mathbf{var}\left[\frac{1 - v^{T_{xy}}}{\delta}\right] = \frac{1}{\delta^2} \mathbf{var}\left(v^{T_{xy}}\right)$$

$$= \frac{1}{\delta^2}\left[{}^2\bar{A}_{xy} - \left(\bar{A}_{xy}\right)^2\right]$$

where ${}^2A$ is evaluated at an interest rate j such that $(1+i)^2 = 1+j$.

---

5. [UK CT5 exam, Sept 2006] A life insurance company issues a 10-year decreasing term assurance to a man aged 50 exact. The death benefit is \$100,000 in the first year, \$90,000 in the 2nd year, and decreases by \$10,000 each year so that the benefit in the 10th year is \$10,000. The death benefit is payable at the end of the year of death.

Level premiums are payable annually in advance for the term of the policy, ceasing on earlier death.

Provide a formula using the usual assurance and annuity functions for the annual premium. Calculate the annual premium under AMC00 select at 5% interest.

Solution

The benefit is equivalent to a temporary insurance of \$110,000, less an assurance of \$10,000, increasing by \$10,000 each year. The annual premium is therefore

$$\frac{110000 A^1_{[50]:\overline{10}|} - 10000 IA^1_{[50]:\overline{10}|}}{\ddot{a}_{[50]:\overline{10}|}} = \$149.60.$$

6. [UK CT5 exam, Apr 2009] A population is subject to two modes of decrement α and β where $q^\beta_x = \frac{1}{3} + \frac{1}{4}q^\alpha_x$.
Derive from first principles aq^β_x. State clearly any assumptions you make.

Solution

Assume that the decrement α operates uniformly over the year. Then the exposure of the population to decrement β is $1 - \frac{1}{2}q^\alpha_x$. Thus

$$aq^\beta_x = q^\beta_x \left(1 - \frac{1}{2}q^\alpha_x\right)$$

$$= \left(\frac{1}{3} + \frac{1}{4}q^\alpha_x\right)\left(1 - \frac{1}{2}q^\alpha_x\right).$$

CHAPTER TEN

Pricing and reserving in theory (CT5: §5)

10.1. Introduction

The most important applications of life contingency valuation are:

- *pricing*: setting the price of a premium for a *new* financial contract involving insurances or annuities, allowing for expenses and profit loadings;
- *reserving*: assessing what funds should be held to support future obligations on an *existing* financial contract.

10.2. Pricing

Premiums are *always* determined using the principle of equivalence

$$\text{Value of premiums} = \text{Value of benefits less other costs.}$$

Ignore practical things like costs for the moment. Consider the simplest case of a lifetime insurance for an individual aged x, with constant premiums payable yearly in advance for the lifetime of the insured:

- If the premium is denoted P_x, then we have

$$P_x \ddot{a}_x = A_x$$

- so the yearly premium can be evaluated easily as

$$P_x = \frac{A_x}{\ddot{a}_x} = \frac{1}{\ddot{a}_x} - d.$$

10.3. Premium for an endowment insurance

It is almost as easy to price an endowment insurance:

$$P_{x:\overline{n}|} \ddot{a}_{x:\overline{n}|} = A_{x:\overline{n}|}$$

so that

$$P_{x:\overline{n}|} = \frac{A_{x:\overline{n}|}}{\ddot{a}_{x:\overline{n}|}} = \frac{1}{\ddot{a}_{x:\overline{n}|}} - d$$

and similarly for an insurance with limited term:

$$P_{x:\overline{n}|} = \frac{A^1_{x:\overline{n}|}}{\ddot{a}_{x:\overline{n}|}} = \frac{1 - v^n \frac{\ell_{x+n}}{\ell_x}}{\ddot{a}_{x:\overline{n}|}} - d$$

and so on for other types of benefit.

10.4. The insurer's risk

Though the insurer sets the premium on the basis of the equivalence principle, this does not mean that they are free from risk. Their surplus (profit/loss) at the start of a lifetime insurance contract is a random variable:

$$S = P_x \ddot{a}_{\overline{K_x+1}|} - v^{K_x+1}$$
$$= P_x \frac{1 - v^{K_x+1}}{d} - v^{K_x+1}$$
$$= \frac{P_x}{d} - v^{K_x+1}\left(\frac{P_x}{d} + 1\right).$$

- The premium P_x is a constant that has been determined so that there is no expected surplus $E(S) = 0$.
- However, the variance of surplus on the contract is not zero:

$$\mathbf{var}(S) = \left(\frac{P_x}{d} + 1\right)^2 \mathbf{var}\left(v^{K_x+1}\right)$$
$$= \left(\frac{P_x}{d} + 1\right)^2 \left[^2A_{x:\overline{n}|} - \left(A_{x:\overline{n}|}\right)^2\right]$$

- and similarly with other types of benefit.

10.5. Reserving

Suppose that:
- a contract has been in force for t years
- the investment income on premiums received has been exactly that assumed, at rate i.

Questions that arise are:
- What funds (assets) are expected to have accumulated at time t? These are known as *retrospective* reserves.
- What funds are required in order to meet future promises under the contract? These are known as *prospective* reserves.
- Are *retrospective* and *prospective* reserves the same?

10.6. Prospective reserves

These are similar to the concept as the insurer's surplus at the outset of a contract. However, because we are measuring the funds required, the relevant concept is the insurer's expected *deficiency*, where

Deficiency $=$ Value of future benefits $-$ Value of future premiums.

- In the lifetime insurance case, we have

$$D = v^{K_{x+t}+1} - P_x \ddot{a}_{\overline{K_{x+t}+1}|}.$$

- The expected deficiency is therefore

$$_tV_x = E(D)$$
$$= A_{x+t} - P_x \ddot{a}_{x+t}$$
$$= 1 - d\ddot{a}_{x+t} - \frac{\ddot{a}_{x+t}}{\ddot{a}_x} + d\ddot{a}_{x+t}$$
$$= 1 - \frac{\ddot{a}_{x+t}}{\ddot{a}_x}.$$

- Prospective reserves are generally positive, because premiums are usually set to more than cover the cost of insurance initially.

10.7. Retrospective reserves

These reserves are assessed on a 'backward looking' basis, by accumulating assets from year to year. We assume that the experience with mortality and investments follows precisely the assumptions made.
- Suppose assets accumulated to time t are $_tF_x$.
- At this time, $\frac{\ell_{x+t}}{\ell_x}$ of the original individuals insured are still alive.
- Then at the start of the following year we have a premium of P_x payable for those still alive.

- Of those alive at the start of year t, a proportion q_{x+t} will die during the year and receive a benefit of 1 at the end of year.
- Thus the *equation of value* for the build–up of assets is

$$_{t+1}F_x = (1+i)\left({_tF_x} + \frac{\ell_{x+t}}{\ell_x}P_x\right) - q_{x+t}\frac{\ell_{x+t}}{\ell_x}.$$

We now consider the reserve, or assets *per individual still alive*, that is $_t\overline{F}_x = {_tF_x}\frac{\ell_x}{\ell_{x+t}}$.
- This obeys the simpler relationship:

$$_{t+1}\overline{F}_x\frac{\ell_{x+t+1}}{\ell_{x+t}} = {_{t+1}\overline{F}_x}\left(1 - q_{x+t}\right)$$

$$= (1+i)\left({_t\overline{F}_x} + P_x\right) - q_{x+t}$$

- or equivalently

$$_{t+1}\overline{F}_x p_{x+t} + q_{x+t} = (1+i)\left({_t\overline{F}_x} + P_x\right).$$

This is known as the *equation of equilibrium*. What this says is that the reserves for individuals at a point of time, when accumulated with premiums and interest over the next year, must be sufficient to pay expected claims q_{x+t} for those dying during the year and to set up reserves for the survivors $_{t+1}\overline{F}_x p_{x+t}$ at the end of year.

The equation of equilibrium for retrospective reserves is a *difference equation*, that is a linear equation relating $_t\overline{F}_x$ and $_{t+1}\overline{F}_x$. To solve this equation, we write it first in the form:

$$_t\overline{F}_x = v \cdot {_{t+1}\overline{F}_x}\frac{\ell_{x+t+1}}{\ell_{x+t}} + vq_{x+t} - P_x.$$

This equation connects $_t\overline{F}_x$ and $_{t+1}\overline{F}_x$. We can then also connect $_{t+1}\overline{F}_x$ and $_{t+2}\overline{F}_x$:

$$_{t+1}\overline{F}_x = v \cdot {_{t+2}\overline{F}_x}\frac{\ell_{x+t+2}}{\ell_{x+t+1}} + vq_{x+t+1} - P_x$$

and then apply this relation again to $_{t+1}\overline{F}_x$:

$$_t\overline{F}_x = v^2 \cdot {_{t+2}\overline{F}_x}\frac{\ell_{x+t+2}}{\ell_{x+t}} + \left(vq_{x+t} + v^2 q_{x+t+1}\frac{\ell_{x+t+1}}{\ell_{x+t}}\right) - P_x\left(1 + v\frac{\ell_{x+t+1}}{\ell_{x+t}}\right).$$

You can see that we can keep on substituting the relation for $_{t+2}\overline{F}_x$, $_{t+3}\overline{F}_x \ldots$ to get

$$_t\overline{F}_x = v^n \cdot {}_{t+n}\overline{F}_x \frac{\ell_{x+t+n}}{\ell_{x+t}} + \left(vq_{x+t} + v^2 q_{x+t+1} \frac{\ell_{x+t+1}}{\ell_{x+t}} + \ldots + v^n q_{x+t+n-1} \frac{\ell_{x+t+n-1}}{\ell_{x+t}} \right)$$
$$- P_x \left(1 + v \frac{\ell_{x+t+1}}{\ell_{x+t}} + v^2 \frac{\ell_{x+t+2}}{\ell_{x+t}} + \cdots + v^{n-1} \frac{\ell_{x+t+n-1}}{\ell_{x+t}} \right).$$

As n becomes very large, we will eventually have $\ell_{x+t+n} = 0$ or $v^n \to 0$. Hence the retrospective reserve is

$$_t\overline{F}_x = \sum_{n=1}^{\infty} \left[v^n q_{x+t+n-1} \frac{\ell_{x+t+n-1}}{\ell_{x+t}} - P_x v^{n-1} \frac{\ell_{x+t+n-1}}{\ell_{x+t}} \right]$$
$$= A_{x+t} - P_x \ddot{a}_{x+t}.$$

10.8. Equality of prospective and retrospective reserves

This is exactly the same expression as for the prospective reserve $_tV_x$! This result is very general, and applies to all types of benefits, but only when:

- The actual mortality experienced in the past is exactly the same as assumed for the future.
- The actual investment experience is exactly the same as assumed. So the next question is:
- What happens when experience is *not exactly* as assumed?
- How do we manage that?

10.9. Mortality profit/loss

Because the prospective and retrospective reserves are equal when future experience is the same as the past, then it is traditional to use the same symbol $_tV_x$ to denote either type of reserve. Recall the equation of equilibrium for (retrospective) reserves:

$$_{t+1}\overline{F}_x p_{x+t} + q_{x+t} = (1+i)\left({}_t\overline{F}_x + P_x \right).$$

The equation of equilibrium can be written prospectively for a sum insured S in year t as

$$_{t+1}V_x + q_{x+t}(S - {}_{t+1}V_x) = (1+i)({}_tV_x + P_x).$$

Because the prospective and retrospective reserves are equal when future experience is the same as the past, then it is traditional to use the same symbol $_tV_x$ to denote either type of reserve. Recall the equation of equilibrium for (retrospective) reserves:

$$_{t+1}\overline{F}_x p_{x+t} + q_{x+t} = (1+i)({}_t\overline{F}_x + P_x).$$

The equation of equilibrium can be written prospectively for a sum insured S in year t as

$$_{t+1}V_x + q_{x+t}(S - {}_{t+1}V_x) = (1+i)({}_tV_x + P_x).$$

Now suppose for this year:

- Reserves are always determined prospectively on the same interest and mortality basis.
- But deaths during the year may be different from what we expect from q_{x+t}—suppose the actual deaths are at a rate of $\bar{q}_{x+t}$.
- How much does the insurer gain or lose as a result?

To answer this question, it is necessary to define what 'profit/loss' is. This is how the insurer would approach it.

- For each individual insured at time t, a reserve of $_tV_x$ must be held in the form of assets.
- For each individual insured at time $t+1$, a reserve of $_{t+1}V_x$ must be found.

Consider an individual who survives the year, so there is no payout. In this case the insurer

- collects the premium at the start of year
- earns interest on the start-of-year reserve and premium
- establishes a reserve of $_{t+1}V_x$ at end of year.

In this case, the insurer's profit is

$$(1+i)({}_tV_x + P_x) - {}_{t+1}V_x.$$

Now consider an individual who dies during the year, so there is a payout of S. In this case the insurer:

- collects the premium at the start of year
- earns interest on the start-of-year reserve and premium
- pays a benefit of S at end of year.

In this case, the insurer's profit is

$$(1 + i)({}_tV_x + P_x) - S.$$

If the probability of death is q_{x+t}, as assumed, then the insurer's overall profit is the sum of those who survive or die:

$$\begin{aligned}
\Pr ofit &= p_{x+t}[(1 + i)({}_tV_x + P_x) -{}_{t+1}V_x] \\
&\quad + q_{x+t}[(1 + i)({}_tV_x + P_x) - S] \\
&= (1 + i)({}_tV_x + P_x) - p_{x+t} \cdot_{t+1}V_x - q_{x+t}S \\
&= 0.
\end{aligned}$$

10.10. Death strain at risk

However, if the actual probability of death is $\bar{q}_{x+t}$, then the insurer's overall profit is the sum of those who actually survive or die:

$$\begin{aligned}
\Pr ofit &= \bar{p}_{x+t}[(1 + i)({}_tV_x + P_x) -{}_{t+1}V_x] \\
&\quad + \bar{q}_{x+t}[(1 + i)({}_tV_x + P_x) - S] \\
&= (1 + i)({}_tV_x + P_x) - \bar{p}_{x+t} \cdot_{t+1}V_x - \bar{q}_{x+t}S \\
&= p_{x+t} \cdot_{t+1}V_x + q_{x+t}S - \bar{p}_{x+t} \cdot_{t+1}V_x - \bar{q}_{x+t}S \\
&= \left(q_{x+t} - \bar{q}_{x+t}\right)(S -_{t+1}V_x).
\end{aligned}$$

Thus the quantity $S -_{t+1}V_x$ is called the *death strain at risk*.

10.11. Thiele's equation

The equation of equilibrium for retrospective reserves has an analog in continuous time, where it is known as *Thiele's equation*. The derivation is almost identical to that in discrete time:

- For a lifetime insurance for life x in continuous time, suppose the assets accumulated to time t are $F(x, t)$.
- At this time, $\frac{\ell(x+t)}{\ell(x)}$ of the original individuals insured are still alive.
- Then during a small time interval $[t, t + dt]$ we have a premium of $P_x dt$ payable for those still alive.

- Of those alive at the time t, a proportion $\mu_{x+t}dt$ will die during the year and receive a benefit of $1.dt$ during the interval.
- Thus the *equation of value* for the build-up of assets is

$$F\left(x, t + dt\right) = \left(1 + \delta \cdot dt\right) F\left(x, t\right) + \frac{\ell(x+t)}{\ell(x)} P_x \cdot dt - \frac{\ell(x+t)}{\ell(x)} \mu_{x+t} dt.$$

Note that we do not have to include interest on premiums $\delta \cdot dt \frac{\ell(x+t)}{\ell(x)} P_x \cdot dt$, because this is of second-order dt^2.

- If we express the equation of value in terms of the assets per head of survivors at time t, that is $V(x, t) = F(x, t) \frac{\ell(x)}{\ell(x+t)}$, we getTake the limit as $dt \to 0$, and set

$$\frac{\partial V}{\partial t} = \lim_{dt \to 0} \frac{V\left(x, t + dt\right) - V\left(x, t\right)}{dt} :$$

- Then we get

$$\frac{\partial V}{\partial t} = \mu_{x+t}[V\left(x, t\right) - 1] + \delta V\left(x, t\right) + P_x.$$

- In a similar way, the quantity $1 - V(x, t)$ is known as the death strain at risk, in continuous time.

Thiele's equation is a differential equation that can be solved numerically over time. Thiele's equation may also be written as

$$\frac{\partial V}{\partial t} - \left(\mu_{x+t} + \delta\right) V\left(x, t\right) = -\mu_{x+t} + P_x.$$

This is an example of a linear differential equation that can be solved using an *integrating factor*:

- Multiply Thiele's equation by a function $M(t)$:

$$M \frac{\partial V}{\partial t} - \left(\mu_{x+t} + \delta\right) V\left(x, t\right) M = M\left(-\mu_{x+t} + P_x\right).$$

- We want to choose $M(t)$ so that

$$\frac{\partial M}{\partial t} = -\left(\mu_{x+t} + \delta\right) M$$

or

$$\frac{\partial \ln M}{\partial t} = -\left(\mu_{x+t} + \delta\right).$$

- Thus

$$\ln M = -\int_0^t \mu_{x+s}ds - \delta t,$$

and thus

$$\frac{\partial}{\partial t}(MV) = M(-\mu_{x+t} + P_x).$$

Integrating between t and ∞,

$$M(t)\,V(t) = -\int_t^\infty M(s)\,[-\mu_{x+s} + P_x]\,ds.$$

Exercise

Show that the solution of Thiele's equation in this case becomes simply

$$V(x, t) = \overline{A}_{x+t} - P_x \overline{a}_{x+t}.$$

10.11.1 Exercises

1. It was shown that the reserves $V(x, t)$ for a lifetime assurance in continuous time obeys Thiele's equation

$$\frac{\partial V}{\partial t} - (\mu_{x+t} + \delta)\,V(x, t) = -\mu_{x+t} + P_x$$

and that this may be solved using an integrating factor $M(t)$ that satisfies

$$\ln M = -\int_0^t \mu_{x+s}ds - \delta t$$

by means of

$$M(t)\,V(x, t) = -\int_t^\infty M(s)\,[\mu_{x+s} + P_x]\,ds$$

Show that this leads to the solution

$$V(x, t) = \overline{A}_{x+t} - P_x \overline{a}_{x+t}.$$

Solution
Since $\mu_{x+s} = -\frac{1}{\ell_{x+s}}\frac{d\ell_{x+s}}{ds} = -\frac{d\ln\ell_{x+s}}{ds}$, we have

$$\ln M = \int_0^t \frac{d \ln \ell_{x+s}}{ds} ds - \delta t$$

$$= \ln \frac{\ell_{x+t}}{\ell_x} - \delta t$$

so that

$$M(t) = \frac{\ell_{x+t}}{\ell_x} e^{-\delta t}.$$

This means that

$$\frac{\ell_{x+t}}{\ell_x} e^{-\delta t} V(x,t) = \int_t^\infty \frac{\ell_{x+s}}{\ell_x} e^{-\delta s} [\mu_{x+s} - P_x] ds$$

and so

$$V(x,t) = \int_t^\infty \frac{\ell_{x+s}}{\ell_{x+t}} e^{-\delta(s-t)} [\mu_{x+s} - P_x] ds$$

$$= \int_t^\infty e^{-\delta(s-t)} {}_{s-t}p_{x+t} \, ds - P_x \int_t^\infty \frac{\ell_{x+s}}{\ell_{x+t}} e^{-\delta(s-t)} ds$$

$$= \overline{A}_{x+t} - P_x \overline{a}_{x+t}.$$

2. [UK CT5 exam, Sept 2008] Write down an alternative expression for each of the following statements. Use notation as set out in the Appendix *International Actuarial Notation* where appropriate and express your answer as concisely as possible.

   a. **prob**$[\max(T_x, T_y) \le n]$
   b. **E**$[F(K_x)]$ where $F(K_x) = v^{K_x+1}$ for $K_x < n$ and 0 for $K_x \ge n$
   c. **prob**$[n < T_x \le m]$
   d. $\lim_{dt \to 0} \frac{\mathbf{prob}[\min(T_x, T_y) \le t + dt | T_x > t, T_y > t]}{dt}$
   e. **E**$\left[a_{\min(n-1, K_x)} + 1 \right].$

Solution

   a. Both lives must die before time n, and so ${}_n q_x \cdot {}_n q_y$.
   b. The benefit of 1 is payable only on death before time n, and so $A^1_{x:\overline{n}|}$.
   c. The life x must survive to time n and die before a further $m - n$ years, so ${}_n p_x \cdot {}_{m-n} q_{x+n}$.

d. Both lives having survived to time t, the failure rate of at least one life. Thus $\mu_{x+n,y+n}$.

e. The annuity has at most n payments whilst x is alive. Thus $\ddot{a}_{x:\overline{n}|}$.

3. [UK CT5 exam, Sept 2007] Calculate $_{t+1}V_x$ given the following:

   - $P_x = 0.017$
   - $_tV_x = 0.468$
   - $i = 0.03$
   - $q_{x+t} = 0.024$.

Solution

We have

$$_{t+1}V_x \cdot p_{x+t} + q_{x+t} = (1+i)\left(_tV_x + P_x\right).$$

Therefore

$$
\begin{aligned}
_{t+1}V_x &= \frac{(1+i)\left(_tV_x + P_x\right) - q_{x+t}}{p_{x+t}} \\
&= \frac{1.03\,(0.468 + 0.017) - 0.024}{1 - 0.024} \\
&= 0.487.
\end{aligned}
$$

4. [UK CT5, Apr 2009] The random variable T_{xy} represents the time to failure of the joint-life status xy. The life x is subject to a constant force of mortality of 0.02 and y is subject to a constant force of mortality of 0.03. Assume x and y are independent with respect to mortality. Calculate the value of $\mathbf{E}[T_{xy}]$.

Solution

We have the pdf of T_x as $0.02e^{-0.02t}$ and of T_y as $0.03e^{-0.03t}$. Thus the pdf of $T_{xy} = \min(T_x, T_y) = t$ is the probability that both lives survive to time t, followed by the mortality rate of x or y at that time. This is $e^{-0.02t}e^{-0.03t}(0.02 + 0.03) = 0.05e^{-0.05t}$.

Thus

$$\mathbf{E}[T_{xy}] = \int_0^\infty 0.05t e^{-0.05t}\,dt$$

$$= te^{-0.05t}\Big|_0^\infty - \int_0^\infty e^{-0.05t}dt$$

$$= 20.$$

5. [UK CT5 exam, Sept 2006] A pure endowment policy on lives aged x at commencement for a term of n years is payable by a single premium (i.e. the total premium is paid at commencement).

   a. Derive Thiele's differential equation for $V(t)$; the reserve for this policy at time t for $0 \le t \le n$.

   b. Explain the effect of each term in your answer in (a).

   c. State the boundary condition needed to solve the equation in (a).

Solution

In the time interval $[t, t + dt]$, the reserve at the start, when accumulated with interest, must be sufficient to pay claims as well as provide the reserve for the survivors at the end of the interval. [No premium is paid for $t > 0$.] Thus

$$V(t + dt)\left[1 - \mu_{x+t}dt\right] = (1 + \delta dt)\, V(t)$$

and so

$$\frac{V(t + dt) - V(t)}{dt} = \delta V(t) + \mu_{x+t} V(t + dt).$$

In the limit as $dt \to 0$ as then have

$$\frac{dV}{dt} = \delta V(t) + \mu_{x+t} V(t).$$

In words, this says that the rate of change in reserve must be financed by interest earnings on the reserve, and the release from deaths $\mu_{x+t} V(t)$. This is an ordinary differential equation that can be solved, with the boundary condition that $V(n) = 0$. The reserve at time 0 will give the single premium payable.

CHAPTER ELEVEN

Pricing in practice (CT5: §6, §7)

11.1. How an insurance company works

An insurer:
- sells policies
- collects premiums
- pays claims
- invests funds
- sets aside reserves
- distributes profits.

11.2. Practical issues

In practice, insurers have to allow for several other issues besides the theoretical value of benefits. These include:
- expenses incurred in running an insurance operation, covering:
  - solicitation of new business
  - administration
  - infrastructure of the business (IT, IP)
- allowance for risks incurred in practice, especially investment risks. This usually takes the form of
  - designing the contract to participate in the insurer's profitability
  - adding a contingency margin in pricing and reserving.

11.3. Types of expense

An insurer's expenses may be:
- *fixed* – not related to the volume of business, e.g.
  - IT systems
  - office buildings
- *variable* – related to business volume
  - commissions to agents for selling policies
  - underwriting
  - claims processing
  - investment

- the distinction is fuzzy, and is made only for the purpose of pricing to recoup costs.

11.4. Expense recovery

It is an economic principle that each insurance contract should be priced to recoup the costs associated with the contract:
- from the viewpoint of 'equity' between policyholders
- to avoid 'Ponzi' schemes.

Thus expenses are reflected in loadings to premiums, which may be:
- on a 'per policy basis', regardless of policy size
- in proportion to the amount insured
- in proportion to premium.

Those loadings are derived by way of an *expense analysis*, which seeks to match the amount of loadings with the way that expenses actually arise.

11.5. Premium assessment

Expense loadings, however they are determined, are usually valued in the same way as benefits: that is, allowing for the time that they arise. The general principle of equivalence is

Value of premiums = Value of benefits and Value of other costs.

Suppose that:
- Each contract incurs a fixed initial cost f as well as a cost e as a percentage of sum insured.
- Recurrent costs are h as a percentage of sum insured and g of annual premium.

Then the equation of value for a sum insured S is

$$\overline{P}_x \ddot{a}_x = (f + eS) + (1 + h) SA_x + g\overline{P}_x \ddot{a}_x$$

or

$$\overline{P}_x \ddot{a}_x = \frac{f}{1 - g} + \frac{e + (1 + h) A_x}{1 - g} S.$$

Here, $\overline{P}_x$ stands for the gross premium for the contract, that is the amount inclusive of expense loadings.

Question

How would you actually charge this premium $\overline{P}_x$, bearing in mind that it is not strictly proportional to S?

11.6. Bonus loadings

The other practical issue with insurance contracts is an allowance for profit sharing. This is another type of loading or margin in pricing, which the insurer rewards if the experience turns out to be good. The most common form of bonus loading works by assuming:

- in pricing that the amount insured increases at a compound rate of, say, b pa
- the actual increase will depend on the experience of all such contracts.

11.7. The with-profit gross premium

In the example above with expense loadings on a lifetime insurance, the only adjustment is to value the insurance with an exponentially increasing amount insured.

We found this in a previous lecture for increasing insurances $B(K_x) = (1+b)^{K_x}$, and showed the simple result

$$\mathbf{E}\left[v^{K_x+1}B(K_x)\right] = \frac{1}{1+b}A_x^j$$

where A_x^j is calculated at an interest rate j such that $1+j = \frac{1+i}{1+b}$.

The premium inclusive of all expense and profit loadings is therefore

$$\overline{P}_x \ddot{a}_x = \frac{f}{1-g} + \frac{e + \frac{1+h}{1+b}A_x^j}{1-g}S.$$

11.7.1 Exercises

[UK CT5 exam, Sept 2007] A life insurance company issues a 35-year endowment assurance contract to a life aged 30 exact. The sum assured of $200,000 is payable at maturity or at the end of the year of death if earlier. Level premiums are payable annually in advance for the duration of the contract.

Show that the annual premium is approximately $1,850, using the following basis:

Interest: 6% pa

Mortality: AMC00 Ultimate

Expenses: Initial: $300 plus 50% of the annual premium

Renewal: 2% of the second and subsequent annual premiums

Claim: $600 on death; $200 on maturity.

Write down the gross premium future loss random variable after 25 years, immediately before the premium then due is paid.

Calculate the retrospective policy reserve after 25 years, using the same basis as in (i), but with 4% pa interest.

Calculate the prospective reserve if the gross premium had been calculated at 4% pa interest, and comment.

Solution

Using the principle of equivalence, the gross annual premium $\overline{P}$ is given by

$$\overline{P}\ddot{a}_{30:\overline{35}|} = 300 + 0.48\overline{P} + 0.02\overline{P}\ddot{a}_{30:\overline{35}|} + 200,600A_{30:\overline{35}|} - 400v^{35}\frac{\ell_{65}}{\ell_{30}}$$

$$\overline{P} = \frac{1}{0.48 + 0.98\ddot{a}_{30:\overline{35}|}}\left[300 + 200,600A_{30:\overline{35}|} - 400v^{35}\frac{\ell_{65}}{\ell_{30}}\right]$$

$$= \frac{1}{0.48 + 0.98 \times 15.186}[300 + 200,600 \times 0.140 - 400 \times 0.119]$$

$$= \$1850.$$

If K_{55} denotes the curtate lifespan when the insured has reached age 55, then the future loss to the insurer is the value of benefits and expenses, less the value of gross premiums payable from that time if $K_{55} < 10$:

$$Loss = 200,600v^{K_{55}+1} + 0.02\overline{P}\ddot{a}_{\overline{K_x}|} - \overline{P}\ddot{a}_{\overline{K_x}|}.$$

And if $K_{55} \geq 10$,

$$Loss = 200,200v^{10} + 0.02\overline{P}\ddot{a}_{\overline{10}|} - \overline{P}\ddot{a}_{\overline{10}|}.$$

If the insurer decides to change the interest basis to 4% pa when the insured is aged 55 the retrospective reserve $_{25}\overline{V}_{55:\overline{10}|}$ is that which would have accumulated if interest had always been 4% pa, but with the gross premium $\overline{P}$ calculated at 6% pa paid. This would be the same as the prospective reserve if the premium had been originally calculated on 4% pa interest. The present value of this reserve must be equal to the present value of premiums less benefits and expenses payable over the 25 years:

$$_{25}\overline{V}_{55:\overline{10}|} \cdot v^{25}\frac{\ell_{55}}{\ell_{30}} = \overline{P}\ddot{a}_{30:\overline{25}|} - 300 - 0.48\overline{P} - 0.02\overline{P}\ddot{a}_{30:\overline{25}|}$$

$$- 200,600A^1_{30:\overline{25}|}$$

$$0.364 \times_{25}\overline{V}_{55:\overline{10}|} = 1850 \times (0.98 \times 16.120 - 0.48) - 300 - 200,600$$

$$\times (0.380 - 0.364),$$

and thus

$$_{25}\overline{V}_{55:\overline{10}|} = \$75,145.$$

If the premium had been assessed at 4% pa, it would have been

$$\overline{P} = \frac{1}{0.48 + 0.98 \times 19.123}[300 + 200,600 \times 0.264 - 400 \times 0.231]$$

$$= \$2,768.$$

The reserve would thus be

$$_{25}\overline{V}_{55:\overline{10}|} = 200,600A_{55:\overline{10}|} + 0.02\overline{P}\ddot{a}_{55:\overline{10}|} - \overline{P}\ddot{a}_{55:\overline{10}|} - 400v^{10}\frac{\ell_{65}}{\ell_{55}}$$

$$= 200,600 \times 0.624 - 0.98 \times 9.788 \times 2768 - 400 \times 0.636$$

$$= \$98,277.$$

This is higher than the retrospective reserve, as the gross premium calculated at 4% pa is higher than that calculated at 6% pa.

CHAPTER TWELVE

Multiple decrement models (CT5: §10.2, §13)

So far, you have been given the theory behind valuation of benefits for the purposes of pricing and reserving.

But even though we have allowed for practical issues like expenses and profit margins, we have not modelled the reality of an insurance company perfectly.

Why not? Because in reality:

- Insurance contracts may not run for their full term—they can be surrendered voluntarily by the insured, in which event a *surrender value* is payable. This itself is also part of the contract.
- The insurer has to maintain reserves, over which there may be investment restrictions.

12.1. Multiple decrement tables

To be more realistic, we need to allow for means of exit *other* than death. This is where *multiple decrement* tables become useful. A multiple decrement table is similar to a life table but allows exit from the population in several ways:

- $a\ell_x$ is used to denote the population at age x.
- ad_x^k is used to denote exits (decrements) through cause k for those aged x.
- Thus

$$a\ell_{x+1} = a\ell_x - \sum_k ad_x^k.$$

- The rate $aq_x^k = \frac{ad_x^k}{a\ell_x}$ is called the *dependent* rate for decrement k.
- It is dependent because it is measured with the presence of other decrements operating.

12.2. Dependent and independent rates of decrement

Suppose we have two decrements for a life contract: death and withdrawal (surrender).

- At a given age x, suppose that q_x^d is the death rate in the absence of withdrawals,
- and q_x^w is the withdrawal rate in the absence of deaths.
- These are *independent* rates.

What are the dependent rates aq_x^d and aq_x^w associated with the independent ones? Consider a population of 1 at age x:

- Without withdrawals, there would be q_x^d deaths during the year.
- Suppose deaths occur uniformly over the year.
- The average population during the year is therefore $1 - \frac{1}{2}q_x^d$.
- The number of withdrawals is therefore approximately $q_x^w\left(1 - \frac{1}{2}q_x^d\right)$,
- so $aq_x^w \simeq q_x^w\left(1 - \frac{1}{2}q_x^d\right)$.
- Similarly, $aq_x^d \simeq q_x^d\left(1 - \frac{1}{2}q_x^w\right)$ if withdrawals occur uniformly.

We can easily extend this approximation to more than two decrements:

$$aq_x^k \simeq q_x^k\left(1 - \frac{1}{2}q_x^{-k}\right)$$

where q_x^{-k} denotes the sum of q_x^i other than for $i = k$.

However, it is only an approximation! Here is a more exact approach. In continuous time:

- Let μ_x^k be the instantaneous rate of decrement k at exact age x.
- Let $\ell^k(x+t)$ be the single table for decrement k, with $\ell^k(x) = 1$.
- Uniform distribution of decrements between ages $[x, x+1]$ means that for $0 \leq t \leq 1$:

$$\ell^k(x+t) = 1 - tq_x^k.$$

- Hence the instantaneous rates of decrement are

$$\mu^k(x+t) = -\frac{1}{\ell^k}\frac{d\ell^k}{dt} = \frac{q_x^k}{1 - tq_x^k}.$$

So that the differential equation for $al(x+t)$ should satisfy

$$-\frac{1}{al(x+t)}\frac{d}{dt}al(x+t) = \sum_k \mu^k(x+t) = \sum_k \frac{q_x^k}{1 - tq_x^k}.$$

- Hence in the multiple decrement table $al(x+t)$, we have

$$al(x+t) = \prod_k \ell^k(x+t)$$

$$= \prod_k \left(1 - tq_x^k\right).$$

- We thus have

$$aq_x^k = \int_0^1 a\ell\,(x+t) \cdot \mu^k\,(x+t)\,dt$$

$$= q_x^k \int_0^1 \prod_{i \neq k} \left(1 - tq_x^i\right) dt.$$

This is a more exact approximation for dependent decrement rates. For example, with three decrements, $k = 1, 2, 3$, we have

$$aq_x^1 = q_x^1 \int_0^1 \left(1 - tq_x^2\right)\left(1 - tq_x^3\right) dt$$

$$= q_x^1 \left[1 - \frac{1}{2}\left(q_x^2 + q_x^3\right) + \frac{q_x^2 q_x^3}{3}\right].$$

12.2.1 Exercises

1. [UK CT5 exam, Sept 2008] A certain population is subject to three modes of decrement: α, β and γ.
   a. Write down an expression for aq_x^α in terms of the single decrement table probabilities q_x^α, q_x^β and q_x^γ, assuming each of the three modes of decrement is uniformly distributed over the year of age x to $x+1$ in the corresponding single decrement table.
   b. Suppose now that in the single decrement table $_tp_x^\alpha = 1 - t^2 q_x^\alpha$ for $0 \leq t \leq 1$, while decrements β and γ remain uniformly distributed. Derive a revised expression for aq_x^α in terms of the single decrement table probabilities q_x^α, q_x^β and q_x^γ.

Solution

The formula for aq_x^α derived in lectures, for a uniform distribution of decrements, is

$$aq_x^\alpha = q_x^\alpha \left[1 - \frac{1}{2}\left(q_x^\beta + q_x^\gamma\right) + \frac{1}{3}q_x^\beta q_x^\gamma\right].$$

If, however, $_tp_x^\alpha = 1 - t^2 q_x^\alpha$, then $a\ell\,(x+t) = \left(1 - t^2 q_x^\alpha\right)\left(1 - tq_x^\beta\right)\left(1 - tq_x^\gamma\right)$. Also $\mu_{x+t}^\alpha = \frac{2tq_x^\alpha}{1 - t^2 q_x^\alpha}$. Thus

$$aq_x^\alpha = \int_0^1 \mu_{x+t}^\alpha \, a\ell\,(x+t)\,dt$$

$$= \int_0^1 2t q_x^\alpha \left(1 - t q_x^\beta\right)\left(1 - t q_x^\gamma\right) dt$$

$$= q_x^\alpha \left[1 - \frac{2}{3}\left(q_x^\beta + q_x^\gamma\right) + \frac{1}{2} q_x^\beta q_x^\gamma\right].$$

2. **[UK CT5 exam, Apr 2009]** A life insurance company issues a 3-year savings contract to unmarried male lives that offers the following benefits:

- On death during the 3 years a sum of $15,000 payable immediately on death.
- On surrender during the 3 years a return of premiums paid, payable immediately on surrender.
- On marriage during the 3 years a return of premiums paid accumulated with compound interest at 4% per annum, payable immediately on marriage.
- On survival to the end of the 3 years a sum of $5000.

The contract ceases on payment of any benefit.

Calculate the level premium payable annually in advance for this contract for a life aged 40 exact.

Basis:

- independent rates of mortality $q_{40}^d = 0.937$, $q_{41}^d = 1.014$, $q_{42}^d = 1.104$ per mille
- independent rate of surrender $q_x^w = 0.1$ per annum
- independent rate of marriage $q_x^m = 0.05$ per annum
- interest 5% per annum
- expenses 0.5% of each premium.

Solution

Denote the independent decrements on death, surrender and marriage as q_x^d, $q_x^w = 0.1$ and $q_x^m = 0.05$. Then the dependent decrements under the assumption of uniform deaths can be calculated as

$$aq_x^d = q_x^d \left[1 - \frac{1}{2}\left(q_x^w + q_x^m\right) + \frac{1}{3} q_x^w q_x^m\right]$$

and similarly for aq_x^w, aq_x^m. This gives the dependent rates:

age x	q_x^d	q_x^w	q_x^m	aq_x^d	aq_x^w	aq_x^m
40	0.000937	0.1	0.05	0.000868	0.097455	0.047478
41	0.001014	0.1	0.05	0.00094	0.097451	0.047476
42	0.001104	0.1	0.05	0.001023	0.097447	0.047474

and the multiple decrement table:

age x	$a\ell$	ad_x^d	ad_x^w	ad_x^m
40	1.000000	0.000868	0.097455	0.047478
41	0.854199	0.000803	0.083243	0.040554
42	0.729599	0.000746	0.071097	0.034637
43	0.623119			

Hence we can calculate benefit values as follows:

t	$a\ell$	d	w	m	v
0	1.0000	0.0009	0.0975	0.0484	1.0000
1	0.8542	0.0008	0.1665	0.0844	0.9524
2	0.7296	0.0007	0.2133	0.1103	0.9070
PV	2.4753	0.0023	0.4386	0.2233	

Take $a\ell_{40} = 1$ and $a\ell_x = a\ell_{x-1} - ad_x^d - ad_x^w - ad_x^m$. The level premium $\overline{P}$ satisfies the equation of value:

$$0.995\overline{P}\sum_{t=0}^{2} v^t \cdot a\ell_{40+t}$$

$$= \sum_{t=0}^{2} v^{t+\frac{1}{2}}\left[15000 ad_{40+t}^d + \overline{P}(t+1)\, ad_{40+t}^w + \overline{P}\ddot{s}_{\overline{t}|}ad_{40+t}^m\right]$$

$$+ 5000v^3 \cdot a\ell_{43}.$$

Hence

$$\overline{P} = \frac{5000v^3 \cdot a\ell_{43} + 15000 \sum_{t=0}^{2} v^{t+\frac{1}{2}} ad_{40+t}^d}{\sum_{t=0}^{2}\left[0.995 v^t \cdot a\ell_{40+t} - (t+1)\, ad_{40+t}^w - \ddot{s}_{\overline{t+1}|}ad_{40+t}^m\right]}$$

$$= \frac{2691 + 34}{2.475 - 0.439 - 0.223}$$

$$= \$1513.$$

CHAPTER THIRTEEN

Defined benefit superannuation (CT5: §14)

One of the most important applications of multiple decrement models is to employee benefit schemes, which provide different types of benefit, depending on the cause of exit.

The best example of this is the *defined benefit* superannuation fund, typically a fund:

- established by an employer for the benefit of employees and their dependants
- with a set of benefit rules that spell out how much and what type of benefit is payable on
  - retirement (say, from age 55 on)
  - resignation (withdrawal)
  - death
  - permanent disability
  - temporary disability
- with benefits that are usually related to an employee's current salary
- and with contributions from both employees and the employer
- administered by a separate *trustee.*

13.1. Trusts

A trust is a legal structure (not a company) that is used in the English-speaking world for retirement benefits (though there are counterparts in Europe – the *Treuhandanstalt*).

It has the following features:

- It is subject to *trust law* that has developed since the crusades.
- It is managed by a *trustee,* which is a board of people, or a company.
- There is a *trust deed* that describes the rights, entitlements and obligations of *beneficiaries* in the trust, as well as the obligations of the trustee.
- Under trust law, the trustee must administer the trust deed for the sole benefit of beneficiaries.

13.2. Defined benefits

For such funds, the important questions are:
- How much in assets should the fund have to support benefits relating to service completed?
- What contributions should be payable in future to support benefits?

The multiple decrement model is perfect for describing the various causes of benefit payment.

But how should salary increases be modelled?

13.3. The salary scale

Salary increases can be of two types:
- from general wage inflation (e.g. AWOTE – Average Weekly Ordinary Time Earnings)
- from promotional or seniority.

It is neatest to model such increases by taking a salary scale s_x, being the notional salary of an employee aged x. The ratio $\frac{s_{x+t}}{s_x}$ is the salary increase within a period of t years.

13.4. Benefit rules

The rules specifying benefits can vary enormously. They can differ in:
- whether benefits are lump sums or pensions
- how closely they are related to current salary
- how they increase with increasing service
- how they depend on the age at commencement of service.

13.5. An example of defined benefits

Here is one of the simplest examples of a set of benefit rules.

Example 13.1.

Cause of exit	*Benefit payable*
retirement or resignation	*20% of current salary for each year of service at exit*
death or disability	*20% of current salary for each potential year of service at age 60*

How do we model such benefits? As there are just two causes of exit, we need two decrements, denoted r (retirement/resignation) and d (death/disability).

For a given employee currently aged x, let:

- PS be the number of (fractional) years of service completed
- S be the employee's current salary.

Then $60 - x$ is the number of potential years of service to age 60 if $x < 60$.

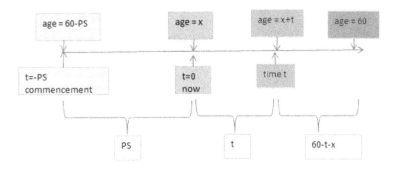

We also have the following benefits:

- If retirement/resignation occurs at time t years, hence the benefit payable is

$$0.2\,(PS + t)\,\frac{s_{x+t}}{s_x}\,S.$$

- If death/disability occurs t years, hence the benefit payable is

$$0.2\,(PS + 60 - x)\,\frac{s_{x+t}}{s_x}\,S$$

if $x < 60$.

- Otherwise it is the same as the retirement/resignation benefit.

We can value these benefits using a multiple decrement table $a\ell_x$.

13.6. Accrued defined benefits

However, this would give the value of all benefits, including those for service in future. For assessing what assets we should have now, we need to specify what amount of any benefit, payable at some future time t, is attributable to service completed *as of now*. These are called *accrued benefits*:

- The process used is called *attribution* under the accounting standards.
- For retirement/resignation benefits, it is clear that the accrued benefit should be based on 20% of *PS* but calculated on future salary.
- For death/disability benefits, which are a constant multiple of salary throughout an employee's service, it is not so clear.
- For death/disability benefits, we can take for simplicity the retirement benefit that would be accrued when death occurs, at time *t* in the future.
- However, there is a more complicated way of attributing death/disability benefits. If this occurs at time *t*, when service is $PS + t$, take the ratio

$$0.2\,(PS + 60 - x)\,\frac{PS}{PS + t}.$$

To comply with convention, we will use the latter method for death/disability benefits.

What we need is the value of benefits for service completed *up to now*. These benefits are:

- if retirement/resignation occurs at time *t* years, hence the *accrued* benefit payable is

$$0.2PS\frac{s_{x+t}}{s_x}S.$$

- If death/disability occurs *t* years, hence the *accrued* benefit payable is

$$0.2\,(PS + 60 - x)\,\frac{PS}{PS + t}\,\frac{s_{x+t}}{s_x}\,S$$

if $x < 60$. Otherwise it is the same as the retirement/resignation benefit.

13.7. The value of accrued defined benefits

Using the multiple decrement table $a\ell_x$:

- The value of accrued retirement/resignation benefits is

$$\sum_{t=0}^{\infty} v^{t+\frac{1}{2}}\frac{ad^r_{x+t}}{a\ell_x} \cdot 0.2PS\frac{s_{x+t+\frac{1}{2}}}{s_x}S.$$

- The value of accrued death/disability benefits is

$$\sum_{t=0}^{\infty} v^{t+\frac{1}{2}}\frac{ad^d_{x+t}}{a\ell_x} \cdot 0.2\,(PS + 60 - x)\,\frac{PS}{PS + t + \frac{1}{2}}\,\frac{s_{x+t+\frac{1}{2}}}{s_x}S.$$

Note that where a decrement occurs in year t, it is assumed to occur on average at exact time $t + \frac{1}{2}$.

The total value of accrued benefits can be compared with the current asset value of assets to see whether the fund has sufficient assets to support accrued benefits.

13.8. Future contributions

Suppose that the current asset value is *exactly* equal to the value of accrued benefits. What contribution should be paid in future, to support benefit accruing for future service? The benefits accruing for potential future service are:

- If retirement/resignation occurs in year t, hence the *future service* benefit payable is

$$0.2 \left(t + \frac{1}{2} \right) \frac{s_{x+t}}{s_x} S.$$

- If death/disability occurs in year t, hence the *future service* benefit payable is

$$0.2 \left(PS + 60 - x \right) \frac{t + \frac{1}{2}}{PS + t + \frac{1}{2}} \frac{s_{x+t}}{s_x} S.$$

13.9. Value of future service benefits

In a similar way, the future service benefits can be valued:

- The value of future service retirement/resignation benefits is

$$\sum_{t=0}^{\infty} v^{t+\frac{1}{2}} \frac{ad^r_{x+t}}{a\ell_x} \cdot 0.2 \left(t + \frac{1}{2} \right) \frac{s_{x+t+\frac{1}{2}}}{s_x} S.$$

- The value of future service death/disability benefits is

$$\sum_{t=0}^{\infty} v^{t+\frac{1}{2}} \frac{ad^d_{x+t}}{a\ell_x} \cdot 0.2 \left(PS + 60 - x \right) \frac{t + \frac{1}{2}}{PS + t + \frac{1}{2}} \frac{s_{x+t+\frac{1}{2}}}{s_x} S.$$

13.10. Future contributions

To assess a future contribution, we assume it is payable as a constant percentage of salary. The value of future salary payable is

$$\sum_{t=0}^{\infty} v^{t+\frac{1}{2}} \frac{a\ell_{x+t+\frac{1}{2}}}{a\ell_x} \cdot \frac{s_{x+t+\frac{1}{2}}}{s_x} S.$$

Hence the appropriate contribution *rate c* is

$$c = \frac{\text{Value of future service benefits on retirement or death/disability}}{\text{Value of future salaries}}$$

$$= \frac{\sum\limits_{t=0}^{\infty} v^{t+\frac{1}{2}} \frac{ad^r_{x+t}}{a\ell_x} \cdot 0.2\left(t+\frac{1}{2}\right) \frac{s_{x+t+\frac{1}{2}}}{s_x} S + \sum\limits_{t=0}^{\infty} v^{t+\frac{1}{2}} \frac{ad^d_{x+t}}{a\ell_x} \cdot 0.2\,(PS+60-x) \frac{t+\frac{1}{2}}{PS+t+\frac{1}{2}} \frac{s_{x+t+\frac{1}{2}}}{s_x} S}{\sum\limits_{t=0}^{\infty} v^{t+\frac{1}{2}} \frac{a\ell_{x+t+\frac{1}{2}}}{a\ell_x} \cdot \frac{s_{x+t+\frac{1}{2}}}{s_x} S}$$

This formula looks horrendous, but it is easily calculated on a spreadsheet.

13.11. A more complex defined benefit fund

The previous example was simple in that there were only two decrements, and benefits were related simply to current salary. Here is a more complex, but more common, example. In this case, benefits are related to Final Average Salary (*FAS*), being defined as the average of the salaries paid in the 3 years before exit from service.

Here are the benefits:

Cause of exit	Value of benefits
retirement *r*	15% of FAS for each year of service at exit
resignation *w*	Accumulation of contributions of 10% of salary
death *d*	15% of FAS for each *potential* year of service at age 60
disability *i*	a lifetime pension of 60% of FAS

The 'accumulation' of contributions in the resignation benefit is at an interest rate equal to the valuation rate i (not to be confused with the disability decrement i).

13.12. Final average salary

Since benefits are related to FAS, it is convenient to introduce a special symbol for this quantity:

$$z_x = \frac{s_{x-1} + s_{x-2} + s_{x-3}}{3}.$$

13.13. Accrued benefits

Just like in the previous example, the value of accrued benefits is easily assessed:

Cause of exit	Value of accrued benefits
retirement	$\sum_{t=0}^{\infty} v^{t+\frac{1}{2}} \frac{ad^r_{x+t}}{a\ell_x} \cdot 0.15 PS \frac{z_{x+t+\frac{1}{2}}}{s_x} S$
resignation	$\sum_{t=0}^{\infty} \frac{ad^w_{x+t}}{a\ell_x} \cdot AC$
death	$\sum_{t=0}^{\infty} v^{t+\frac{1}{2}} \frac{ad^d_{x+t}}{a\ell_x} \cdot 0.15 \, (PS + 60 - x) \frac{PS}{PS+t+\frac{1}{2}} \frac{z_{x+t+\frac{1}{2}}}{s_x} S$
disability	$\sum_{t=0}^{\infty} v^{t+\frac{1}{2}} \frac{ad^i_{x+t}}{a\ell_x} \cdot 0.60 \bar{a}_{x+t+\frac{1}{2}} \frac{PS}{PS+t+\frac{1}{2}} \frac{z_{x+t+\frac{1}{2}}}{s_x} S$

13.14. Value of accrued benefits

Some comments about the benefit valuation formulas:

- The retirement and death benefits are the same (apart from using FAS) as in the previous example.
- In the resignation benefit, we use AC to denote the members accumulated 10% contributions. This has to be supplied as data! Why does the interest discount $v^{t+\frac{1}{2}}$ not appear in the value of the accrued resignation benefit?
- The disability pension value $\bar{a}_{x+t+\frac{1}{2}}$ has to be calculated on a single decrement table. In general, the mortality of pensioners is different from that of active employees. [Why?]
- The total benefit on disability is $0.60\bar{a}_{x+t+\frac{1}{2}}$ a proportion of current FAS. We pro-rate this by $\frac{PS}{PS+t+\frac{1}{2}}$, i.e. service at the time of disability to total service at age 60.

13.15. Value of future service benefits

Benefits for future service can be similarly valued:

Cause of exit	Value of future service benefits
retirement	$\sum_{t=0}^{\infty} v^{t+\frac{1}{2}} \frac{ad^r_{x+t}}{a\ell_x} \cdot 0.15 \left(t+\frac{1}{2}\right) \frac{z_{x+t+\frac{1}{2}}}{s_x} S$
resignation	$\sum_{t=0}^{\infty} v^{t+\frac{1}{2}} \frac{ad^w_{x+t}}{a\ell_x} \cdot 0.10 \cdot FC_{x:t} \cdot S$
death	$\sum_{t=0}^{\infty} v^{t+\frac{1}{2}} \frac{ad^d_{x+t}}{a\ell_x} \cdot 0.15 \left(PS + 60 - x\right) \frac{t+\frac{1}{2}}{PS+t+\frac{1}{2}} \frac{z_{x+t+\frac{1}{2}}}{s_x} S$
disability	$\sum_{t=0}^{\infty} v^{t+\frac{1}{2}} \frac{ad^i_{x+t}}{a\ell_x} \cdot 0.60 \bar{a}_{x+t+\frac{1}{2}} \frac{t+\frac{1}{2}}{PS+t+\frac{1}{2}} \frac{z_{x+t+\frac{1}{2}}}{s_x} S$

Here, the only thing complicated is the value of future contributions:

$$FC_{x:t} = \sum_{u=0}^{t-1} \frac{s_{x+u+\frac{1}{2}}}{s_x} (1+i)^{t-u} + \frac{1}{2} \frac{s_{x+t+\frac{1}{2}}}{s_x}.$$

This does not involve decrements. [Why not?]

13.15.1 Exercises

[UK CT5 exam, Apr 2008] A defined benefit pension scheme provides a pension, payable continuously, on exit for any reason of $\frac{1}{60}$ of FAS for each year of service (with proportion for fractional years of service). FAS is average salary over the 3 years immediately preceding retirement.

Provide a formula for the cost of providing *future service* benefits for a new member aged 40 exact as a constant percentage of salary, in terms of the decrement table $a\ell_x$ and the salary scale s_x.

Solution

The value of the benefit payable, in respect of future service, for exit at time $t+\frac{1}{2}$ is $\frac{t+\frac{1}{2}}{60} \bar{a}_{x+t+\frac{1}{2}} S \frac{z_{x+t+\frac{1}{2}}}{s_x}$. The amount of salary payable in year t is $S \frac{s_{x+t+\frac{1}{2}}}{s_x}$. Hence the contribution rate c for future service benefits is

$$c = \frac{\text{Value of future benefits}}{\text{Value of future salary}}$$

$$= \frac{\sum_{t=0}^{\infty} v^{t+\frac{1}{2}} \frac{t+\frac{1}{2}}{60} \bar{a}_{x+t+\frac{1}{2}} \frac{z_{x+t+\frac{1}{2}}}{s_x} \frac{ad_{40+t}}{a\ell_{40}}}{\sum_{t=0}^{\infty} v^{t+\frac{1}{2}} \frac{s_{x+t+\frac{1}{2}}}{s_x} \frac{a\ell_{40+t+\frac{1}{2}}}{a\ell_{40}}}.$$

CHAPTER FOURTEEN

Life insurance modelling (CT5: §10; §11)

14.1. Profit testing

Another important application of multiple decrement models is in *profit testing*:

- We have established a theoretical basis for pricing and reserving an insurance contract.
- We now have come up with another, more realistic basis for what will happen, allowing for
  - payment of expenses
  - setting aside reserves
  - withdrawals from the contract.
- How profitable will the contract be?

14.2. A model of an insurer

Suppose for a lifetime insurance contract of amount S on a life x:

- Gross premiums have been set at rate $\overline{P}$.
- Initial expenses are at rate e of the gross premium.
- Renewal expenses are at rate f of the gross premium.
- Reserves at time t are required to be held on a net premium basis of $S \cdot {}_t V_x = S \left(1 - \frac{\ddot{a}_{x+t}}{\ddot{a}_x}\right)$ on some agreed basis.
- Realistic decrements of aq_x^d and aq_x^w for death and withdrawal are expected.
- On withdrawal a benefit is payable equal to the amounts of gross premium paid (without interest), at the end of the year of withdrawal.
- At time t, we have a surviving sum insured of $S_t = \frac{a\ell_{x+t}}{a\ell_x}$.

14.3. The profit vector

We can model the operation of the contract in terms of the insurer's cash flows, for a unit of sum insured for each year, as follows:

Year:	1	2	...	t
Transfer in	0	$_1V_x$	...	$_{t-1}V_x$
Premium	$\overline{P}$	$\overline{P}$	...	$\overline{P}$
Expenses	$-e\overline{P}$	$-f\overline{P}$	...	$-f\overline{P}$
Withdrawal	$-aq_x^w\overline{P}$	$-aq_{x+1}^w\left(2\overline{P}\right)$	...	$-aq_{x+t-1}^w\left(t\overline{P}\right)$
Death	$-aq_x^d$	$-aq_{x+1}^d$	...	$-aq_{x+t-1}^d$
Interest	$i\left[\overline{P}(1-e)\right]$	$i\left[_1V_x+\overline{P}\left(1-f\right)\right]$	...	$i\left[_{t-1}V_x+\overline{P}\left(1-f\right)\right]$
Transfer out	$-_1V_x\cdot\frac{a\ell_{x+1}}{a\ell_x}$	$-_2V_x\cdot\frac{a\ell_{x+2}}{a\ell_{x+1}}$	...	$-_tV_x\cdot\frac{a\ell_{x+t}}{a\ell_{x+t-1}}$
Profit	sum of above	sum of above	...	sum of above

14.4. The profit signature

Alternatively, we can allow for the reduction of policies through time, by taking the *depleted* sum insured $S_t=\frac{a\ell_{x+t}}{a\ell_x}$.

Year:	1	2	...	t
Transfer in	0	$S_1\cdot{}_1V_x$	...	$S_{t-1}\cdot{}_{t-1}V_x$
Premium	$S\overline{P}$	$S_1\overline{P}$	...	$S_{t-1}\overline{P}$
Expenses	$-eS\overline{P}$	$-fS_1\overline{P}$	...	$-fS_{t-1}\overline{P}$
Withdrawal	$-aq_x^w\left(S\overline{P}\right)$	$-aq_{x+1}^w\left(2S_1\overline{P}\right)$	...	$-aq_{x+t-1}^w\left(tS_{t-1}\overline{P}\right)$
Death	$-aq_x^d S$	$-aq_{x+1}^d S_1$	...	$-aq_{x+t-1}^d S_{t-1}$
Interest	$i\left[\overline{P}(1-e)\right]S$	$i\left[_1V_x+\overline{P}\left(1-f\right)\right]S_1$	...	$i\left[_{t-1}V_x+\overline{P}\left(1-f\right)\right]S_{t-1}$
Transfer out	$-S_1\cdot{}_1V_x$	$-S_2\cdot{}_2V_x$	...	$-S_t\cdot{}_tV_x$
Profit	sum of above	sum of above	...	sum of above

CHAPTER FIFTEEN

Profit signature

The series of expected profits on a single policy, allowing for decrements over the years, is called the *profit signature*. It is important to note that it depends on four main things:

- the design of the contract (benefits and relevant decrements)
- the basis used for pricing
- the basis used for reserving
- the actual experience assumed.

15.1. Profit signature

Why is the profit signature important? It allows insurers to:

- assess the emergence of profit on particular contracts
- compare profitability between different types of contract
- assess whether capital (in the form of reserves) is used efficiently
- assess premiums in a realistic way to allow a given level of profitability.

Here are some typical measures of profitability on a contract, where PS_t is the profit signature:

- the NPV of profits at a risk adjusted discount rate r:

$$NPV = \sum_{t=1}^{\infty} \frac{PS_t}{(1+r)^t}$$

- the ratio of NPV to the NPV of expected premium income $\overline{P} \sum_{t=0}^{\infty} \frac{a\ell_{x+t}}{a\ell_x} \frac{1}{(1+r)^t}$ at the same discount rate
- the *IRR* of the PS_t, which is known as the *return on transfers*. This is an indication of how fast the business can grow.

15.2. The return on transfers

Suppose the number of policies grows at rate g. Then the profits can be projected with the growth of policies as follows:

Profit signature	1	2	3	$\ldots$	t
1	PS_1	PS_2	PS_3	$\ldots$	PS_t
2		$(1+g)\,PS_1$	$(1+g)\,PS_2$	$\ldots$	$(1+g)\,PS_{t-1}$
3			$(1+g)^2\,PS_1$	$\ldots$	$(1+g)^2\,PS_{t-2}$
3					$(1+g)^3\,PS_{t-3}$
$\vdots$					$\vdots$
n					$(1+g)^n\,PS_{t-n}$

Thus as t becomes very large, the total profit in that year is zero (and so the business is self sustaining) when

$$PS_t + (1+g)\,PS_{t-1} + (1+g)^2\,PS_{t-2} + \ldots + (1+g)^{t-1}\,PS_1 = 0$$

or equivalently,

$$PS_1 + \frac{PS_2}{1+g} + \frac{PS_3}{(1+g)^2} + \ldots + \frac{PS_t}{(1+g)^{t-1}} = 0.$$

This is exactly the definition of an *IRR*!

15.3. Unit linked insurances

The insurances discussed so far in this unit have been traditional—the benefits are expressed in nominal terms. Once declared, benefits are guaranteed.

- This has obvious advantages for the insured.
- However, the disadvantage is that the insured does not fully enjoy the upside of the investment return on the underlying assets.
- If the insurance is without profit, then the insured does not enjoy it all.
- Even for with profit insurances, the insurer can be conservative in releasing the investment surplus.

A way around this is for most of the premium to be invested in a fund that is *unitised*, i.e. the value of the investment fluctuates with the market value of the underlying assets. The balance of the premium is then used to pay for insurance.

Here's how it often works in Australia:

- Premiums are either allocated to the unit fund or are paid as unallocated to a cash (i.e. nonunit) fund.
- The cash fund also enjoys payment of asset based and unit transaction fees.

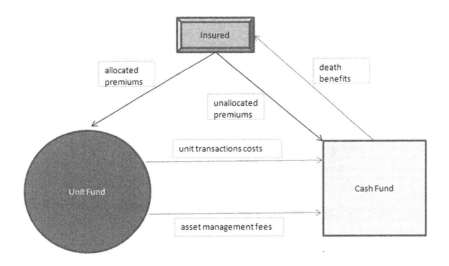

- In turn, it has to pay the death benefits agreed on the policy, which may take the form of a guaranteed minimum benefit (after allowing for the value of units in the unit fund).

The unallocated premium (that is not invested in the unit fund) can be made equal to the cost of death benefits for that year. In this way, all the insurer is providing is a 1-year temporary insurance, and there is no need to set up reserves. However, there is no reason why the unallocated premiums should be equal to the cost of providing 1 year's insurance cover. Unallocated premiums can be made higher later on during the term of the policy. This is common in the UK.

How can profit testing deal with this type of insurance?

- The policy contract will specify how much of any premium $\overline{P}$ will be allocated to the unit fund during year t of the policy. Suppose this is a proportion α_t.
- Suppose also the value of units in the unit fund can be modelled, and at time t, they are worth U_t (this is an investment modelling exercise, not part of this subject).
- Suppose asset management fees are a percentage κ of the unit value at the end of each year.
- And unit transaction base costs are λ of allocated premiums.
- The cash fund's administration costs are e per contract.
- Suppose that the guaranteed minimum benefit on death is S.

15.4. Testing unit linked insurances

Then profit testing during year t can be undertaken as follows:

Year:	t
Unallocated premium	$(1 - \alpha_t)\overline{P}$
Transaction costs	$\lambda \alpha_t \overline{P}$
Asset based fees	κU_{t+1}
Expense	$-e$
Death	$-a q_x^d (S - U_{t+1})$
Interest	$i\left[(1 - \alpha_t) P + \lambda \alpha_t \overline{P} - e\right]$
Profit	sum of above

15.5. Reserves under profit testing

Profit vectors for unit-linked contracts can be used for determining reserves in the cash fund. These reserves may be needed to support upfront expenses, as well as over-allocations of premium to the unit fund.

- Suppose the profit vector is written as C_t from the profit testing conducted previously.
- This can be converted into a profit signature $PS_t = \frac{\ell_{x+t-1}}{\ell_x} C_t$.
- Then it is typical for $PS_t < 0$ in the early years of the contract.
- And $PS_t > 0$ in the later years, when assets and asset fees build up (and death benefit payments decline).
- However, it is not prudent to assume that later profits will be realised, as the insured may simply decide to withdraw!

15.6. Zeroisation

Here is a procedure, called *zeroisation*, that provides a conservative approach to establishing reserves. The idea is to make an adjustment ΔPS_t to the profits so that the present value of profits is unchanged:

$$\sum_{t=1}^{\infty} v^t \Delta PS_t = 0.$$

- The adjusted profits $PS_t + \Delta PS_t \geq 0$, except possible for $t = 1$.
- The adjustments ΔPS_t are as small in magnitude as possible, and represent (if negative) an injection of reserves to support negative cash flows in future years.

For a particular year $t = m$, where $PS_m < 0$, and all future profits are positive, this can be achieved by taking

$$\Delta PS_m = -PS_m \text{ and } \Delta PS_{m-1} = -v\Delta PS_m.$$

This can be extended to years earlier than m, and is best illustrated by example.

Example 15.1. *Take the profit signature* $PS_t = (-375.4, 100, -136.2, 118.0)$ *with interest at 5.5% pa.*

t	PS_t	ΔPS_m	$PS_t + \Delta PS_t$	ΔPS_m	$PS_t + \Delta PS_t$	ΔPS_m
0						**−382.0**
1	−375.4		−375.4	**−27.6**	−403.0	403.0
2	100.0	**−129.1**	−29.1	29.1	0.0	
3	−136.2	136.2	0.0		0.0	
4	118.0		118.0		118.0	

The required reserves are (the negative) of the bolded figures.

15.6.1 Exercises

1. [UK CT5 exam, Sept 2008] The profit signature of a 3-year assurance contract issued to a life aged 57 exact, with a premium payable at the start of each year of $500 is $(-250, 150, 200)$.
   Calculate the profit margin (the NPV of profit to that of premiums) of the contract.
   Basis:
   Mortality *AMC00* ultimate
   Lapses None
   Risk discount rate 12% per annum.

Solution
The NPV of profits is $$\sum_{t=1}^{3} \frac{PS_t}{1.12^t} = 38.7$$

and of premiums is

$$P\sum_{t=0}^{2}\frac{{}_tp_{57}}{1.12^t} = 1340.$$

Thus the profit margin is $38.7/1340 = 2.9\%$.

2. [UK CT5 exam, Sept 2007] A 12-year life insurance contract has the following profit signature before any nonunit reserves are created:

$$(+1, -1, +1, +1, +1, -1, 0, -1, +1, -1, +1, +1).$$

Nonunit reserves are to be set up to zeroise the negative cash. Write down the revised profit signature, ignoring interest.

Solution

The contract is self-supporting after year 10. Use a transfer from year 9 to year 10 to zeroise the loss of -1 in year 10:

year	1	2	3	4	5	6	7	8	9	10	11	12
signature	1	-1	1	1	1	-1	0	-1	1	-1	1	1
transfer									-1	1		
result	1	-1	1	1	1	-1	0	-1	0	0	1	1
							-1	1				
						-1	1					
transfers					-2	2						
				-1	1							
	-1	1										
result	0	0	1	0	0	0	0	0	0	0	1	1

3. [UK CT5 exam, Apr 2009] A life insurance company issues a 5-year with profits endowment assurance policy to a life aged 60 exact. The policy has a basic sum assured of $10,000. Simple reversionary bonuses are added at the start of each year, including the first. The sum assured (together with any bonuses attaching) is payable at maturity or at the end of year of death, if earlier. Level premiums are payable annually in advance throughout the term of the policy.

   a. Show that the annual premium is approximately $2,382.
      Basis:
      Mortality: AMC00 *Select*

Interest: 6% per annum

Initial expenses: 60% of the first premium

Renewal expenses: 5% of the second and subsequent premiums

Bonus Rates: A simple reversionary bonus will declared each year at a rate of 4% per annum

b. The office holds net premium reserves using a rate of interest of 4% per annum and AMC00 *Ultimate* mortality. In order to profit test this policy, the company assumes that it will earn interest at 7% per annum on its funds, mortality follows the AMC00 *Ultimate* table, and expenses and bonuses will follow the premium basis.

Calculate the expected profit margin on this policy using a risk discount rate of 9% per annum.

Solution

The gross premium $\overline{P}$ satisfies the equation of value

$$0.95\overline{P}\ddot{a}_{[60]:\overline{5}|} = 0.55\overline{P} + 10000\left(0.96\overline{A}_{[60]:\overline{5}|} + 0.04I\overline{A}_{[60]:\overline{5}|}\right)$$

and hence

$$\overline{P} = 10000\frac{0.96 \times 0.7501 + 0.04 \times 3.6973}{0.95 \times 4.4145 - 0.55}$$

$$= 2382$$

The net premium reserves are based on the following:

Net premium reserves

		Interest	4%		
t	x	q_x	ℓ_x		Reserve per unit initial sum
0	60	0.0061	1.0000		0.0000
1	61	0.0068	0.9939		0.2123
2	62	0.0077	0.9872		0.4337
3	63	0.0086	0.9796		0.6649
4	64	0.0097	0.9712		0.9067
5	65		0.9618		1.1600

This gives

$a_{60\,:\overline{5}|}$	$A_{60:\overline{5}|}$	$IA_{60:\overline{5}|}$	**Premium**
4.5694	0.8243	4.0585	0.2087

Thus profits can be calculated as follows:

	Profit signature					
Year	**1**	**2**	**3**	**4**	**5**	**NPV**
survival to end of year	0.99557	0.98914	0.98156	0.97311	0.96369	
death probability	0.00443	0.00646	0.00766	0.00861	0.00968	
sum insured	1	1.04	1.08	1.12	1.16	
reserve per initial unit at end	0.2123	0.4337	0.6649	0.9067	1.1600	
reserve start	0	2113	4290	6526	8823	
premium	2382	2372	2356	2338	2318	9989
expense	−1429	−119	−118	−117	−116	
death benefits	−44	−67	−82	−95	−109	
interest	67	306	457	612	772	
reserve end	−2113	−4290	−6526	−8823	−11179	
profit	−1138	315	377	442	509	157

The profit margin is therefore $\frac{157}{9989} = 1.57\%$.

CHAPTER SIXTEEN

Multiple decrements and multiple states (CT5: §10)

In continuous time, we have so far considered only one decrement—death, at the instantaneous rate $\mu_x = -\frac{1}{\ell(x)} \frac{d\ell(x)}{dx}$.

- It is not hard to extend this to multiple decrements α, with corresponding rates $\mu^\alpha(x)$.
- In continuous time, we do not have the problem of interaction between decrements, so that independent and dependent decrements are the same.
- This means that the aggregate population $a\ell(x)$ simply satisfies the equation

$$\frac{1}{a\ell(x)} \frac{d}{dt} a\ell(x+t) = -\sum_\alpha \mu^\alpha(x+t).$$

This simplification allows us to extend the model in another direction.

16.1. Multiple decrements and multiple states in continuous time

So far, we have considered only two *states*: active and inactive (i.e. dead or terminated service).

What if there are other states, for example, sickness—from which a recovery might be possible?

The decrement rates then have to be described by two states in general:
- the state which one *departs*, denoted α
- the state which one *enters*, denoted β.

It is assumed that there is only one means of going from state α to β (unlike for pension funds, for which there may be many means—retirement, death, etc.). This is not a severe restriction in practice, as we can create a different 'inactive' state for each means of decrement.

16.2. Multiple states

If we allow multiple states, we can analyse a larger class of problems. Generally, we are interested in:

Actuarial Principles
https://doi.org/10.1016/B978-0-32-390172-7.00020-8

- the probability of being in a particular state
- how frequently transitions between states can occur
- but not what *causes* transitions to occur.

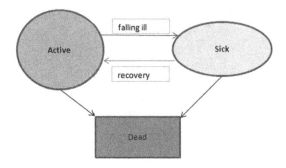

16.3. Transition intensities

The instantaneous decrement rate of moving from state α to β is denoted $\mu^{\alpha\beta}(x)$ when $\alpha \neq \beta$. This is usually called the *transition intensity* with multi-state models. It is also convenient to define

$$\mu^{\alpha\alpha}(x) = -\sum_{\beta \neq \alpha} \mu^{\alpha\beta}(x).$$

What is the probability of movement between states in finite time? It is useful to define:

- $p^{\alpha\beta}(x,t) = \mathbf{prob}\left[\beta \text{ at age } x+t | \alpha \text{ at age } x\right]$
- $p^{\overline{\alpha\alpha}}(x,t) = \mathbf{prob}\left[\alpha \text{ continuously from age } x \text{ to } x+t\right].$

Note that in $p^{\alpha\beta}(x,t)$ we are interested only in the states at the endpoints of $[x, x+t]$—there may be many ways of getting from one to the other.

16.4. Kolmogorov forward equations

The *Kolmogorov forward equations* allow us to solve for these probabilities. Consider a small time interval $[t, t+dt]$, and suppose we know what $p^{\overline{\alpha\alpha}}(x,t)$ is.

- Then the probability of not moving from state α in the time interval is

$$1 - \sum_{\beta \neq \alpha} \mu^{\alpha\beta}(x+t)\,dt,$$

and hence

$$p^{\overline{\alpha\alpha}}\left(x, t + dt\right) = p^{\overline{\alpha\alpha}}\left(x, t\right)\left[1 - \sum_{\beta \neq \alpha}\mu^{\alpha\beta}\left(x + t\right)dt\right]$$

and as $dt \to 0$:

$$\frac{\partial}{\partial t}p^{\overline{\alpha\alpha}}\left(x, t\right) = -p^{\overline{\alpha\alpha}}\left(x, t\right)\sum_{\beta \neq \alpha}\mu^{\alpha\beta}\left(x + t\right)$$

or

$$\frac{\partial}{\partial t}\ln\left[p^{\overline{\alpha\alpha}}\left(x, t\right)\right] = -\sum_{\beta}\mu^{\alpha\beta}\left(x + t\right) = \mu^{\alpha\alpha}\left(x + t\right).$$

This gives us a single differential equation for each $p^{\overline{\alpha\alpha}}\left(x, t\right)$, which we can solve if we know $\mu^{\alpha\beta}\left(x + t\right)$. In fact, it can be integrated directly as

$$p^{\overline{\alpha\alpha}}\left(x, t\right) = \exp\left[\int_0^t \mu^{\alpha\alpha}\left(x + s\right)ds\right].$$

Similarly, for the transition probabilities $p^{\alpha\beta}\left(x, t\right)$:
- If state α applies at age x, then any of the states γ can apply at age $x + t$.
- The probability of moving from $\gamma \neq \beta$ at age $x + t$ to β at age $x + t + dt$ is $\mu^{\gamma\beta}\left(x + t\right)dt$.
- If the state is $\gamma = \beta$ at age $x + t$, then the probability of remaining in this state to age $x + t + dt$ is

$$1 - \sum_{\gamma}\mu^{\beta\gamma}\left(x + t\right)dt.$$

- Thus the probability of being in state β at age $x + t + dt$ is

$$p^{\alpha\beta}\left(x, t + dt\right) = \sum_{\substack{\gamma \neq \beta \\ \alpha \to \gamma}}p^{\alpha\gamma}\left(x, t\right)\cdot\underset{\gamma \to \beta}{\mu^{\gamma\beta}}\left(x + t\right)dt$$

$$+ p^{\alpha\beta}\left(x, t\right)\left[1 - \sum_{\gamma \neq \beta}\mu^{\beta\gamma}\left(x + t\right)dt\right]$$

- and as $dt \to 0$:

$$\frac{\partial}{\partial t} p^{\alpha\beta}(x, t) = \sum_{\gamma \neq \beta} p^{\alpha\gamma}(x, t) \cdot \mu^{\gamma\beta}(x+t) - p^{\alpha\beta}(x, t) \sum_{\gamma \neq \beta} \mu^{\beta\gamma}(x+t)$$

$$= \sum_{\gamma} p^{\alpha\gamma}(x, t) \cdot \mu^{\gamma\beta}(x+t).$$

This gives us a *system* of differential equations for $p^{\alpha\beta}(x, t)$, which we can solve if we know $\mu^{\alpha\beta}(x+t)$. These equations can be written in matrix form as follows:

- Define $\mathbf{P} = \left[p^{\alpha\beta}(x, t) \right]$.
- Define $\mathbf{M} = \left[\mu^{\alpha\beta}(x+t) \right]$.
- Then the rows of $\mathbf{M}$ sum to zero.
- Kolmogorov's equation can then be written simply as

$$\frac{\partial}{\partial t} \mathbf{P} = \mathbf{PM}$$

where $\mathbf{P}(t=0) = \mathbf{I}$.

This can be solved if we can diagonalise $\mathbf{M}$ using eigenvectors, that is

$$\mathbf{M} = \mathbf{V} \boldsymbol{\Lambda} \mathbf{V}^{-1}$$

where $\boldsymbol{\Lambda}$ is a diagonal matrix of the eigenvalues. In this case,

$$\frac{\partial}{\partial t} \left(\mathbf{V}^{-1} \mathbf{P} \mathbf{V} \right) = \mathbf{V}^{-1} \mathbf{P} \mathbf{V} \boldsymbol{\Lambda}$$

or putting $\mathbf{Q} = \mathbf{V}^{-1} \mathbf{P} \mathbf{V}$:

$$\frac{\partial}{\partial t} \mathbf{Q} = \mathbf{Q} \boldsymbol{\Lambda}.$$

This has the solution $\mathbf{Q} = e^{t\Lambda}$, so that

$$\mathbf{P} = \mathbf{V} e^{t\Lambda} \mathbf{V}^{-1}.$$

Where $\mathbf{M}$ is not diagonalisable, it is still possible to solve the equation with a sub-diagonal matrix $\boldsymbol{\Lambda}$. See the Appendix *Useful mathematical techniques* for details.

16.5. A sickness example

Example 16.1. *In the sickness insurance model, we have three states:*

1. *active*
2. *sick*
3. *dead.*

The transition intensities are constant

$$\mu^{12} = \sigma, \ \mu^{13} = \mu \ \mu^{21} = \rho, \ \mu^{23} = v \ \textit{All other transitions have zero intensity (why?)}$$

Then the matrix **M** *has the elements*

$$\mathbf{M} = \begin{bmatrix} -\mu - \sigma & \sigma & \mu \\ \rho & -\rho - v & v \\ 0 & 0 & 0 \end{bmatrix}.$$

The eigenvalues are $\lambda_1 = 0$ and

$$\lambda_2 = \frac{1}{2}\left[\sqrt{(\mu + \sigma - \rho - v)^2 + 4\rho\sigma} - (\mu + \sigma + \rho + v)\right]$$

$$\lambda_3 = \frac{1}{2}\left[-\sqrt{(\mu + \sigma - \rho - v)^2 + 4\rho\sigma} - (\mu + \sigma + \rho + v)\right]$$

with eigenvectors:

$$\mathbf{V} = \begin{bmatrix} 1 & \sigma & \sigma \\ 1 & \lambda_2 + \mu + \sigma & \lambda_3 + \mu + \sigma \\ 1 & 0 & 0 \end{bmatrix}.$$

16.6. A sickness example with no recovery

In the special case $\rho = v = 0$, this simplifies considerably:

$$\Lambda = \begin{bmatrix} 0 & 0 & 0 \\ 0 & 0 & 0 \\ 0 & 0 & -\mu - \sigma \end{bmatrix}$$

and

$$\mathbf{V} = \begin{bmatrix} 1 & \sigma & \sigma \\ 1 & \mu + \sigma & 0 \\ 1 & 0 & 0 \end{bmatrix}.$$

Hence

$$\mathbf{P}=\mathbf{V}e^{t\Lambda}\mathbf{V}^{-1}$$

$$
=\begin{bmatrix} 1 & \sigma & \sigma \\ 1 & \mu+\sigma & 0 \\ 1 & 0 & 0 \end{bmatrix}
\begin{bmatrix} 1 & 0 & 0 \\ 0 & 1 & 0 \\ 0 & 0 & e^{-(\mu+\sigma)t} \end{bmatrix}
\begin{bmatrix} 0 & 0 & 1 \\ 0 & \frac{1}{\mu+\sigma} & -\frac{1}{\mu+\sigma} \\ \frac{1}{\sigma} & -\frac{1}{\mu+\sigma} & -\frac{\mu}{\sigma(\mu+\sigma)} \end{bmatrix}
$$

$$
=\begin{bmatrix} 1 & \sigma & \sigma e^{-(\mu+\sigma)t} \\ 1 & \mu+\sigma & 0 \\ 1 & 0 & 0 \end{bmatrix}
\begin{bmatrix} 0 & 0 & 1 \\ 0 & \frac{1}{\mu+\sigma} & -\frac{1}{\mu+\sigma} \\ \frac{1}{\sigma} & -\frac{1}{\mu+\sigma} & -\frac{\mu}{\sigma(\mu+\sigma)} \end{bmatrix}
$$

$$
=\begin{bmatrix} e^{-(\mu+\sigma)t} & \frac{\sigma}{\mu+\sigma}\left(1-e^{-(\mu+\sigma)t}\right) & 1-\frac{\sigma}{\mu+\sigma}-\frac{\mu}{\mu+\sigma}e^{-(\mu+\sigma)t} \\ 0 & 1 & 0 \\ 0 & 0 & 1 \end{bmatrix}.
$$

16.7. Using transition probabilities

Example 16.2. *A friendly society offers a 3-year contract, under which:*
- *A weekly benefit of $500 is payable during sickness.*
- *A funeral benefit of $3,000 is payable immediately on death.*
- *Premiums are payable weekly but are waived on sickness.*

   What is the weekly premium for a healthy individual aged x, under the three-state model with recovery?

Solution

- If the premium is P, the value of the sickness benefit, with waiver of premiums, is

$$52\,(500)\int_0^3 e^{-\delta t}p^{12}\,(x,t)\,dt.$$

- The value of the funeral benefit is

$$3000\int_0^3 e^{-\delta t}\left[p^{11}\,(x,t)\,\mu^{13}\,(x+t)+p^{12}\,(x,t)\,\mu^{23}\,(x+t)\right]dt.$$

- The value of the premiums is

$$52P\int_0^3 e^{-\delta t}p^{11}\,(x,t)\,dt.$$

Hence

$$52P \int_0^3 e^{-\delta t} p^{11}(x,t)\, dt = 52\,(500) \int_0^3 e^{-\delta t} p^{12}(x,t)\, dt$$

$$+ 3000 \int_0^3 e^{-\delta t} \left[\begin{array}{c} p^{11}(x,t)\,\mu^{13}(x+t) \\ +p^{12}(x,t)\,\mu^{23}(x+t) \end{array} \right] dt.$$

16.7.1 Exercises

1. [UK CT5 exam, Sept 2008] A certain population is subject to three modes of decrement: α, β and γ.
   a. Write down an expression for aq_x^α in terms of the single decrement table probabilities q_x^α, q_x^β and q_x^γ, assuming each of the three modes of decrement is uniformly distributed over the year of age x to $x+1$ in the corresponding single decrement table.
   b. Suppose now that in the single decrement table $_t p_x^\alpha = 1 - t^2 q_x^\alpha$ for $0 \le t \le 1$, while decrements β and γ remain uniformly distributed. Derive a revised expression for aq_x^α in terms of the single decrement table probabilities q_x^α, q_x^β and q_x^γ.

Solution

The formula for aq_x^α derived in lectures, for a uniform distribution of decrements, is

$$aq_x^\alpha = q_x^\alpha \left[1 - \frac{1}{2}(q_x^\beta + q_x^\gamma) + \frac{1}{3} q_x^\beta q_x^\gamma \right].$$

If, however, $_t p_x^\alpha = 1 - t^2 q_x^\alpha$, then $a\ell(x+t) = (1 - t^2 q_x^\alpha)(1 - tq_x^\beta)(1 - tq_x^\gamma)$. Also, $\mu_{x+t}^\alpha = \frac{2tq_x^\alpha}{1 - t^2 q_x^\alpha}$. Thus

$$aq_x^\alpha = \int_0^1 \mu_{x+t}^\alpha a\ell(x+t)\, dt$$

$$= \int_0^1 2tq_x^\alpha (1 - tq_x^\beta)(1 - tq_x^\gamma)\, dt$$

$$= q_x^\alpha \left[1 - \frac{2}{3}(q_x^\beta + q_x^\gamma) + \frac{1}{2} q_x^\beta q_x^\gamma \right].$$

2. [UK CT5 exam, Apr 2009] A life insurance company issues a 3-year savings contract to unmarried male lives that offers the following benefits:

- On death during the 3 years a sum of $15,000 payable immediately on death.
- On surrender during the 3 years a return of premiums paid, payable immediately on surrender.
- On marriage during the 3 years a return of premiums paid accumulated with compound interest at 4% per annum, payable immediately on marriage.
- On survival to the end of the 3 years a sum of $5000.

The contract ceases on payment of any benefit.

Calculate the level premium payable annually in advance for this contract for a life aged 40 exact.

Basis:

- Independent rates of mortality $q_{40}^d = 0.937$, $q_{41}^d = 1.014$, $q_{42}^d = 1.104$ per mille
- Independent rate of surrender $q_x^w = 0.1$ per annum
- Independent rate of marriage $q_x^m = 0.05$ per annum
- Interest 5% per annum
- Expenses 0.5% of each premium.

Solution

Denote the independent decrements on death, surrender and marriage as q_x^d, $q_x^w = 0.1$ and $q_x^m = 0.05$. Then the dependent decrements under the assumption of uniform deaths can be calculated as

$$aq_x^d = q_x^d \left[1 - \frac{1}{2} \left(q_x^w + q_x^m \right) + \frac{1}{3} q_x^w q_x^m \right]$$

and similarly for aq_x^w, aq_x^m. This gives the dependent rates:

age x	q_x^d	q_x^w	q_x^m	aq_x^d	aq_x^w	aq_x^m
40	0.000937	0.1	0.05	0.000868	0.097455	0.047478
41	0.001014	0.1	0.05	0.00094	0.097451	0.047476
42	0.001104	0.1	0.05	0.001023	0.097447	0.047474

and the multiple decrement table:

age x	$a\ell$	add_x^d	ad_x^w	ad_x^m
40	1.000000	0.000868	0.097455	0.047478
41	0.854199	0.000803	0.083243	0.040554
42	0.729599	0.000746	0.071097	0.034637
43	0.623119			

Hence we can calculate benefit values as follows:

t	$a\ell$	d	w	m	v
0	1.0000	0.0009	0.0975	0.0484	1.0000
1	0.8542	0.0008	0.1665	0.0844	0.9524
2	0.7296	0.0007	0.2133	0.1103	0.9070
PV	2.4753	0.0023	0.4386	0.2233	

Take $a\ell_{40} = 1$ and $a\ell_x = a\ell_{x-1} - ad_x^d - ad_x^w - ad_x^m$. The level premium $\overline{P}$ satisfies the equation of value:

$$0.995\overline{P}\sum_{t=0}^{2} v^t \cdot a\ell_{40+t}$$

$$= \sum_{t=0}^{2} v^{t+\frac{1}{2}}\left[15000 ad_{40+t}^d + \overline{P}(t+1)\, ad_{40+t}^w + \overline{P}\ddot{s}_{\overline{t}|}ad_{40+t}^m\right]$$

$$+ 5000 v^3 \cdot a\ell_{43}.$$

Hence

$$\overline{P} = \frac{5000 v^3 \cdot a\ell_{43} + 15000 \sum_{t=0}^{2} v^{t+\frac{1}{2}} ad_{40+t}^d}{\sum_{t=0}^{2}\left[0.995 v^t \cdot a\ell_{40+t} - (t+1)\, ad_{40+t}^w - \ddot{s}_{\overline{t+1}|}ad_{40+t}^m\right]}$$

$$= \frac{2691 + 34}{2.475 - 0.439 - 0.223}$$

$$= \$1513.$$

CHAPTER SEVENTEEN

More complex benefits on multiple lives (CT5: §9)

Recall the joint life insurance that was introduced in previous chapters, with the curtate joint lifetime K_{xy}:

$$A_{xy} - \mathbf{E}\left(v^{K_{xy}+1}\right) = \sum_{t=0}^{\infty} v^{t+1} \cdot \mathbf{prob}\left(K_{xy} = t\right).$$

We are now going to look at insurances where the benefit depends on the order in which deaths occur. These are known as *contingent* insurances. These are the most complex (and, thankfully, rarest) type of benefit.

17.1. More complex contingent insurances

An example is a lifetime insurance payable on the death of x if this occurs *before* that of y, or the failure of the joint status $\overset{1}{x}: y$. Thus the benefit is payable at time $K_x + 1$ provided that $K_x \leq K_y$. Its value is

$$A_{xy}^1 = \sum_{t=0}^{\infty} v^{t+1} \cdot \mathbf{prob}\left(K_x = t\right) \cdot \mathbf{prob}\left(K_y \geq t\right)$$

$$= \sum_{t=0}^{\infty} v^{t+1} \frac{\ell_{x+t} - \ell_{x+t+1}}{\ell_x} \frac{\ell_{y+t}}{\ell_y}$$

$$= \sum_{t=0}^{\infty} v^{t+1} \frac{\ell_{x+t}\ell_{y+t}}{\ell_x\ell_y} - \sum_{t=0}^{\infty} v^{t+1} \frac{\ell_{x+t+1}\ell_{y+t}}{\ell_x\ell_y}.$$

Note that this is only approximate, as in the case that $K_x = K_y$, we cannot be sure which one dies first! This has to be dealt with in continuous time. However, assuming in half of the cases where $K_x = K_y$ that x dies first, a better approximation would be

$$A_{xy}^1 = \sum_{t=0}^{\infty} v^{t+1} \cdot \mathbf{prob}\left(K_x = t\right) \cdot \left[\mathbf{prob}\left(K_y > t\right) + \frac{1}{2}\mathbf{prob}\left(K_y = t\right)\right]$$

Actuarial Principles
https://doi.org/10.1016/B978-0-32-390172-7.00021-X

$$= \sum_{t=0}^{\infty} v^{t+1} \frac{\ell_{x+t} - \ell_{x+t+1}}{\ell_x} \left[\frac{\ell_{y+t+1}}{\ell_y} + \frac{1}{2} \frac{\ell_{y+t}}{\ell_y} \left(1 - \frac{\ell_{y+t+1}}{\ell_{y+t}} \right) \right]$$

$$= \sum_{t=0}^{\infty} v^{t+1} \frac{\ell_{x+t} - \ell_{x+t+1}}{\ell_x} \left[\frac{\ell_{y+t} + \ell_{y+t+1}}{2\ell_y} \right].$$

This can be written more neatly as

$$A_{xy}^1 = \sum_{t=0}^{\infty} v^{t+1} \cdot \mathbf{prob}\,(K_x = t) \cdot \mathbf{prob}\left(K_y > t + \frac{1}{2}\right).$$

It should not be surprising that

$$A_{xy}^1 + A_{xy}^1 = A_{xy}.$$

A similar insurance is one payable on the death of x, if that occurs *after* that of y, denoted A_{xy}^2. This can be computed from

$$A_{xy}^1 + A_{xy}^2 = A_x$$

since

$$A_{xy}^2 = \sum_{t=0}^{\infty} v^{t+1} \cdot \mathbf{prob}\,(K_x = t) \cdot \mathbf{prob}\left(K_y \le t + \frac{1}{2}\right)$$

$$= \sum_{t=0}^{\infty} v^{t+1} \frac{\ell_{x+t} - \ell_{x+t+1}}{\ell_x} \left[1 - \frac{\ell_{y+t} + \ell_{y+t+1}}{2\ell_y} \right].$$

17.2. Contingent insurances as double summations

There is a simpler way of looking at A_{xy}^1:
- Suppose we have specific values for the pair (K_x, K_y).
- This occurs with probability $\mathbf{prob}\,(K_x) \cdot \mathbf{prob}\,(K_y)$.
- Then a benefit is payable at time $K_x + 1$ of amount:
  - 1 if $K_x < K_y$,
  - $\frac{1}{2}$ if $K_x = K_y$,
  - 0 otherwise.

Hence A_{xy}^1 can be found as the double summation:

$$A_{xy}^1 = \sum_{s,t} v^{s+1} \mathbf{prob}\,(K_x = s) \cdot \mathbf{prob}\,(K_y = t)\, B_{st}$$

where

- $B_{st} = 1$ if $s < t$,
- $B_{st} = \frac{1}{2}$ if $s = t$, and
- $B_{st} = 0$ if $s > t$.

Example 17.1. *In Excel, suppose you are given a column range KX denoting the values of K_x and another column range PX = **prob**(K_x) for the probability distribution of K_x. Let a row range KY with probability PY = **prob**(K_y) do the same for K_y. What is an array formula for the value A^1_{xy}?*

Answer: Hence an array formula for the value of the contingent insurance is

$$= \left\{ sum \left(\begin{array}{c} (if(KX < KY, 1, 0) + if(KX = KY, 0.5, 0)) \\ *v\hat{} - (KX + 1) * PX * PY \end{array} \right) \right\}.$$

17.3. Contingent insurances dependent on term

Here is an example of a limited contingent insurance.

Example 17.2. *Suppose a benefit of 1 is payable in the year of the death of x, provided it occurs within n years and before the death of y. This has the value*

$$A^1_{xy:\overline{n}|} = \sum_{t=0}^{n-1} v^{t+1} \cdot \textbf{prob}\,(K_x = t) \cdot \textbf{prob}\left(K_y \geq t + \frac{1}{2}\right)$$

$$= \sum_{t=0}^{n-1} v^{t+1} \frac{\ell_{x+t} - \ell_{x+t+1}}{\ell_x} \left[\frac{\ell_{y+t} + \ell_{y+t+1}}{2\ell_y}\right].$$

This can be computed in Excel with the array formula:

$$= \left\{ sum \left(\begin{array}{c} (if(KX < KY, 1, 0) + if(KX = KY, 0.5, 0)) \\ *v\hat{} - (KX + 1) * PX * PY * if(KX < N, 1, 0) \end{array} \right) \right\}.$$

17.4. Even more complex contingent insurances

It should now be obvious that the superscript 1 or 2 above the life in the insurance determines the death upon which the benefit is to be payable. For example,

$$A^2_{xyz} = \sum_{t=0}^{\infty} v^{t+1} \cdot \textbf{prob}\,(K_x = t) \cdot$$

$$\left[\begin{array}{l} \mathbf{prob}\left(K_y < t + \tfrac{1}{2}\right) \cdot \mathbf{prob}\left(K_z > t + \tfrac{1}{2}\right) \\ +\mathbf{prob}\left(K_z < t + \tfrac{1}{2}\right) \cdot \mathbf{prob}\left(K_y > t + \tfrac{1}{2}\right) \end{array} \right].$$

If we require that one of the other lives must specifically die first, we put a 1 below that life. For example,

$$A^2_{\underset{1}{xyz}} = \sum_{t=0}^{\infty} v^{t+1} \cdot \mathbf{prob}\left(K_x = t\right) \cdot \left[\mathbf{prob}\left(K_y < t + \frac{1}{2}\right) \cdot \mathbf{prob}\left(K_z > t + \frac{1}{2}\right)\right].$$

17.5. Contingent annuities

Most contingent annuities can be computed from contingent insurances. The simplest type of continent annuity is one that commences in the year that x dies, and then is payable for the lifetime of y. This has the value:

$$\ddot{a}_{x|y} = \ddot{a}_y - \ddot{a}_{xy}$$

with $\ddot{a}_y$ and $\ddot{a}_{xy}$ being computed from $A_{xy} = 1 - d\ddot{a}_{xy}$, etc.

Example 17.3. *A more complex contingent annuity is one commencing on the death of x, and payable for a further n years after the death of y. The value of this benefit is*

$$\ddot{a}_{x|y} + A^2_{yx}\ddot{a}_{\overline{n}}.$$

17.5.1 Exercises

1. It was shown that

$$A^1_{xy} = \sum_{t=0}^{\infty} v^{t+1} \cdot \mathbf{prob}\left(K_x = t\right) \cdot \left[\mathbf{prob}\left(K_y > t\right) + \frac{1}{2}\mathbf{prob}\left(K_y = t\right)\right].$$

An approximation was made in the case that $K_y = K_y$ to find that probability that y dies after x.

Why is this? Because K_y, K_y denote the curtate lifespans (the integer year just before death). The fact that $K_y = K_y = t$ merely indicates that x and y die in the same year, without telling us who will die first. To do this precisely, we need to analyse probabilities in continuous time.

Suppose a benefit of 1 is paid to x at the end of year t. For this to happen:

*   both x and y must survive to time t

- x must die before time $t+1$
- y must die after x (i.e. y must be alive when x dies).

This probability can be written as

$$_tp_x \cdot _tp_y \int_0^1 {}_sp_{x+t} \cdot {}_sp_{y+t} \cdot \mu_{x+t+s} ds.$$

Under the assumption that deaths occur uniformly in year t, show that this probability is equal to

$$\mathbf{prob}\,(K_x = t) \cdot \left[\mathbf{prob}\,(K_y > t) + \frac{1}{2}\mathbf{prob}\,(K_y = t) \right]$$

as appears in the formula for A_{xy}^1.

Is there a simpler explanation of this result?

Solution

The exact probability that y dies after x in continuous time is given by the probability that both x and y survive to time s followed shortly by the death of x:

$$\int_0^1 {}_sp_{x+t} \cdot {}_sp_{y+t} \cdot \mu_{x+t+s} ds.$$

The UDD assumption implies that the probability, that x or y survive for a fraction s of a year (having survived to time t), is

$$_sp_{x+t} = 1 - s q_{x+t}$$
$$_sp_{y+t} = 1 - s q_{y+t}.$$

Hence

$$\mu_{x+t+s} = -\frac{1}{{}_sp_{x+t}} \frac{\partial}{\partial s} {}_sp_{x+t} = \frac{q_{x+t}}{1 - s q_{x+t}}$$

and the required probability is

$$_tp_x \cdot _tp_y \int_0^1 {}_sp_{x+t} \cdot {}_sp_{y+t} \cdot \mu_{x+t+s} ds$$

$$= {}_tp_x \cdot {}_tp_y \int_0^1 (1 - s q_{x+t}) \cdot (1 - s q_{y+t}) \cdot \frac{q_{x+t}}{1 - s q_{x+t}} ds$$

$$= {}_tp_x \cdot {}_tp_y \cdot q_{x+t} \left(1 - \frac{1}{2} q_{y+t} \right)$$

$$= \mathbf{prob}\,(K_x = t) \cdot {}_t p_y \cdot \left(1 - \frac{1}{2}q_{y+t}\right)$$

$$= \mathbf{prob}\,(K_x = t) \cdot \left[{}_t p_y \left(1 - q_{y+t}\right) + \frac{1}{2}{}_t p_y q_{y+t}\right]$$

$$= \mathbf{prob}\,(K_x = t) \cdot \left[\mathbf{prob}\,(K_y > t) + \frac{1}{2}\mathbf{prob}\,(K_y = t)\right].$$

This result can be explained much more simply as follows.

The benefit is payable at time $t+1$ if $K_x = t$ and $K_y > t$, which has a probability of $\mathbf{prob}\,(K_x = t) \cdot \mathbf{prob}\,(K_y > t)$.

However, it is also payable when $K_x = K_y = t$. For a uniform distribution of deaths, the time of death of either x or y is therefore uniformly distributed, and since the deaths are independent, the probability that x dies first is $\frac{1}{2}$. Thus there is an extra probability of $\frac{1}{2}\mathbf{prob}\,(K_x = t) \cdot \mathbf{prob}\,(K_y = t)$ that the benefit is payable.

2. [UK CT5 exam, Sept 2007] A policy provides a benefit of $500,000 at the end of the year of death of y if she dies after x.

   a. Write down an expression in terms of K_x and K_y (random variables denoting the complete future lifetimes of x and y, respectively) for the present value of the benefit under this policy. State all assumptions.

   b. Write down an expression for the expected present value of the benefit in terms of a sum.

   c. Suggest, with a reason, the most appropriate term for regular premiums to be payable under this policy.

Solution

The assurance may be denoted A^2_{xy}. A benefit is payable at time $K_x + 1$ of amount:

- 1 if $K_x < K_y$,
- $\frac{1}{2}$ if $K_x = K_y$,
- 0 otherwise.

These amounts must be discounted by v^{K_x+1} to get present values. The expected present value of the policy is therefore

$$500000 A_{xy}^2 =$$

$$500000 \sum_{t=0}^{\infty} v^{t+1} \mathbf{prob}\,(K_x = t) \cdot \left[\mathbf{prob}\,(K_y < t) + \frac{1}{2}\mathbf{prob}\,(K_y = t) \right].$$

The regular premiums could be payable to the death of x or y, or the first death or the last death. If payable to the last death, and y dies first, then no benefit would be payable, so policy would lapse; similarly if the premium is payable to the death of x.
Hence the premium payment period could be to the death of y, or to the first death.

3. [UK CT5 exam, Sept 2008] Two lives, a female aged 60 exact and a male aged 65 exact, purchase a policy with the following benefits:
(i) an annuity deferred 10 years, with \$20,000 payable annually in advance for as long as either of them is alive
(ii) a lump sum of \$100,000 payable at the end of the policy year of the first death, should this occur during the deferred period
Level premiums are payable monthly in advance throughout the deferred period or until earlier payment of the death benefit.
Give a formula for the monthly premium.
Basis:
Interest 4% per annum
Expenses Initial \$350
Renewal 2.5% of each monthly premium excluding the first.

Solution

The value of the deferred annuity on a last survivor basis is

$$20000 \,{}_{10|}\ddot{a}_{\overline{65:60}} = 20000 v^{10} \cdot {}_{10}p_{65:60} \left(\ddot{a}_{75} + \ddot{a}_{70} - \ddot{a}_{75:70} \right).$$

The value of the lump sum payable on failure of the joint life status is

$$100000 A_{\overline{65:60:\overline{10}|}}$$

and the value of premiums is $12\overline{P}\ddot{a}^{(12)}_{65:60:\overline{10}|}$.
Hence the equation of value is

$$0.975 \times 12\overline{P}\ddot{a}^{(12)}_{65:60:\overline{10}|} + 0.025\overline{P} = 350 + 20000 \,{}_{10|}\ddot{a}_{\overline{65:60}} + 100000 A_{\overline{65:60:\overline{10}|}}$$

4. What does this probability in (1) become when there is a constant mortality rate during year t?

Solution

In this case,

$$_sp_{x+t} = p^s_{x+t}$$
$$_sp_{y+t} = p^s_{y+t}$$

and

$$\mu_{x+t+s} = -\frac{1}{_sp_{x+t}} \frac{\partial}{\partial s} {}_sp_{x+t} = -\ln(p_{x+t})$$

and thus

$$_tp_x \cdot {}_tp_y \int_0^1 {}_sp_{x+t} \cdot {}_sp_{y+t} \cdot \mu_{x+t+s} ds$$

$$= -{}_tp_x \cdot {}_tp_y \ln(p_{x+t}) \int_0^1 p^s_{x+t} \cdot p^s_{y+t} ds$$

$$= {}_tp_x \cdot {}_tp_y \cdot \frac{\ln(p_{x+t})}{\ln(p_{x+t}) + \ln(p_{y+t})} \left[1 - p_{x+t}p_{y+t}\right]$$

$$= \mathbf{prob}(K_{xy} = t) \frac{\ln(p_{x+t})}{\ln(p_{x+t}) + \ln(p_{y+t})}.$$

CHAPTER EIGHTEEN

Risk factors in mortality

18.1. Life tables

This last topic takes us back to the start of this unit—the life table.

- How are life tables constructed, and why are different life tables used in practice?
- To answer this question, it is necessary to examine the *factors* that affect mortality.

18.2. Mortality factors

Some obvious candidates for factors that affect mortality are:

- occupation
- education
- living standards (nutrition, housing, income)
- geography
- genetics.

This list is not exhaustive, and the factors may be interdependent, e.g.

- some occupations allow a higher living standard
- poorer people tend to live in less affluent suburbs (or countries).

18.2.1 Occupation

Occupation is usually regarded as an important indicator of mortality because:

- some are naturally hazardous (e.g. mining, small aircraft pilots, emergency workers)
- some are naturally stressful (psychiatry, surgery, share trader)
- some tend to attract a relaxed lifestyle (landscape gardener, park ranger).

18.2.2 Education

Education is interdependent on occupation, but may itself affect mortality directly through:

- knowledge of a healthier lifestyle
- avoidance of risks (e.g. smoking, promiscuity, financial speculation).

Actuarial Principles
https://doi.org/10.1016/B978-0-32-390172-7.00022-1

18.2.3 Living standards

These tend to affect:
- the quality of diet (which may be too rich or too poor in nutrition)
- the quality of accommodation (which may quarantine from diseases)
- the ability to exercise and to use leisure effectively.

18.2.4 Geography

Though location is often thought to be a risk factor (and in the UK, pensioner mortality may be location based), it is often a proxy for other factors such as:
- occupation (and income)
- living standards.

However, geography may directly affect the mortality rates between countries because of:
- tropical diseases
- propensity for natural disasters (earthquake, storms, famines, drought, flood)
- political stability.

18.2.5 Genetics

- This refers to the intrinsic propensity to certain diseases or conditions as a result of heredity.
- Only a small (though growing) number of conditions can be identified (e.g. breast cancer).
- There is no requirement in law for an insured to be genetically tested.
- However, if an insured has access to such information, it must be disclosed to the insurer.
- The wholescale application of genetic testing would violate the whole principle of insurance, i.e. pooling of risk.

18.3. Selection

Selection is the term used to describe how one group of people may have different mortality characteristics from others.
- We met this term in the use of 'select' life tables, where a group of insureds have undergone an underwriting process (and are therefore expected to be healthier than those who have not). This is known as *temporary initial selection*.

Other forms of selection are:

- *class* selection – where there are *permanent* risk factors, such as sex, education, genetics (or even race).
- *time* selection – people in the 14th century experienced much higher mortality than today. More generally, medical advances mean people are living longer (though not necessarily better).
- *adverse* selection – the ability of people to act against an insurer by exploiting information not available to the insurer. A classic example is for an insurer who does not discriminate against smokers. It is likely it will end up insuring mostly smokers.
- *spurious* selection – this is not really a form of selection at all, but refers to mortality factors which are suspected incorrectly. An example is using geography as a risk factor, when it is only a proxy for occupation and income.

18.4. How selection operates in practice

In life insurance, the *underwriting process* is the key to mortality experience. This mitigates adverse selection, and can take account of:

- occupation
- sex and other class characteristics
- individual characteristics such as genetics, risky activities (e.g. paragliding, rock climbing)
- the results of a medical screening (i.e. questionnaire and examination).

In superannuation and pensions, underwriting of risks is much less common (because the possibility of adverse selection is much lower).

In this case, different groups of members may show different mortality simply as a result of their life experience:

- active employees would show mortality consistent with their occupational and income levels
- disability pensioners would show the effects of disabling conditions
- some members who experience less than disabling conditions would resign to pursue less demanding work
- retired pensioners may be healthier as they have 'survived' the stress of a long career.

CHAPTER NINETEEN

Types of life tables

As a result of these different risk factors, it is appropriate that different life tables be used for different purposes. These might cover:
- the population at large (e.g. ALT2005–07)
- insured lives for endowment insurances (AMC00)
- insured lives for temporary insurances (TMC00)
- annuitants (IML00, those who buy an annuity from a life insurer—rare in Australia)
- retired pensioners (RMC00)
- disability pensioners.

See https://www.actuaries.org.uk/learn-and-develop/continuous-mortality-investigation/cmi-mortality-and-morbidity-tables/00-series-tables.

19.1. Life table construction

It is not the main purpose of this unit to construct a life table in detail (this belongs to ETC2430). However:
- It is based on observing deaths in the population that is being studied.
- We have to have a time period over which deaths are observed (the observation period).
- Suppose this is a single year.

Ideally, we would like to perform a laboratory experiment like the following:
- At the start of the year, find 1000 people aged x exact.
- Track all the people throughout the year.
- Count the actual number of deaths θ_x.
- Calculate the raw mortality rate $q_x = \frac{\theta_x}{1000}$.
- Notice that if deaths occur on average halfway during the year, then $1000 - \frac{1}{2}\theta_x$ is the number of lives that are exposed during the year.
- In this case, $m_x = \frac{\theta_x}{1000 - \frac{1}{2}\theta_x}$ is called the central mortality rate.

Unfortunately life does not provide such ideal experiments.

19.2. Construction of a life table

In practice:

- A population of people with different ages is observed.
- There will be movements in and out of the population (other than through death).

Since we have to classify mortality rates by age x, we need to define the number of lives who are 'exposed' to death during the year.

19.3. Exposures to death

Consider a typical person who is:
- aged x at their last birthday at the start of the year
- or aged exact $x + h$ at the start of the year, where h is a fraction of a year
- and is in the population for the whole year.

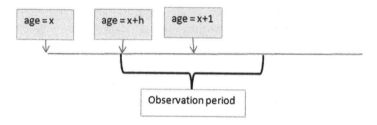

Then:
- The exposure of the person to death after age x during the year is $E_x = 1 - h$ years.
- The exposure of the person to death after age $x + 1$ during the year is $E_{x+1} = h$ years.

The exposures are more complicated for a person who exits the population during the year. Suppose he leaves at time t during the year. Then:
- The exposure of the person to death after age x during the year is $E_x = \min(1 - h, t)$ years.
- The exposure of the person to death after age $x + 1$ during the year is $E_{x+1} = \max(t - 1 - h, 0)$ years.

You can work out in a similar way the exposures for a person who enters the population during the year.

19.4. Assessing mortality rates in practice

Having worked out the exposures for each person (whether active, exiting or entering during the year), then:

- Sum the exposures E_x for each age x over all persons.
- Collate the number of deaths θ_x that occur during the observation period for those aged x at their birthday before death.
- Work out the central mortality rate $m_x = \frac{\theta_x}{E_x}$.

Note: This is not a standard mortality rate q_x, because deaths that occur during the year are given exposure only for the period up to the date of death. In calculating q_x, we need to allow deaths a full year's exposure, so that approximately

$$q_x = \frac{\theta_x}{E_x + \frac{1}{2}\theta_x}.$$

19.5. Mortality comparisons

It is sometimes useful to calculate a single statistic that summarises the mortality of a whole population, so as to enable populations to be compared.

- One such statistic is the crude population mortality rate:

$$m = \frac{\sum_x \theta_x}{\sum_x E_x} = \frac{\sum_x m_x E_x}{\sum_x E_x} = \frac{\Theta}{E}.$$

However, this is simply a weighting of the age-based mortality rates m_x by the population exposures E_x.

- On this basis, it is possible that an old population shows a higher mortality rate than a young population, simply because mortality rates are higher at high ages than at low ages.
- This may overlook the fact that the aged-based mortality rates in the old population are lower (say, as a result of higher income).

19.6. Comparing mortality of two different populations

One way out of this difficulty is to standardise a population's overall mortality rate:

- This does not apply the actual exposures E_x of the population, but those of a life table or some other reference population.
- If a lifetable were used, then the exposures for age x are

$$\overline{E}_x = \frac{\ell_x + \ell_{x+1}}{2}.$$

- This allows deaths in the year starting at age x only a $\frac{1}{2}$ year exposure, consistent with how E_x is calculated.
- So the standardised mortality rate is

$$\overline{m} = \frac{\sum_x m_x \overline{E}_x}{\sum_x \overline{E}_x}.$$

19.7. Indirect standardisation

Standardisation:

- removes the effect of the age structure of a population
- and allows the underlying mortality of two different populations to be compared.

In practice, however, we may not even have sufficient information to assess the age-based mortality rates m_x of a population. For example, we may know the total number of deaths $\Theta = \sum_x \theta_x$ but not the ages when those deaths occurred θ_x.

Here is a rough rule of thumb can that be used.

- We can still calculate the crude mortality rate of the population $m = \frac{\Theta}{E}$.
- We adjust it by considering the ratio

$$F = \frac{\overline{m}}{m}$$

$$= \frac{\sum_x m_x \overline{E} / \sum_x \overline{E}_x}{\sum_x m_x E_x / \sum_x E_x}.$$

We may not know the actual population mortality rates m_x, so we approximate them by those of the standard life table: $\overline{m}_x = \frac{\ell_x - \ell_{x+1}}{\overline{E}_x}$

- Hence a reasonable approximation to the standardised mortality rate is

$$\overline{m} \approx m \frac{\sum_x \overline{m}_x \overline{E} / \sum_x \overline{E}_x}{\sum_x \overline{m}_x E_x / \sum_x E_x} = mF^*.$$

The factor

$$F^* = \frac{\sum_x \overline{m}_x \overline{E} / \sum_x \overline{E}_x}{\sum_x \overline{m}_x E_x / \sum_x E_x}$$

is called an area comparability factor. F^* requires a knowledge of the structure of the population E_x but does not require a detailed analysis of deaths.

19.7.1 Exercises

1. [UK CT5 exam, Sept 2008] A life insurance company has reviewed its mortality experience. For each age, it has pooled all the deaths and corresponding exposures from its entire portfolio over the previous 10 years and derived a single mortality table.

   List three types of selection which might be likely to produce heterogeneity of mortality characteristics in this particular investigation. In each case, explain the nature of the heterogeneity and how it could be caused, and state how the heterogeneity could be dealt with.

Solution

Class selection

People with same age definition will have different underlying mortality due to particular permanent attributes, e.g. sex or education. The existence of such classes would be certainly found in these data: e.g. male/female smoker/nonsmoker, people having different occupational and/or social backgrounds, etc.

The solution would be to subdivide the data according to the nature of the attribute.

Time selection

Where mortality is changing over calendar time, people of the same age could experience different levels of mortality at different times. This might well be a problem here, as data from as much as 10 years apart are being combined.

The solution would be to subdivide the data into shorter time periods.

Temporary initial selection

Mortality changes with policy duration and the combination of subgroups of policyholders with different durations into a single sample will cause heterogeneity. Lives accepted for insurance have passed a medical screening process. The longer that has elapsed since screening (i.e. since entry), the greater the proportion of lives who may have developed impairments since the screening date, and hence the higher the mortality. Mortality rates would then be expected to rise with policy duration, and hence result in heterogeneous data.

The solution would be to perform a select mortality investigation, that is, one in which the data are subdivided by policy duration as well as by age.

Adverse selection

By purchasing a particular product type, policyholders are putting themselves in a particular group. People expecting lighter than normal mortality might purchase annuities and experience better mortality rates than, for example, term assurance buyers.

The solution would be to subdivide the data by product type.

2. [UK CT5 exam, Apr 2009] 'Selection' is a term used most often in the context of mortality. However, it can also be used to describe the withdrawal experience of a life insurer.

   Explain, in the context of the lapse (i.e. withdrawal) rates of life insurance policies, what is meant by:

   a. class selection
   b. temporary initial selection
   c. time selection

   Give an example in each case.

Solution

Different groups or classes of policyholders may have naturally higher or lower lapse rates across all major risk factors (age, duration, gender, etc.) than other classes. An example would be for classes of policyholders who purchased their policies through a particular sales outlet (e.g. broker versus newspaper advertising).

Lapse rates may vary by policy duration as well as age for shorter durations. At shorter durations, lapse rates may be the result of "misguided" purchase by policyholder whereas at longer durations the policy has become more stable.

Lapse rates vary with calendar time for all major risk factors, e.g. economic prosperity varies over time and this results in a similar variation in lapse rates. Another example is the effect of HIV/AIDS on mortality claims.

3. In a mortality investigation for a particular population, E_x is defined as the central exposure of those people aged exactly x last birthday.

   The observation period is one year, and a new entrant enters at age $x + h$ at time t during the year, where h is a fraction of a year.

   What is the new entrant's contribution to E_x and E_{x+1}?

Solution

The new entrant's next birthday is at age $x+1$, which is at time $1-h$.
Thus:
- if $t > h$, the entrant's exposure is solely at age x, and $E_x = 1 - t$
- if $t \leq h$, the entrant's exposure at age x, and $E_x = 1 - h$ and $E_{x+1} = h - t$

so that in general $E_x = 1 - \max(t, h)$ and $E_{x+1} = \max(h - t, 0)$.

---

4. [UK CT5 exam, Apr 2007] You are given the following statistics in relation to the mortality experience of Actuaria and its province Giro:

Age group	Actuaria Exposure	Actuaria Deaths	Giro Exposure	Giro Deaths
0–19	300,000	25	12,000	2
20–39	275,000	35	10,000	3
40–59	200,000	100·	9000	6
60–79	175,000	500	8000	50

a. Explain, giving a formula, the term Standardised Mortality Ratio (SMR). Define all the symbols that you use.
b. Comment on the relative mortality of the province, by calculating the SMR for Giro.

Solution

The SMR is the overall central mortality rate of a local population, assessed by weighting aged-based rates with the exposures of the aggregate population. In symbols,

$$\overline{m} = \frac{\sum_x m_x \overline{E}_x}{\sum_x \overline{E}_x}$$

where $\overline{m}$ is the SMR, m_x are aged-based rates for the local population, and $\overline{E}_x$ are exposures for the aggregate population.
The SMR for Giro can be computed as:

Age group	Actuaria $\overline{E}_x$	$\overline{\theta}_x$	Giro E_x	θ_x	Giro m_x
0–19	300,000	25	12,000	2	0.000167
20–39	275,000	35	10,000	3	0.0003
40–59	200,000	100	9,000	6	0.000667
60–79	175,000	500	8,000	50	0.00625
Total	950,000	660	39,000	61	
Actuaria population mortality	0.000695				
SMR for Giro	0.001431				

Thus the overall mortality for Giro is more than twice that for Actuaria.

CHAPTER TWENTY

Constructing a life table

The aim of all mortality models is to estimate mortality rates from data.
- In practice, however, data can be observed under different conditions and constraints.
- The people whose mortality is being measured may change over the period of observation.
- The period of observation may not be static or the same for all persons observed.
- Assumptions may need to be made about the 'shape' of mortality rates over time or over ages.

20.1. Lifetime distribution

The symbol T denotes the lifetime of an individual (just born) in continuous time.
- Its distribution function is $F(t) = prob(T \leq t)$.
- How do we estimate $F(t)$ from real data?
- In practice, there are difficulties from imperfect data.

20.2. Censoring

In practice, data observations are censored (i.e. truncated). Observations always take place over a specific time period. However:
- Observations are *right* censored if they cease being observed before the end of the period.
- Observations are *left* censored if they commence being observed after the start of the period.

20.3. Censoring examples

Right censoring occurs when:
- people withdraw from a mortality investigation
- people emigrate between censuses
- members of superannuation fund retire or withdraw.

Left censoring occurs when:

Actuarial Principles
https://doi.org/10.1016/B978-0-32-390172-7.00024-5

- new people are drawn into an investigation following diagnosis of a medical condition
- people immigrate between censuses.

Both left and right censoring are examples of interval censoring, where we have lack of complete data about the time of occurrence of an event, e.g. death.

20.4. Information from censoring

Censoring is *informative* when it tells us something about the people being observed.

For example:

- Members who become disabled from a super fund are likely to suffer higher mortality than those who do not.
- Immigrants are more likely to be in better health than the population at large.

Censoring is *noninformative* when it tells us nothing about the people being observed.

Therefore the truncated observation is statistically independent of the mortality of the person observed.

20.5. Censoring and truncation

We have been using the terms 'censoring' and 'truncation' inter-changeably. However, the statistical definition of 'truncation' is that design of observations does not allow some observations to be made. An example is in insurance claims, which take several years to be reported (IBNR claims). If the observation period is too short, such claims cannot be observed.

CHAPTER TWENTY-ONE

Maximum likelihood estimation

The method of *maximum likelihood* (**MLE**) is by far the most popular technique for deriving estimates of unknown parameters.

- It can be applied to estimating the parameters underlying a life table, when a particular distribution of the life table has been adopted.
- You will see various applications of this technique, applied to various life table models.
- In these notes, we illustrate the technique by means of a relatively simple example for observations from a normally distributed population. But the technique applies to any distribution.

21.1. Background

Assume that $X_1, X_2, \ldots, X_n$ are independently and identically distributed normal random variables with unknown mean μ and unknown variance σ^2. That is,

$$X_i \sim N(\mu, \sigma^2), \quad i = 1, 2, \ldots n.$$

Suppose that we have a sample of n observations $(x_1, x_2, \ldots x_n)$ and we wish to estimate the unknown parameters μ and σ^2. That is, in our sample,

$$X_1 = x_1, X_2 = x_2, \ldots, X_n = x_n.$$

Notice that we are using X_i to denote the ith random variable and x_i to denote a realisation of the ith random variable.

The method of MLE works as follows:

- It selects as estimates of μ and σ^2 those values of μ and σ^2 that maximise the probability of observing the sample that we actually obtained.
- That is, the maximum likelihood estimator (**MLE**) selects as estimates of μ and σ^2 those values that maximise the probability of the actual observations.
- Intuition suggests that using as estimates of the unknown parameters those values of the parameters that maximise the probability of the observed sample occurring ought to lead to "good" estimates.

Actuarial Principles
https://doi.org/10.1016/B978-0-32-390172-7.00025-7

- Formal analysis confirms this intuition by demonstrating that, in general, the method of ML produces estimators that have excellent statistical properties.

  The first step in deriving the MLE is to write down the joint probability density function (pdf) of the random variables $X_1, X_2, ..., X_n$. Let

$$f(x_1, x_2, \ldots, x_n | \mu, \sigma^2)$$

denote the joint pdf of the random variables $X_1, X_2, ..., X_n$, evaluated at their sample values. This notation emphasises that the probability of observing the sample that we actually obtained depends on the unknown parameters μ and σ^2. We can write the joint pdf, evaluated at the sample values of the $X's$, more compactly as

$$f(\mathbf{x} | \mu, \sigma^2),$$

where

$$\mathbf{x} \equiv (x_1, x_2, ..., x_n).$$

The assumption that the $X's$ are independently distributed implies that the joint pdf may be expressed as the product of the marginal density functions. That is,

$$f(\mathbf{x} | \mu, \sigma^2) = f(x_1 | \mu, \sigma^2) f(x_2 | \mu, \sigma^2)....f(x_n | \mu, \sigma^2),$$

where $f(x_i | \mu, \sigma^2)$ denotes the marginal density function of X_i evaluated at $X_i = x_i$. Under the assumption that the $X's$ are normally distributed,

$$f(x_i | \mu, \sigma^2) = \frac{1}{(2\pi\sigma^2)^{1/2}} \exp\left[-\frac{1}{2}\frac{(x_i - \mu)^2}{\sigma^2}\right], \quad i = 1, 2, ..., n.$$

Substituting for the marginal density function, we obtain

$$f(\mathbf{x} | \mu, \sigma^2) = \frac{1}{(2\pi\sigma^2)^{n/2}} \exp\left[-\frac{1}{2\sigma^2}\sum_{i=1}^{n}(x_i - \mu)^2\right].$$

In the above, we treat $x_1, x_2, ..., x_n$ as the independent variables in the function and we treat μ and σ^2 as fixed numbers.

However, if instead we treat $x_1, x_2, ..., x_n$ as fixed numbers and we treat μ and σ^2 as the variables in the function, we obtain what is referred to as the *likelihood function* for our problem:

$$L(\mu, \sigma^2|\mathbf{x}) = \frac{1}{(2\pi\sigma^2)^{n/2}} \exp\left[-\frac{1}{2\sigma^2}\sum_{i=1}^{n}(x_i - \mu)^2\right]. \qquad (21.1)$$

21.2. Likelihood function

The likelihood function and the joint pdf are mathematically identical. They differ only in the way that we interpret them. In the latter, we regard μ and σ^2 as variables and x as fixed, while the converse is assumed in the former.

The MLEs of the unknown parameters are the values of μ and σ^2 that maximise (21.1). However, in practice, it is usually easier to maximise the natural logarithm of the likelihood function. Taking natural logarithms on both sides, we obtain

$$l(\mu, \sigma^2|\mathbf{x}) = -\frac{n}{2}\ln 2\pi - \frac{n}{2}\ln\sigma^2 - \frac{1}{2\sigma^2}\sum_{i=1}^{n}(x_i - \mu)^2.$$

This is referred to as the *log-likelihood function*. Because the logarithm of any variable, y, is a monotonically increasing function of y, the values of μ and σ^2 that maximise the log likelihood, also maximise the likelihood function.

21.3. Maximising the log likelihood

Maximising the log likelihood by choice of μ and σ^2 is a standard unconstrained optimisation problem. We can solve by taking its first and second derivatives. The first-order conditions (FOC) for a local maximum of $l(\mu, \sigma^2|\mathbf{x})$ are $\nabla l = 0$, that is,

$$\frac{\partial l(\mu, \sigma^2|\mathbf{x})}{\partial \mu} = \frac{1}{\sigma^2}\sum_{i=1}^{n}(x_i - \mu) = 0$$

$$\frac{\partial l(\mu, \sigma^2|\mathbf{x})}{\partial \sigma^2} = -\frac{n}{2\sigma^2} + \frac{1}{2\sigma^4}\sum_{i=1}^{n}(x_i - \mu)^2 = 0.$$

Denoting the values of μ and σ^2 that solve these equation, we have

$$\hat{\mu} = \frac{1}{n} \sum_{i=1}^{n} x_i \equiv \bar{x}$$

and   (21.2)

$$\hat{\sigma}^2 = \frac{1}{n} \sum_{i=1}^{n} (x_i - \bar{x})^2.$$

21.4. Second-order conditions

To confirm that $l(\hat{\mu}, \hat{\sigma}^2 | x)$ is a local maximum, we need to check the SOC:

$$\frac{\partial}{\partial \mu} \left(\frac{\partial l(\mu, \sigma^2 | \mathbf{x})}{\partial \mu} \right) = -\frac{n}{\sigma^2}$$

$$\frac{\partial}{\partial \sigma^2} \left(\frac{\partial l(\mu, \sigma^2 | \mathbf{x})}{\partial \sigma^2} \right) = \frac{n}{2\sigma^4} - \frac{1}{\sigma^6} \sum_{i=1}^{n} (x_i - \mu)^2$$

$$\frac{\partial}{\partial \mu} \left(\frac{\partial l(\mu, \sigma^2 | \mathbf{x})}{\partial \sigma^2} \right) = -\frac{1}{\sigma^4} \sum_{i=1}^{n} (x_i - \mu).$$

Therefore, the Hessian matrix of second-order partial derivatives is given by

$$\mathbf{H} = \nabla^2 l = \begin{bmatrix} -\frac{n}{\sigma^2} & -\frac{1}{\sigma^4} \sum_{i=1}^{n} (x_i - \mu) \\ -\frac{1}{\sigma^4} \sum_{i=1}^{n} (x_i - \mu) & \frac{n}{2\sigma^4} - \frac{1}{\sigma^6} \sum_{i=1}^{n} (x_i - \mu)^2 \end{bmatrix}.$$

When we evaluate $\mathbf{H}$ at $\mu = \bar{x}$, $\sigma^2 = \hat{\sigma}^2$, we obtain

$$\hat{\mathbf{H}} = \begin{bmatrix} -\frac{n}{\hat{\sigma}^2} & -\frac{1}{\hat{\sigma}^4} \sum_{i=1}^{n} (x_i - \bar{x}) \\ -\frac{1}{\hat{\sigma}^4} \sum_{i=1}^{n} (x_i - \bar{x}) & \frac{n}{2\hat{\sigma}^4} - \frac{1}{\hat{\sigma}^6} \sum_{i-1}^{n} (x_i - \bar{x})^2 \end{bmatrix}.$$

Since

$$\sum_{i=1}^{n} (x_i - \bar{x}) = 0,$$

it follows that

$$\hat{\mathbf{H}} = \begin{bmatrix} -\frac{n}{\hat{\sigma}^2} & 0 \\ 0 & \frac{n}{2\hat{\sigma}^4} - \frac{n\hat{\sigma}^2}{\hat{\sigma}^6} \end{bmatrix}$$

$$= \begin{bmatrix} -\frac{n}{\widehat{\sigma}^2} & 0 \\ 0 & -\frac{n}{2\widehat{\sigma}^4} \end{bmatrix}.$$

21.5. Conditions for a local maximum

It is easily shown that $l(\widehat{\mu}, \widehat{\sigma}^2 | x)$ is a strict local maximum if

$$\left| \widehat{H}_1 \right| < 0, \quad \left| \widehat{H} \right| > 0. \tag{21.3}$$

Since

$$\left| \widehat{H}_1 \right| = -\frac{n}{\widehat{\sigma}^2} < 0, \quad \left| \widehat{H} \right| = \frac{n^2}{2\widehat{\sigma}^6} > 0,$$

$l(\widehat{\mu}, \widehat{\sigma}^2 | x)$ is a strict local maximum. In fact, for this problem it can be shown that $l(\widehat{\mu}, \widehat{\sigma}^2 | x)$ is the unique, global maximum.

21.6. General conditions for a local maximum

In general we require $H = \nabla^2 l$ to be *negative-definite*, that is,

$$\mathbf{x}^T \mathbf{H} \mathbf{x} < 0$$

for any vector $\mathbf{x} \neq \mathbf{0}$. This is so when the eigenvalues of H are all negative, as in the case above. The matrix $I = -H$ is called the *Fisher information matrix*, and is very significant in other fields, e.g. physics. It is easily shown that $l(\widehat{\mu}, \widehat{\sigma}^2 | x)$ is a strict local maximum if

$$\left| \widehat{H}_1 \right| < 0, \quad \left| \widehat{H} \right| > 0. \tag{21.4}$$

Since

$$\left| \widehat{H}_1 \right| = -\frac{n}{\widehat{\sigma}^2} < 0, \quad \left| \widehat{H} \right| = \frac{n^2}{2\widehat{\sigma}^6} > 0,$$

$l(\widehat{\mu}, \widehat{\sigma}^2 | x)$ is a strict local maximum. In fact, for this problem it can be shown that $l(\widehat{\mu}, \widehat{\sigma}^2 | x)$ is the unique, global maximum.

Why do we require $H = \nabla^2 l$ to be *negative-definite*? If l were one-dimensional, then it may be written as a Taylor series:

$$l(x + \Delta x) = l(x) + \Delta x \frac{d}{dx} l(x) + (\Delta x)^2 \frac{d^2}{dx^2} l(x) + \dots$$

However, if l were multidimensional, then the Taylor series is

$$l(\mathbf{x} + \Delta\mathbf{x}) = l(\mathbf{x}) + \Delta\mathbf{x} \cdot \nabla l(\mathbf{x}) + \underset{<0}{\Delta\mathbf{x}^T H \Delta\mathbf{x}} + \ldots$$

for any vector $\mathbf{x} \neq \mathbf{0}$. This is so when the eigenvalues of H are all negative, as in the case above. The matrix $I = -H$ is called the *Fisher information matrix*, and is very significant in other fields, e.g. physics.

21.7. Properties of ML estimators

Estimators of distribution parameters (such as μ and σ^2) under the MLE technique enjoy many desirable characteristics. Suppose in general β is the true parameter with an estimator $\widehat{\beta}$ under MLE. Then the MLE estimator is:

- consistent, i.e. $\widehat{\beta} \to \beta$ as the observed sample size $n \to \infty$, with convergence in probability
- asymptotically normal with variance I^{-1}
- asymptotically efficient, in the sense that it approaches the best possible.

CHAPTER TWENTY-TWO

Binomial and Poisson models (CT4: §10)

The simplest model is to consider:
- a given period for observation for a group of people
- each member of the group is identical in their mortality risk in the period
- the mortality of each person is independent from others.

Suppose the 'true' (but unknown) mortality rate for the group is denoted q. How can we estimate q from an observation of deaths?

22.1. Estimating q

The ideal approach is to observe the group throughout the whole period: Each member of the group has a probability q of dying and of $1 - q$ of surviving the period. If $\theta = 1$ if the member dies, and $\theta = 0$ if he survives, then

$$E(\theta) = q$$

and

$$\begin{aligned} \mathbf{var}(\theta) &= q(1 - q)^2 + (1 - q)(-q)^2 \\ &= q(1 - q). \end{aligned}$$

Suppose we observe n such members and count the total number of deaths:

$$\Theta = \theta_1 + \theta_2 + \cdots + \theta_n.$$

Then, as the θ_i are independent and identically distributed,

$$E(\Theta) = nq$$

and

$$\mathbf{var}(\Theta) = nq(1 - q).$$

So an estimate of q is

$$\hat{q} = \frac{\Theta}{n}$$

Actuarial Principles
https://doi.org/10.1016/B978-0-32-390172-7.00026-9

and this has variance

$$\mathbf{var}\left(\hat{q}\right) = \frac{q\left(1-q\right)}{n}.$$

22.2. The MLE for q

It is easy to show that the MLE for q is the same as $\hat{q} = \frac{\Theta}{n}$. The likelihood of observing $\theta_1, \theta_2, \ldots, \theta_n$ is

$$\mathcal{L} = \prod_{i=1}^{n} q^{\theta_i}\left(1-q\right)^{1-\theta_i}.$$

Taking logarithms, this is maximised when

$$\frac{d}{dq}\ln\mathcal{L} = \frac{1}{q}\sum_{i=1}^{n}\theta_i - \frac{1}{1-q}\sum_{i=1}^{n}(1-\theta_i) = 0$$

or when

$$\frac{1-q}{q} = \frac{n-\Theta}{\Theta}$$

so that

$$\hat{q} = \frac{\Theta}{n}.$$

22.3. Different observation periods

The above experiment is rare in practice, as people enter and leave observation for various reasons. How do we cope with this difficulty? It is necessary then to allow for a different period of observation for each member. Suppose member i is observed in the age interval

$$\left[x+a_i, x+b_i\right]$$

where $0 \le a_i < b_i \le 1$.

- This means that all members are observed only between ages x and $x+1$.

- If they are observed outside this range, then that would belong to a separate mortality investigation for the $[x-1, x]$ or $[x+1, x+2]$ age bracket.

Since we are dealing with different observation periods, it is also necessary to define a mortality law that can apply to such periods. We adopt the general notation:

$$_t q_z$$

as the probability of death for a person aged z exact over a period of length t. Hence $_{b_i - a_i} q_{x+a_i}$ is the probability of death for the observation of member i.

22.4. Likelihood function

If θ_i denotes as before the observed death of member i, then

$$E(\theta_i) = {}_{b_i - a_i} q_{x+a_i}.$$

The probability of observing $\theta_1, \theta_2, \dots \theta_n$ is

$$\mathcal{L} = \prod_{i=1}^{n} {}_{b_i - a_i} q_{x+a_i}^{\theta_i} \left(1 - {}_{b_i - a_i} q_{x+a_i}\right)^{1-\theta_i}.$$

This is called the *likelihood function* for the observation of deaths $\theta_1, \theta_2, \dots \theta_n$.

22.5. The Balducci assumption

We have first to simplify $_t q_z$ in order to get a mortality estimate. This can be done by making the *Balducci assumption* for specifying how mortality varies within a year of age:

$$_{1-t} q_{x+t} = (1-t) \, q_x.$$

This assumption reduces the mortality law to a single mortality rate q_x. Thus for member i, we get

$$\underbrace{{}_{b_i - a_i} q_{x+a_i}}_{} = {}_{1-a_i} q_{x+a_i} - {}_{1-b_i} q_{x+b_i} \cdot {}_{b_i - a_i} p_{x+a_i}$$

$$= (1 - a_i) \, q_x - \left(1 - b_i\right) q_x \cdot \left(1 - {}_{b_i - a_i} q_{x+a_i}\right)$$

$$= \left(b_i - a_i\right) q_x + \left(1 - b_i\right) q_x \cdot \underbrace{{}_{b_i - a_i} q_{x+a_i}}_{}$$

and hence

$$_{b_i-a_i}q_{x+a_i} = \frac{\left(b_i - a_i\right) q_x}{1 - \left(1 - b_i\right) q_x}.$$

Hence for $\Theta = \theta_1 + \theta_2 + \cdots + \theta_n$, we have

$$E\left(\Theta\right) = \sum_{i=1}^{n} \frac{\left(b_i - a_i\right) q_x}{1 - \left(1 - b_i\right) q_x}.$$

Hence an estimator for q_x is $\hat{q}_x$ satisfying

$$\Theta = \hat{q}_x \sum_{i=1}^{n} \frac{\left(b_i - a_i\right)}{1 - \left(1 - b_i\right) \hat{q}_x},$$

which has to be solved for $\hat{q}_x$ numerically.

22.6. The Balducci estimator

An alternative method of estimating q_x is to consider

$$_{b_i-a_i}q_{x+a_i} = \left(b_i - a_i\right) q_x + \left(1 - b_i\right) q_x \cdot {}_{b_i-a_i}q_{x+a_i}$$

and approximate $_{b_i-a_i}q_{x+a_i}$ on the right-hand side by the observed θ_i. On this basis,

$$E\left(\Theta\right) = \sum_{i=1}^{n} \left(b_i - a_i\right) q_x + \left(1 - b_i\right) q_x \theta_i.$$

The estimator $\hat{q}_x$ can be found to be that satisfying

$$\Theta = \hat{q}_x \sum_{i=1}^{n} \left(b_i - a_i\right) + \left(1 - b_i\right) \theta_i$$

or

$$\hat{q}_x = \frac{\Theta}{\sum_{i=1}^{n} \left(b_i - a_i\right) + \left(1 - b_i\right) \theta_i}$$

$$= \frac{\Theta}{\sum_{i=1}^{n} \left(1 - a_i\right) + \left(1 - b_i\right) \left(\theta_i - 1\right)}$$

$$= \frac{\Theta}{\sum_{i=1}^{n} \left(1 - a_i\right) - \sum_{\theta_i=0} \left(1 - b_i\right)}.$$

22.7. Initial and central risk exposures

The denominator of the Balducci estimator is

$$E = \sum_{i=1}^{n} (1 - a_i) - \sum_{\theta_i=0} \left(1 - b_i\right).$$

In this expression:
- Member i contributes a period of $b_i - a_i$ if he survives.
- If he dies, he contributes $1 - a_i$.
- Thus a member who dies is deemed to contribute the whole of the period to the end of the year.

Why is this reasonable? Because they can only cease being observed on the date of death—exit is not voluntary! When deaths are given exposure only to the point of death, we have simply

$$\overline{E} = \sum_{i=1}^{n} (1 - a_i) - \sum_{i=1}^{n} \left(1 - b_i\right)$$

$$= \sum_{i=1}^{n} \left(b_i - a_i\right).$$

This is called the *central* risk exposure. If deaths occur on average halfway during the year, then

$$E \simeq \overline{E} + \frac{1}{2}\Theta.$$

CHAPTER TWENTY-THREE

The Poisson model

The binomial model of mortality operates in discrete time: that is, only finite time periods are considered in which deaths occur.

- What happens when smaller and smaller time periods are allowed?
- How do we ensure that the mortality over two consecutive periods is consistent with the mortality over each one of these periods?

If we deal with these issues, we come to the *Poisson model* of mortality. This says that in a given period, the number of deaths for a group of n identical persons is Θ, where

$$prob\left(\Theta = k\right) = e^{-\mu n}\frac{(\mu n)^k}{k!}.$$

It is easy to show that

$$E\left(\Theta\right) = \mathbf{var}\left(\Theta\right) = \mu n$$

so that $\mu = \frac{E(\Theta)}{n}$ is called the force of mortality. The parameter μn is called the *Poisson parameter*.

23.1. Properties of the Poisson model

Note that the population size n can be replaced by:

- the combined population in each of two periods, that is, $2n$, if each of the periods has population n
- more generally, by the central exposure of life-years in a period, if people move into and out of the population.

This property of additivity of the Poisson parameter over periods is unique to the Poisson model (why?)

23.2. The MLE for the Poisson model

Suppose we observe Θ deaths in a population of size n. How do we estimate μ? Since

$$E\left(\Theta\right) = \mathbf{var}\left(\Theta\right) = \mu n$$

Actuarial Principles
https://doi.org/10.1016/B978-0-32-390172-7.00027-0

it may be concluded that an estimator for μ is

$$\hat{\mu} = \frac{\Theta}{n}.$$

This is also the MLE for μ (why?)

23.3. Choosing between the binomial and Poisson models

Both models estimate the mortality rate within a given period as the ratio of observed deaths to the observed population. How does one choose between them?

- The binomial model operates in discrete time, the Poisson in continuous time.
- The binomial model allows at most one death for a given member, the Poisson multiple deaths.
- The Poisson model is extendible to multiple periods in a consistent way.

Thus the choice of model depends on the purpose of your modelling, in particular:

- the timeframe of the model
- whether analysis of deaths within sub-periods is important
- whether other risk factors (e.g. sickness) are to be included.

CHAPTER TWENTY-FOUR

The Kaplan–Meier estimator (CT4: §8)

24.1. Mortality investigation with censoring

Consider the observation of N persons for a given period under the following rules:

- The N persons are selected with some common trait, e.g of the same age or with the same medical condition.
- There is only right censoring.
- Censoring is noninformative, e.g. commencement or cessation of observation is independent of the mortality status of the person.
- Although deaths can occur anywhere in continuous time, we can observe events only in discrete time.

24.2. Notation for the investigation

Let the observation period be divided into discrete intervals ending at times $t = 1, 2, \ldots k$. Define the following:

- d_t is the number of deaths occurring in the interval ended time t.
- c_t are the number of persons who are censored in the interval ended time t and, therefore, die at a time $> t$.
- All persons are eventually censored (perhaps in the last interval ended time k).
- $m = d_1 + d_2 + \ldots + d_k$ is the total number of deaths.
- $N - m = c_1 + c_2 + \ldots + c_k$ is the remaining number of persons observed who did not die.

24.3. The likelihood function

Suppose that:

- The probability of survival to time t is $G(t)$ (the survival function).
- Exits occur only at the end of each time interval.
- The mortality of each person is independent from other persons.

Then the probability of observing d_t deaths and c_t exits for time intervals $t = 1, 2 \ldots k$ is

$$\mathcal{L} = \prod_{t=1}^{k} [G(t-1) - G(t)]^{d_t} \cdot \prod_{t=1}^{k} G(t)^{c_t}.$$

This can be simplified using the following notation. Let λ_t be the probability of death at time t for those who have survived to time $t-1$, that is,

$$\lambda_t = \frac{G(t-1) - G(t)}{G(t-1)}$$

and so

$$1 - \lambda_t = \frac{G(t)}{G(t-1)}$$

and

$$G(t) = \prod_{i=1}^{t} (1 - \lambda_i)$$

and let n_t be the number of survivors to time t, that is,

$$n_t = n_{t-1} - d_t - c_t$$
$$= N - \sum_{i=1}^{t} (d_i + c_i).$$

Then $\mathcal{L}$ can be written as

$$\mathcal{L} = \prod_{t=1}^{k} [G(t-1) - G(t)]^{d_t} \cdot \prod_{t=1}^{k} G(t)^{c_t}$$

$$= \prod_{t=1}^{k} \lambda_t^{d_t} G(t-1)^{d_t} G(t)^{c_t}$$

$$= \prod_{t=1}^{k} \lambda_t^{d_t} \cdot \prod_{t=1}^{k} \left[\prod_{i=1}^{t-1} (1 - \lambda_i)^{d_t} \prod_{i=1}^{t} (1 - \lambda_i)^{c_t} \right].$$

The term $(1 - \lambda_i)$ appears in this product with exponent:

$$d_{i+1} + d_{i+2} + \ldots + d_k + c_i + c_{i+1} + \ldots + c_k$$
$$= N - (d_1 + d_2 + \ldots + d_i) - (c_1 + c_2 + \ldots + c_{i-1})$$
$$= n_{i-1} - d_i.$$

Thus

$$\mathcal{L} = \prod_{t=1}^{k} \lambda_t^{d_t} (1 - \lambda_t)^{n_{t-1} - d_t}.$$

24.3.1 Exercises

The Weibull distribution is often used to model windspeeds, which is important for locating windfarms (refer http://en.wikipedia.org/wiki/Weibull_distribution).

The density function for windspeed $x \geq 0$ is of the form

$$pdf = \frac{k}{\lambda} \left(\frac{x}{\lambda}\right)^{k-1} e^{-\left(\frac{x}{\lambda}\right)^k}$$

and this has the cumulative density function

$$cdf = 1 - e^{-\left(\frac{x}{\lambda}\right)^k}$$

where k is a shape parameter and λ is a scale parameter.

For a particular location, you have taken 100 observations of windspeeds x_i in $m/\sec$ for $i = 1, 2 \ldots 100$, over a 12-month period (set out on in the accompanying spreadsheet). Your task is to estimate the values of the parameters and their reliability using the method of MLE.

1. Write down the likelihood function in terms of the observations x_i.
2. Derive the first-order conditions for the MLE estimates, and explain why they cannot be solved analytically.
3. In the spreadsheet, calculate the log-likelihood function ℓ for given values of k and λ.
4. Using SOLVER within Excel, estimate k and λ by maximising ℓ numerically.
5. By making small variations in k and λ, estimate the Hessian matrix $\nabla^2 \ell$ and then comment on the reliability of your estimates.

    Hint: the Hessian matrix for F can be approximated for small h as

$$
\begin{bmatrix}
\frac{\partial^2 F}{\partial k^2} & \frac{\partial^2 F}{\partial k \partial \lambda} \\
\frac{\partial^2 F}{\partial k \partial \lambda} & \frac{\partial^2 F}{\partial \lambda^2}
\end{bmatrix}
\simeq
$$

$$
\begin{bmatrix}
\dfrac{F(k+h,\lambda)+F(k-h,\lambda)-2F(k,\lambda)}{h^2} & \dfrac{\begin{array}{c}F(k+h,\lambda+h)+F(k-h,\lambda-h)\\-F(k+h,\lambda-h)-F(k-h,\lambda+h)\end{array}}{4h^2} \\[4ex]
\dfrac{\begin{array}{c}F(k+h,\lambda+h)+F(k-h,\lambda-h)\\-F(k+h,\lambda-h)-F(k-h,\lambda+h)\end{array}}{4h^2} & \dfrac{F(k,\lambda+h)+F(k,\lambda-h)-2F(k,\lambda)}{h^2}
\end{bmatrix}.
$$

Solution

1. $\mathcal{L} = \prod_i \frac{k}{\lambda} \left(\frac{x_i}{\lambda}\right)^{k-1} e^{-\left(\frac{x_i}{\lambda}\right)^k}$
2. The FOCs are

$$-n\frac{k-1}{\lambda} + \frac{k}{\lambda^{k+1}} \sum x_i^k = 0$$

$$\frac{n}{k} - n \ln \lambda + \sum x_i - \frac{k}{\lambda^{k-1}} \sum x_i^{k-1} = 0.$$

These are clearly nonlinear in k and λ.

3. See the log likelihood in the cell shaded green.
4. SOLVER is used to maximise this, giving estimate of $k = 1.82$ and $\lambda = 8.3$. [In fact, the parameters used to simulate the windspeeds were $k = 2$ and $\lambda = 8.4$.]
5. The Hessian is calculated by varying ℓ by variations of $h = 0.001$. The resulting sds of k and λ are 0.57 and 0.08, respectively, which suggests a reasonable fit.

24.4. Kaplan–Meier estimator

The likelihood $\mathcal{L}$ is simple in form, despite having a complicated derivation. However, a much simpler derivation is possible. Note that:

- The experience in any year is independent of all other years.
- At time $t-1$, there are n_{t-1} persons alive who are exposed to death for the interval to time t.
- If λ_t is the probability of death of one person, then the probability of exactly d_t deaths from n_{t-1} persons is

$$\lambda_t^{d_t} (1 - \lambda_t)^{n_{t-1}-d_t}.$$

- Multiplying this probability over k years gives the expression for $\mathcal{L}$ above.

Suppose there are d_t deaths and c_t exits. This allows us to compute the survivors n_{t-1}. The maximum likelihood (MLE) estimator of the probabilities under the distribution function λ_t can be found by differentiating $\ln \mathcal{L}$ with respect to λ_t:

$$\ln \mathcal{L} = \sum_{t=1}^{k} d_t \ln \lambda_t + \left(n_{t-1} - d_t\right) \ln (1 - \lambda_t)$$

$$\frac{\partial}{\partial \lambda_t} \ln \mathcal{L} = \frac{d_t}{\lambda_t} - \frac{n_{t-1} - d_t}{1 - \lambda_t} = 0$$

or

$$d_t(1 - \lambda_t) - (n_{t-1} - d_t)\lambda_t = 0$$

or

$$\hat{\lambda}_t = \frac{d_t}{n_{t-1}}.$$

Thus the MLE estimate of mortality is given by dividing the number of deaths in a time interval by the number of those exposed to death at the start of that interval. This is a trivial result! But note that:

- The time intervals have been taken as uniform $t = 1, 2, \ldots k$, but there is no reason why they should have the same length.
- The c_t exits have been taken to have the same mortality as those who do not exit. The Kaplan–Meier approach can be adapted if this assumption does not hold.

The KM estimate of the survival function $G(t)$ is

$$\hat{G}(t) = \prod_{i=1}^{t} \left(1 - \hat{\lambda}_i\right).$$

Note that this is only an estimate, and has a variance. The variance of $\hat{\lambda}_t$ is from the binomial distribution:

$$\frac{\partial^2}{\partial \lambda_t^2} \ln \mathcal{L} = -\frac{d_t}{\lambda_t^2} - \frac{n_{t-1} - d_t}{(1 - \lambda_t)^2}$$

$$\mathbf{var}\left(\hat{\lambda}_t\right) = \frac{1}{n_{t-1}} \frac{d_t}{n_{t-1}} \left(1 - \frac{d_t}{n_{t-1}}\right)$$

$$= \frac{1}{n_{t-1}} \hat{\lambda}_t \left(1 - \hat{\lambda}_t\right)$$

and hence

$$\mathbf{var}\left(\hat{G}\right) = \prod_{i=1}^{t} \left[\left(1 - \hat{\lambda}_i\right)^2 + \frac{1}{n_{t-1}} \hat{\lambda}_t \left(1 - \hat{\lambda}_t\right)\right] - \hat{G}(t)^2$$

$$= \hat{G}(t)^2 \left[\prod_{i=1}^{t} \left(1 + \frac{1}{n_{t-1}} \frac{\hat{\lambda}_t}{1 - \hat{\lambda}_t}\right) - 1\right].$$

This is often approximated by Greenwood's formula:

$$\mathbf{var}\left(\hat{G}\right) = \hat{G}(t)^2 \sum_{i=1}^{t} \frac{1}{n_{t-1}} \frac{\hat{\lambda}_t}{1 - \hat{\lambda}_t}.$$

24.5. Application of the KM method

Example 24.1 (UK C4 Exam, Sept 2009). *An electronics company developed a revolutionary new battery which it believed would make it enormous profits.*

- *It commissioned a subcontractor to estimate the survival function of battery life for the first 12 prototypes.*
- *The subcontractor inserted each prototype battery into an identical electrical device at the same time and measured the duration elapsing between the time each device was switched on and the time its battery ran out.*
- *The subcontractor was instructed to terminate the test immediately after the failure of the 8th battery, and to return all 12 batteries to the company.*

When the test was complete, the subcontractor reported that he had terminated the test after 150 days. He further reported that:

- two batteries had failed after 97 days
- three further batteries had failed after 120 days
- two further batteries had failed after 141 days
- one further battery had failed after 150 days.

However, he reported that he was only able to return 11 batteries, as one had exploded after 110 days, and he had treated this battery as censored at that duration when working out the Kaplan–Meier estimate of the survival function.

Questions:

1. State, with reasons, the forms of censoring present in this study.
2. Calculate the Kaplan–Meier estimate of the survival function based on the information supplied by the subcontractor.
3. In his report, the subcontractor claimed that the Kaplan–Meier estimate of the survival function at the duration when the investigation was terminated was 0.2727. Explain why the subcontractor's Kaplan–Meier estimate would be consistent with him having stolen the battery he claimed had exploded.

Solution

Censoring took place after the failure of the eighth battery (150 days), and according to the subcontractor, one battery failed after 110 days as a result of explosion (not censored). Censoring is therefore on the right, and allegedly noninformative.

The relevant times for a KM analysis are $t = 0, 97, 110, 120, 141, 150$. The KM estimate of the survival function is as follows:

t	d_t	c_t	n_t	λ_t	$G(t)$
0			12		100.0%
97	2		10	17%	83.3%
110	1		9	10%	75.0%
120	3		6	33%	50.0%
141	2		4	33%	33.3%
150	1	3	0	25%	25.0%

The survival probability for 150 days is 25%, lower than the reported 27%. The subcontractor must have started off with a smaller number of batteries!

24.6. Nelson–Aalen estimator

There is a Poisson version of the Kaplan–Meier estimator. This relies on the 'integrated hazard' $\Lambda(t)$. In practice, deaths can be observed only discretely, so that the estimator for $\Lambda(t)$ is

$$\hat{\Lambda}(t) = \sum_{s \leq t} \frac{d_s}{n_s}.$$

This allows us to estimate the survival function $G(t)$ as

$$\hat{G}(t) = 1 - e^{-\hat{\Lambda}(t)}.$$

24.6.1 Exercises

In the Kaplan–Meier model of mortality, we have:
- N persons selected with some common trait, e.g. of the same age or with the same medical condition
- only right censoring
- d_t as the number of deaths occurring in the interval ended time t
- c_t as the number of persons who are censored in the interval ended time t and, therefore, die at a time $> t$
- all persons are eventually censored (perhaps in the last interval ended time k)

- $m = d_1 + d_2 + \ldots + d_k$ as the total number of deaths
- $N - m = c_1 + c_2 + \ldots + c_k$ as the remaining number of persons observed who did not die.

A mortality investigation is undertaken by an insurance company of people who are temporarily insured. Some persons are right censored because they remain in good health, do not see any purpose of continuing insurance and, therefore, withdraw. Suppose that:

- the probability of survival to time t is $G(t)$ for those who are *not* censored (the survival function)
- censoring is informative—the probability of survival to time t of those who are censored is higher than normal, and is described by a survival function $\sqrt{G(t)}$

Show that the likelihood function is

$$\mathcal{L} = \prod_{t=1}^{k} [G(t-1) - G(t)]^{d_t} \cdot \prod_{t=1}^{k} G(t)^{c_t/2}$$

Derive the Kaplan–Meier estimate for $G(t)$ in this case by the method of maximum likelihood.

Solution

If the probability of survival to time t is $G(t)$ for those who are *not* censored, the probability of death in the period ending time t is $G(t-1) - G(t)$. The probability of survival for those who are censored is $G(t)^{1/2}$. Hence the probability of d_t deaths and c_t exits for periods ending at times $t = 1, 2 \ldots k$ is

$$\mathcal{L} = \prod_{t=1}^{k} [G(t-1) - G(t)]^{d_t} \cdot \prod_{t=1}^{k} G(t)^{c_t/2}.$$

Let λ_t denote the probability of death at time t for those who have survived to time $t - 1$, and have not exited, that is,

$$\lambda_t = \frac{G(t-1) - G(t)}{G(t-1)}.$$

Then

$$\mathcal{L} = \prod_{t=1}^{k} \lambda_t^{d_t} G(t-1)^{d_t} G(t)^{c_t/2}$$

$$= \prod_{t=1}^{k} \lambda_t^{d_t} \cdot \prod_{t=1}^{k} \prod_{i=1}^{t-1} (1-\lambda_i)^{d_t} \prod_{i=1}^{t} (1-\lambda_i)^{c_t/2} .$$

The term $(1-\lambda_i)$ appears in this product with exponent:

$$d_{i+1} + d_{i+2} + \ldots + d_k + \frac{1}{2}(c_i + c_{i+1} + \ldots + c_k)$$

$$= N - (d_1 + d_2 + \ldots + d_i) - (c_1 + c_2 + \ldots + c_{i-1})$$

$$- \frac{1}{2}(c_i + c_{i+1} + \ldots + c_k)$$

$$= n_{i-1} - d_i - \frac{1}{2} C_{i-1}$$

where $C_{i-1} = c_i + c_{i+1} + \ldots + c_k$ are the number of people censored after time i. Thus:

$$\mathcal{L} = \prod_{t=1}^{k} \lambda_t^{d_t} (1-\lambda_t)^{n_{t-1}-d_t-\frac{1}{2}C_{t-1}} .$$

Taking logs, this is maximised when

$$\frac{\partial}{\partial \lambda_t} \ln \mathcal{L} = \frac{d_t}{\lambda_t} - \frac{n_{t-1} - d_t - \frac{1}{2}C_{t-1}}{1-\lambda_t} = 0$$

or when

$$\hat{\lambda}_t = \frac{d_t}{n_{t-1} - \frac{1}{2}C_{t-1}} .$$

This is greater than the uninformative estimate $\hat{\lambda}_t = \frac{d_t}{n_{t-1}}$ because it allows for the higher mortality of those who will withdraw during the investigation. (Note: This assumes that the people censored by the termination of the investigation at time k enjoy the lighter mortality).

CHAPTER TWENTY-FIVE

The Cox regression model (CT4: §9)

All models so far have assumed a homogeneous population of observed lives, i.e. all lives have the same mortality risks. How can we model a group of lives with heterogeneous risks? These risks are called *covariates* or *risk factors*, and might include:

- sex
- weight
- smoking/nonsmoking
- location
- occupation.

They can be denoted as a vector $\mathbf{z} = (z_1, z_2, \ldots z_p)$ for each member of the population.

25.1. The Cox model

The Cox model allowing for covariates is a regression model for mortality, using the covariates as regressors:

$$\lambda(t, \mathbf{z}) = \mu(t) \, e^{\boldsymbol{\beta}^T \mathbf{z}}.$$

Here:

- $\lambda(t, \mathbf{z})$ is the mortality rate for lives with covariates $\mathbf{z}$.
- $\mu(t)$ is the underlying mortality rates without covariates at time t.
- $\boldsymbol{\beta} = (\beta_1, \beta_2, \ldots \beta_p)$ is a vector of regression parameters, just like in a standard regression model.

25.2. Proportional hazards

The Cox model is sometimes called a model of *proportional hazards* because risk factors are allowed for *multiplicatively* in mortality rates.

- Thus the mortality of two individuals, one with and one without a risk factor, is a constant independent of other risks.
- This makes it possible to estimate the regression parameters $\boldsymbol{\beta}$ without knowing what the underlying mortality rates $\mu(t)$ are.

Actuarial Principles
https://doi.org/10.1016/B978-0-32-390172-7.00029-4

25.3. Partial likelihood

The form of the Cox model allows a modification of maximum likelihood to be used. This is known as *partial likelihood*.

- We have $\theta_1, \theta_2, \ldots \theta_m$ deaths as before, but now we consider these ordered in the sequence that they occur in time.
- Let $\mathbf{z}_{\theta_1}, \mathbf{z}_{\theta_2}, \ldots \mathbf{z}_{\theta_m}$ denote the risk factors for the first, second, etc deaths.
- Let $\mathbf{z}_1, \mathbf{z}_2, \ldots \mathbf{z}_n$ denote the risk factors of the total observed population $N = \{1, 2, \ldots n\}$.

Then we consider the likelihood of observing the order of deaths $\theta_1, \theta_2, \ldots \theta_m$, *given that* those deaths have occurred. Consider the time of the first death. Any one of the population of size n could have died, and the total probability of one death is

$$\sum_{i \in N} \mu(t) e^{\boldsymbol{\beta}^T \mathbf{z}_i}.$$

Yet the death that actually occurred is θ_1 with risk factor $\mathbf{z}_{\theta_1}$. So given that a death occurred, the likelihood that this is θ_1 is

$$\frac{e^{\boldsymbol{\beta}^T \mathbf{z}_{\theta_1}}}{\sum_{i \in N} e^{\boldsymbol{\beta}^T \mathbf{z}_i}}.$$

Similarly, for the second death, the likelihood is

$$\frac{e^{\boldsymbol{\beta}^T \mathbf{z}_{\theta_2}}}{\sum_{i \in N \backslash \theta_1} e^{\boldsymbol{\beta}^T \mathbf{z}_i}}$$

and so on.

By multiplying these likelihoods, we get the total likelihood that the sequence of deaths is $\theta_1, \theta_2, \ldots \theta_m$:

$$\mathcal{L} = \frac{e^{\boldsymbol{\beta}^T \mathbf{z}_{\theta_1}}}{\sum_{i \in N} e^{\boldsymbol{\beta}^T \mathbf{z}_i}} \frac{e^{\boldsymbol{\beta}^T \mathbf{z}_{\theta_2}}}{\sum_{i \in N \backslash \theta_1} e^{\boldsymbol{\beta}^T \mathbf{z}_i}} \cdots \frac{e^{\boldsymbol{\beta}^T \mathbf{z}_{\theta_m}}}{\sum_{i \in N \backslash \theta_1 \backslash \cdots \backslash \theta_{m-1}} e^{\boldsymbol{\beta}^T \mathbf{z}_i}}.$$

The symbol $\backslash$ denotes set subtraction, that is $N \backslash \theta_1$ denotes N without the member θ_1. Notice this is a complicated expression involving the $\boldsymbol{\beta} = (\beta_1, \beta_2, \ldots \beta_p)$. However, it can be maximised by varying these parameters.

25.4. Example of Cox model

Example 25.1. *Suppose that there are six male lives all aged 40 exact, some of whom smoke.*

They leave observation either by death or withdrawal during the investigation in the following order.

ID	Smoker?	Age at exit	Means of exit
1	y	41	death
2	n	42	death
3	y	43	withdrawal
4	n	45	withdrawal
5	n	48	death
6	y	50	withdrawal

Let the probability of death at age x be

$$\lambda(x, z) = \mu(x) e^{\beta z}$$

where $z = 1$ for a smoker and $z = 0$ for a nonsmoker.

Then the partial likelihood can be computed as follows:

- At age 41, there were 6 lives exposed to death and one died. The likelihood that the death was that of life 1, given one person died, is

$$\frac{e^{\beta}}{3e^{\beta} + 3}.$$

- Note that $\mu(41)$ does not figure in this likelihood, as all lives are of the same age. Also, there are six lives in total, three of whom smoke, and three do not smoke.
- At age 42, there are only five lives left. The probability that the second death is that of life 2 is

$$\frac{1}{2e^{\beta} + 3}$$

- and similarly at age 48, there are only two lives left: The partial likelihood for the sequence of deaths is thus: $\mathcal{L} = \frac{e^{\beta}}{3e^{\beta}+3} \cdot \frac{1}{2e^{\beta}+3} \cdot \frac{1}{e^{\beta}+1}$. To maximise the partial likelihood, it is convenient (as usual) to take logs and differentiate

$$\ln \mathcal{L} = \beta - 2\ln\left(e^{\beta} + 1\right) - \ln\left(2e^{\beta} + 3\right) + \text{constant}$$

$$\frac{\partial \ln \mathcal{L}}{\partial \beta} = 1 - \frac{2e^\beta}{e^\beta + 1} - \frac{2e^\beta}{2e^\beta + 3}$$

$$= \frac{2e^{2\beta} + 5e^\beta + 3 - 4e^{2\beta} - 6e^\beta - 2e^{2\beta} - 2e^\beta}{\left(e^\beta + 1\right)\left(2e^\beta + 3\right)}$$

$$= \frac{3 - 4e^{2\beta} - 3e^\beta}{\left(e^\beta + 1\right)\left(2e^\beta + 3\right)} = 0.$$

If we denote $u = e^\beta$, this is the solution of the quadratic equation

$$4u^2 + 3u - 3 = 0$$

or

$$e^\beta = \frac{-3 \pm \sqrt{9 + 48}}{8}.$$

25.5. Breslow's approximation

The expression for the partial likelihood on the first death

$$\frac{e^{\beta^T z_{\theta_1}}}{\sum_{i \in N} e^{\beta^T z_i}}$$

assumes that only one death, θ_1, occurs at that time. What if several deaths occur at the same time—say $P = \{\theta_1, \theta_2 \ldots \theta_p\}$? The proper way of dealing with this is to:

- take every combination of p deaths out of n lives
- calculate the likelihood of those deaths being P

In practice, a simpler way of calculating the likelihood of multiple deaths is through

$$\frac{\prod_{i \in P} e^{\beta^T z_{\theta_i}}}{\left[\sum_{i \in N} e^{\beta^T z_i}\right]^p}.$$

This can be applied to each set of multiple deaths. The intuition is that each life in P occurs out of the full N lives possible (not out of the lives reduced by the multiple deaths).

25.6. Example of Breslow's approximation

Suppose that lives 1 and 2 in the previous example died at the same time. Then the likelihood of the first pair of deaths being $P = \{\theta_1, \theta_2\}$ is approximated as

$$\frac{e^\beta}{\left(3e^\beta + 3\right)^2}$$

so the partial likelihood is

$$\mathcal{L} = \frac{e^\beta}{\left(3e^\beta + 3\right)^2} \cdot \frac{1}{e^\beta + 1}.$$

Breslow's approximation allows for the same person to die twice! For the sake of curiosity, the precise likelihood of the death of $P = \{\theta_1, \theta_2\}$ would be

$$\frac{e^\beta}{18e^\beta + 6e^{2\beta} + 6}.$$

This can be justified as follows:
- There are initially three smokers and three nonsmokers.
- If two deaths occur at the same time, there are $6 \times 5 = 30$ ways in which this could have occurred.
- Of these, $3 \times 2 = 6$ ways involve only smokers, or only nonsmokers.
- And there are $3 \times 3 \times 2 = 18$ ways that involve a smoker as the first death, and a nonsmoker as the second death, or vice versa.

25.7. Applying the Cox model

Thus a more precise likelihood is

$$\mathcal{L} = \frac{e^\beta}{18e^\beta + 6e^{2\beta} + 6} \cdot \frac{1}{e^\beta + 1}.$$

Maximising the partial likelihood is not always easy.
- In general, software giving numerical solutions has to be used.
- However, the partial likelihood estimator $\widehat{\beta}$ is consistent and asymptotically normal, just like maximum likelihood estimators in general.
- The information matrix is also given in the usual way as

$$I\left(\widehat{\beta}\right) = - \left.\frac{\partial^2 \ln \mathcal{L}}{\partial \beta^2}\right|_{\beta = \widehat{\beta}}$$

- Fortunately, this is a by-product of numerical maximisation, and gives an estimate of $\mathbf{var}\left(\hat{\boldsymbol{\beta}}\right) = I\left(\hat{\boldsymbol{\beta}}\right)^{-1}$.

25.7.1 Exercises

A pharmaceutical company has developed a drug which it believes will be helpful for preventing the onset of Type 2 diabetes. It has undertaken a clinical trial over a 10-year period of 50 persons who are susceptible to this condition:

- Some of the persons were treated with the drug, whilst a control group were given a placebo.
- Some of the persons were observed to develop diabetes during the trial, whilst others were right censored as a result of voluntary withdrawal or termination of the trial.

The results of the trial are summarised in the second tab, **q2**. Using the Body Mass Index (BMI) of the persons observed as risk factor 1, as well as the treatment by the drug or by placebo as risk factor 2, use the Cox model of proportional hazards to assess the effectiveness of the drug as follows:

1. Explain the calculation of the 'likelihood' in column F of the tab **q2** for given values of β_1, β_2.
2. Use the likelihood column to calculate the partial log likelihood $F = \ln \mathcal{L}$ of the observations.
3. Use the SOLVER routine in Excel to assess the values of β_1, β_2, which maximise the partial log likelihood.
4. Comment on the reliability of your estimates using the information matrix of $\mathcal{L}$.

Hint: the Hessian matrix for F can be approximated for small h as

$$
\begin{bmatrix}
\frac{\partial^2 F}{\partial \beta_1^2} & \frac{\partial^2 F}{\partial \beta_1 \partial \beta_2} \\
\frac{\partial^2 F}{\partial \beta_1 \partial \beta_2} & \frac{\partial^2 F}{\partial \beta_2^2}
\end{bmatrix}
\simeq
$$

$$
\begin{bmatrix}
\frac{F(\beta_1+h,\beta_2)+F(\beta_1-h,\beta_2)-2F(\beta_1,\beta_2)}{h^2} & \frac{F(\beta_1+h,\beta_2+h)+F(\beta_1-h,\beta_2-h)-F(\beta_1+h,\beta_2-h)-F(\beta_1-h,\beta_2+h)}{4h^2} \\
\frac{F(\beta_1+h,\beta_2+h)+F(\beta_1-h,\beta_2-h)-F(\beta_1+h,\beta_2-h)-F(\beta_1-h,\beta_2+h)}{4h^2} & \frac{F(\beta_1,\beta_2+h)+F(\beta_1,\beta_2-h)-2F(\beta_1,\beta_2)}{h^2}
\end{bmatrix}.
$$

Solution

See the solution spreadsheet.

The likelihood in column E is simply $e^{\boldsymbol{\beta}^T \mathbf{z}} = e^{\beta_1 z_1 + \beta_2 z_2}$, where z_1, z_2 are the BMI and treatment factors. Column F is the probability that, where a death occurs, the likelihood that this is for individual i is given by

$$\frac{e^{\boldsymbol{\beta}^T \mathbf{z}_{\theta_i}}}{\sum_{i \in S} e^{\boldsymbol{\beta}^T \mathbf{z}_i}}$$

where S is the set of individuals alive just before that death. The sum of the logs of column F, cell C1, provides the log-likelihood of the sequence of deaths observed.

If SOLVER is used to maximise the log likelihood, the values of the parameters are $\beta_1 = 0.518$, $\beta_2 = -2.762$. This indicates that BMI is a risk factor for diabetes, and that the treatment is effective in preventing it.

The Hessian matrix is

$$H = \begin{bmatrix} -5.6274 & -25.7220 \\ -25.7220 & -260.1269 \end{bmatrix}$$

and the information matrix is

$$I = -H^{-1} = \begin{bmatrix} 0.324260 & -0.032064 \\ -0.032064 & 0.007015 \end{bmatrix}.$$

Hence the standard deviations are of β_1, β_2 are 0.08 and 0.57, respectively, which suggest significance of both risk factors.

CHAPTER TWENTY-SIX

Graduation

In previous sections, you have learned how to estimate:

- decrement (mortality) rates for a specific group (cohort) of people with similar risk characteristics—the binomial or Poisson models
- the survival function for a population of people over time (or age)—the Kaplan–Meier model
- decrement rates from a heterogeneous population with various risk characteristics—the Cox regression model.

The question now becomes: *How do you apply the estimates from such models in real life situations?*

Some possible applications are in:

- pricing insurance products
- managing the funding of superannuation and pension funds
- inventory control of products with limited shelf life
- assessing efficacy of new drugs with usage over time
- replacement of machinery or equipment (can have effectively a survival table for equipment).

26.1. Some issues with raw estimates

The models for estimating raw (crude) decrement rates all suffer from one possible defect: There is measurement error always potentially present.

Such error can arise from:

- the occurrence of abnormal events in the timeframe relevant to the data, for example a single large claim, or a flu epidemic in a year that is not typical of long-term experience
- heterogeneity in the data, for example where the data sampling has been restricted to wealthy or poor neighbourhoods in a biased way
- misstatement on the data itself (if collected by surveys for instance).

Such measurement error can result in undesirable outcomes:

- discontinuities in premium rates
- over- or under-pricing of particular risks (e.g. mileage in motor insurance).

We consider in this chapter mainly mortality rates as they relate to age.

Actuarial Principles
https://doi.org/10.1016/B978-0-32-390172-7.00030-0
149

26.2. Definition of 'graduation'

- **Graduation** is the process of adjusting a set of observed rates of occurrence to produce a relatively smooth pattern, possibly following a certain mathematical formula, to provide a suitable basis for actuarial and demographic calculations of a practical nature.
- Essentially this process is that of **choosing a model** to represent the assumed underlying set of decrement rates.
- We then fit the model to the data, calculating the model parameters which give the best result.
- Thus the graduation process is that of using statistical techniques to improve the estimated rates as produced from the observed data.

26.3. Aim of the graduation process

There are two competing aims of the graduation process:

- Graduation should produce a set of comparatively smooth rates suitable for the relevant purpose:
  - to remove random sampling errors as far as is possible and reasonable
  - to use the information available from adjacent ages to improve the reliability of the estimated rates.
- To be faithful to the data—**fidelity** (also known as **goodness-of-fit**) to the extent that the data can model future experience.

26.4. Do mortality rates progress smoothly?

It is intuitively reasonable to assume that mortality rates will generally progress smoothly from age to age:

- After all, the cohort of people at a particular age x in a time-limited investigation will exhibit many features in common with those at adjacent ages $x - 1$, $x + 1$, etc.
- If we are looking at a mortality investigation over a period of 3 or more years, the same group of individuals will contribute years of exposure at adjacent ages and there will be few reasons to suppose that their experienced mortality will suddenly jump unevenly when they progress from age to age.

There are, however, some notable exceptions—the accident hump and post-retirement mortality.

26.4.1 The accident hump for young lives

- If population members on an age such as their 17th or 18th birthday are suddenly able to drive cars or motorbikes, and to drink alcohol in public places, then, given the 'risk taking tendencies' of young males in particular, a significant discontinuity in experienced rates of mortality may then be experienced.
- This creates a discontinuity in experienced mortality rates known as the *accident hump*.
- This effect is likely to be spread over a number of years, as some males in the experience will suffer from increased accident incidence as young as 15–17, and others at ages past 18.
- Other factors can also interplay, for example incidences of drowning, flying accidents, mountain climbing accidents, etc., which also become more prevalent for young people of similar ages.
- The same effect will also apply for females of similar ages, but perhaps statistically they are less likely to indulge in risk-tasking behaviour.

26.4.2 The retirement effect

- Other discontinuities in mortality can be experienced in practice, for example it is a commonly held belief that mortality rates for males rise suddenly after they retire from the workforce—at ages such as 60 to 65.
- This can be a combination of the effect of increasing ill-health causing their retirement, and also the possibility that some psychological trauma and possible feeling of uselessness affects them after retirement. There is also a possible physical effect of the body reacting adversely to a reduction in their stress levels, bringing out health problems that were possibly 'submerged' previously.
- Countering this of course should be that people after retirement should be able to enjoy a healthier lifestyle and will have more time for exercise.

CHAPTER TWENTY-SEVEN

Graduation techniques (CT4: §12)

Here are some well-known graduation techniques:
- graphical graduation
- mathematical graduation
- standard table graduation
- splines and adjusted average graduation—not covered here.[1]

In what follows,
- $\hat{q}_x$ denotes the raw (or crude) mortality rate observed from a risk exposure E_x,
- and $\overset{\circ}{q}_x$ the graduated rate.

Note the following for the binomial estimate for mortality rates:
- $\hat{q}_x = \frac{\theta_x}{E_x}$ is the observed mortality rate.
- $\hat{q}_x$ is a binomial random variable with parameters $n = E_x$ and $p = q_x$.
- Therefore, if $np = q_x > 5$, $\theta_x \tilde{} N(E_x q_x, E_x q_x p_x)$.
- $\hat{q}_x$ approximately $N(q_x, \frac{q_x}{E_x})$.
- The confidence interval is (approximately)

$$\hat{q}_x \pm 2\sqrt{\frac{\hat{q}_x}{E_x}}.$$

Technique: Draw a curve through the estimated $\hat{q}_x$, within the confidence interval of each estimate.

27.1. Pros and cons of graphical techniques

Graphical techniques:
- can always and quickly be applied
- can be used to capture (subjectively assessed) features of importance
- do not need prior assumption as to shape or form

but
- requires experience
- do not necessarily result in smoothness
- may lack precision.

---

[1] See 'The Analysis of Mortality', Benjamin and Pollard, Chapter 12.

Actuarial Principles
https://doi.org/10.1016/B978-0-32-390172-7.00031-2

27.2. Mathematical graduation methods

What do we graduate? That is, what is our dependent variable? It could be $\hat{q}_x$. It could also be the force of mortality

$$\mu_x \simeq -\ln(1 - \hat{q}_x) = -\ln \hat{p}_x.$$

We specify some mathematical form for the dependent variable, e.g.

$$\hat{q}_x = F(x).$$

Then estimate the parameters of $F(x)$. Common types of curves are used:
- Makeham and Gompertz
- Perk
- Barnett
- Heligman and Pollard
- others.

27.3. Makeham and Gompertz

The following curves are traditional:
Gompertz:

$$\mu_x = Bc^x.$$

Makeham:

$$\mu_x = A + Bc^x.$$

We may approximate μ_x by $\mu_x = -\ln(1 - \hat{q}_x)$.

27.3.1 To estimate the Gompertz curve

1. Plot $-\ln(\mu_x) = -\ln\left[-\ln(1 - \hat{q}_x)\right]$ against x. This should approximate

$$-\ln(\mu_x) = -\ln(B) - \ln(c)x.$$

Does this appear linear?
2. Draw a line through $-\ln\left[-\ln(1 - \hat{q}_x)\right]$ (or estimate by OLS).
3. Read off values for a and b in

$$-\ln(\mu_x) = a + bx$$
$$= -\ln(B) - \ln(c)x$$

obtaining $\hat{c}$ and $\hat{B}$.

4. Plot $\overset{\circ}{q}_x$ where

$$\overset{\circ}{q}_x = 1 - \exp\left(-\hat{B}\hat{c}^x\right).$$

27.4. Example for estimating the Gompertz curve

Example 27.1. *Suppose a population of approx. 370,000 individuals has been surveyed, with the following raw mortality statistics (5-year ages only):*

age x	$\hat{q}_x$	E_x	age x	$\hat{q}_x$	E_x
5	0.0038%	4969	45	0.2261%	4815
10	0.0039%	4966	50	0.3401%	4757
15	0.0752%	4963	55	0.5043%	4673
20	0.0702%	4951	60	0.8829%	4546
25	0.0708%	4931	65	1.0085%	4348
30	0.0929%	4910	70	1.6319%	4040
35	0.0771%	4884	75	3.0503%	3583
40	0.1565%	4854	80	6.1672%	2898

An OLS regression of $-\ln\left[-\ln(1 - \hat{q}_x)\right]$ against x gives the following Excel output:

	b	a
coeff	−0.07573	9.364255
SE	0.003014	0.140503
R2, Sey	0.890052	0.622466
F, df	631.4246	78
SSQ	244.6543	30.2222

Using a and b to plot $\overset{\circ}{q}_x$, we get the following chart:

Is this a good fit? It looks OK at first, but notice that:

- the graduated rates look consistently lower than the raw rates at ages 20–30
- and consistently higher at ages 50–60.

We need a systematic way of testing for goodness-of-fit (see later).

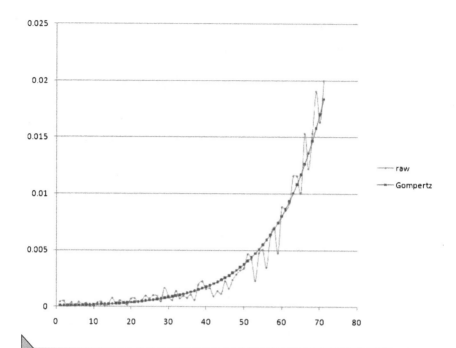

27.5. Perk's curve

There are may other functional forms for graduated rates. In the following, we write $\overset{\circ}{q}_x$ simply as q_x for convenience:

$$\mu_x \text{ or } q_x$$
$$= \frac{A + Bc^x}{1 + Dc^x}$$
$$\text{or}$$
$$= \frac{A + Bc^x}{Kc^{-x} + 1 + Dc^x}.$$

However, this curve:
- does not work very well at all ages
- may, up to 25 be too low, and between 30–35 may be too high.

However, it is very influential in determining alternative functional forms.

27.6. Barnett's formula

$$\frac{q_x}{p_x} = A - Hx + Bc^x$$

$$\Longrightarrow \frac{q_x}{p_x} = f(x)$$

$$\Longrightarrow q_x = \frac{f(x)}{1 + f(x)}$$

$$\Longrightarrow q_x = \frac{A - Hx + Bc^x}{1 + A - Hx + Bc^x}.$$

This has the following features:
- a satisfactory fit for both select and ultimate tables
- allowance for lower mortality at younger ages.

27.7. Heligman–Pollard

$$\frac{q_x}{p_x} = A^{(x+B)^c} + De^{-E(\ln x - \ln F)^2} + GH^x.$$

This model works well but is notoriously hard to fit! It has many parameters, since it is trying to capture:
- child mortality
- accident mortality and
- senescent mortality.

This can be used to graduate ALT2005–07.

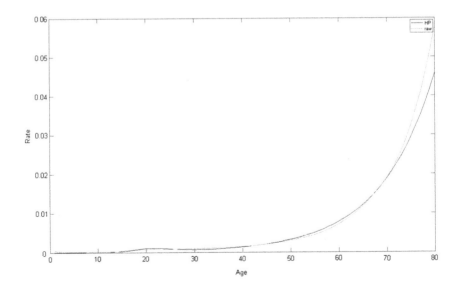

This was fitted using Matlab® and Solver. Interpreting the parameter values:

A	approximates q_1, mortality at year 1.	0.001875
B	no clear interpretation	0.022003
C	early life rate of decline in mortality, Δq_x	1.65195
D	accident hump intensity	0.00083
E	accident hump dispersion	13.95933
F	accident hump location	21.03957
G	level of senescent mortality	3.96E-05
H	change in senescent mortality	1.092218

CHAPTER TWENTY-EIGHT

Methods of estimation of the parameters

The main methods of estimating parameters in any given model are:
- maximum likelihood
- least squares and
- minimum chi-square.

28.1. Maximum likelihood (MLE)

If $\theta_x \sim B(E_x, q_x)$, then

$$P\left(\theta_x | E_x, q_x\right) = \binom{E_x}{\theta_x} q_x^{\theta_x} \left(1 - q_x\right)^{E_x - \theta_x}.$$

Assuming independence, the likelihood function is

$$\mathcal{L}\left[\theta_0, \theta_1, \ldots \theta_N | E_x, q_x\right] = \prod_x \binom{E_x}{\theta_x} q_x^{\theta_x} \left(1 - q_x\right)^{E_x - \theta_x}.$$

Therefore maximise

$$\ln \mathcal{L} = \sum_x \left[\ln \binom{E_x}{\theta_x} + \theta_x \ln q_x + (E_x - \theta_x) \ln p_x \right]$$

or

$$\Lambda = \sum_x \left[\theta_x \ln q_x + (E_x - \theta_x) \ln p_x \right]$$

with respect to the parameters in $q_x = F(x)$. The steps are to:
1. Derive first derivatives of Λ with respect to the parameters in $F(x)$.
2. Set these first derivatives to zero.
3. Solve the resulting equations for the parameters in $F(x)$.

Commonly use computer programs to do this—use numerical approximation. For example, assuming the same set of data we used before, let

$$q_x = F(x) = \frac{\exp\left[a + b(x - 70)\right]}{1 + \exp\left[a + b(x - 70)\right]}.$$

Actuarial Principles
https://doi.org/10.1016/B978-0-32-390172-7.00032-4

Then

$$\ln\left(\frac{q_x}{p_x}\right) = a + b(x - 70).$$

Estimate a and b by MLE.

28.2. Least squares (OLS/WLS)

If we approximate q_x by $\hat{q}_x = q_x + e_x$, with

$$q_x = F(x)$$

then OLS estimates are obtained by minimising

$$SSE = \sum_x w_x \left[\hat{q}_x - F(x)\right]^2$$

by finding $F(x)$. If $w_x = 1$, we are assuming that the variance at all ages are the same, i.e.

$$q_x p_x / E_x = \text{constant}.$$

A more realistic approach allows the variance to vary with age. WLS estimates are obtained by minimising SSE with

$$w_x = \frac{E_x}{q_x}$$

or

$$w_x = \frac{E_x}{q_x^{ST}}$$

where q_x^{ST} is from a standard life table. The steps are to:
1. Derive first derivatives of SSE with respect to the parameters in $F(x)$.
2. Set these first derivatives to zero.
3. Solve the resulting equations for the parameters in $F(x)$.
    For example: Assuming the same set of data we used before and the Makeham curve, let

$$-\ln(p_x) = \alpha + \beta e^{\gamma x} = A + Bc^x.$$

Since $-\ln(p_x) \simeq q_x$, therefore

$$\mathbf{var}\left[-\ln(p_x)\right] \simeq \mathbf{var}(q_x) = \frac{E_x}{q_x}.$$

This is a nonlinear equation and so must be solved numerically.

28.3. Minimum chi-square method (MCSM)

Aims to choose parameter values to minimise the χ^2 statistic. Uses an iterative search for a set of parameters in $q_x = F(x)$ that minimise

$$\chi^2 = \sum_x \frac{(\theta_x - q_x E_x)^2}{q_x(1 - q_x)E_x}.$$

28.4. Which estimation method to use?

As E_x increases, the distribution for q_x can be approximated by the normal. In this case,

$$MLE \equiv OLS \equiv MCSM.$$

That is, all three methods become equivalent.

28.5. Pros and cons of the mathematical approach

Mathematical graduation always produces a smooth curve. We need only to test fidelity.

Advantages.
- The results are always smooth.
- Usually, the total and the accumulated deviations are zero.
- General purpose computer packages make implementation easy.
- Objectivity.

Disadvantages
- It may be difficult to find a suitable curve.
- Less judgement is required.
- A single curve is usually not sufficient.

28.6. Standard table graduation

If we have the following:
- we have scanty data, **and**
- we know that the observations $\hat{q}_x$ comes from a population with characteristics believed similar to a population for which a standard table q_x^{ST} has previously been developed, then we can use q_x^{ST} as a 'base curve' for graduation.

We may observe some relationship in the ratio

$$\frac{\hat{q}_x}{q_x^{ST}}.$$

Lidstone improved this method by using

$$\mu_x = \mu_x^{ST} + c$$

which implies

$$\ln\left(\frac{p_x^{ST}}{\overset{\circ}{p}_x}\right) = \text{constant.}$$

However, more complicated functions of x (age) may work better. For example, a cubic in age,

$$\ln\left(\frac{p_x^{ST}}{\overset{\circ}{p}_x}\right) = c + \alpha x + \beta x^2 + \gamma x^3.$$

We apply this form to the example data.

28.7. Variations of the standard table approach

Functional form	Dependent variable	Independent variables		Weights	
$\hat{q}_x = c + \alpha\, q_x^{ST}$	$\overset{\circ}{q}_x$	q_x^{ST}	1	$\frac{E_x}{q_x^{ST}}$	Linear
$\hat{q}_x = q_x^{ST}(c + \alpha\, x)$	$\frac{\overset{\circ}{q}_x}{q_x^{ST}}$	x	1	$\frac{E_x}{q_x^{ST}}$	Linear Trend
$\hat{q}_x = \alpha\, q_x^{ST1} + \beta q_x^{ST2}$	$\overset{\circ}{q}_x$	q_x^{ST1}	q_x^{ST2}	$\frac{2E_x}{q_x^{ST1} + q_x^{ST2}}$	Linear Mixture

These forms are generally estimated by WLS.

28.8. Summary of the standard table approach

The standard table approach has benefits as well as drawbacks.

Advantages

- It is valuable when data are scanty. Other methods are not much use in this case.

- Standard tables are smooth so the final graduation is smooth $\Rightarrow$ can concentrate on adherence.
- There are no missing values at ends of table.
  Disadvantages
- It is not always possible to find a suitable standard table.

CHAPTER TWENTY-NINE

Assessing a graduation (CT4: §13)

Graduation is a trade-off between:
- smoothness of graduated rates $\overset{\circ}{q}_x$ and
- fidelity to the observed rates $\hat{q}_x$.

How do we assess these characteristics? This can be done using mathematical and statistical techniques.

29.1. Testing for smoothness

Smoothness is a mathematical property that is in the eyes of the observer. However, it is commonly accepted that if the third derivative of a mathematical function is small (relative to the values of the function), then the function has limited curvature, and can be considered 'smooth'.

For graduated rates, which are based on discrete ages, this idea can be implemented by:
- analysing the nth order differences $\Delta^n \overset{\circ}{q}_x$, for $n = 1, 2, 3$
- comparing these differences to $\hat{q}_x$.

29.2. Testing for fidelity

For assessing fidelity in graduated rates, we compare the actual deaths with those predicted by $\overset{\circ}{q}_x$, and consider the *standardised differences*. These can be analysed across the *whole of the age range* for:
- goodness–of–fit using the χ^2 test
- normality (using a different χ^2 test)
- overall bias (low or high graduated rates) using the sign test.

In addition, we can test for fidelity of a graduation over age bands by analysing for:
- normality of *cumulative* standardised differences
- runs of signs (positive or negative) in standardised differences
- serial correlation of standardised differences.

29.3. Standardised mortality differences z_x

If $\overset{\circ}{q}_x$ is an unbiased estimate of the true q_x, and deaths follow a binomial distribution, the following *standardised difference* in deaths should be approximately normal:

$$z_x = \frac{\theta_x - \overset{\circ}{q}_x E_x}{\sqrt{\overset{\circ}{q}_x \left(1 - \overset{\circ}{q}_x\right) E_x}}.$$

This is also known as a *standardised deviation* (a confusing term, which is avoided in this book). Sometimes, when we are testing the suitability of a standard life table, we replace $\overset{\circ}{q}_x$ by q_x^{ST}. We adopt a Poisson distribution of deaths in continuous time with a graduated force of mortality $\overset{\circ}{\mu}_x$ and risk exposures $\overline{E}_x$, then the corresponding standardised difference is

$$z_x = \frac{\theta_x - \overset{\circ}{\mu}_x \overline{E}_x}{\sqrt{\overset{\circ}{\mu}_x \overline{E}_x}}.$$

Either way, we can exploit the approximate normality of z_x to test for fidelity of the graduation. This is shown as follows.

29.4. The χ^2 test for goodness-of-fit

This is a well-known test based on the statistic:

$$\chi^2 = \sum_x z_x^2,$$

which has a χ^2 distribution with m degrees of freedom.

For the appropriate degrees of freedom m, we can compute χ^2 from the data and the graduated rates, and see whether it exceeds a desired confidence level. What m is depends on the method of graduation:

*   If the graduated rates are taken straight from a standard life table, then we have imposed no restrictions and m is the number of age groups N.
*   If the graduated rates are based on a mathematical formula with k estimated parameters, then we have restricted the shape of the graduated rates, and $m = N - k$.
*   If other (subjective) methods of graduation are used, we may need to guess how many constraints k have been imposed.

Though χ^2 is a good measure of overall fidelity, it does not identify the following possible defects:

- The z_x may show skewness or fat-tails (i.e. not normal).
- The z_x may not be random across the whole age spectrum (clumping or runs).
- The z_x may be biased away from zero.

The following tests deal with these issues.

29.5. The χ^2 test for normality

The z_x are assumed to be independent and normally distributed $\tilde{N}(0,1)$. It is therefore possible to use any of the normality tests to confirm this assumption.[1] One of these tests is the familiar Pearson χ^2 test. To implement this:

- Divide the range of observations of z_x into 'bins'.
- The bins are chosen so that the number of observed values of z_x is at least 5.
- Calculate the statistic $\chi^2 = \sum_{bins} \frac{(Actual-Expected)^2}{Expected}$ where for each bin, *Actual* is the observed number of values of z_x, and *Expected* is the number expected if $z_x \tilde{} N(0,1)$.

This statistic χ^2 should follow the χ^2 distribution for $bins - 1$ degrees of freedom.

29.6. The sign test for overall bias

Despite the χ^2 tests above, the graduation may still be biased (the z_x may be predominantly positive or negative, which isn't picked up in the χ^2 test). A simple (nonparametric) way of testing for bias is to consider the sign of the z_x. If $z_x \tilde{} N(0,1)$, then the sign of z_x, that is,

$$\mathbf{signum}(z_x) = \begin{cases} 1 & \text{if } z_x \geq 0 \\ 0 & \text{if } z_x < 0 \end{cases}$$

should have a binomial distribution with parameter $\frac{1}{2}$. Thus if there are N values of z_x, and of these m are positive, then the probability of this

---

[1] http://en.wikipedia.org/wiki/Normality_test.

occurring is

$$\binom{N}{m}\left(\frac{1}{2}\right)^{N}$$

If m is either too large or small in relation to the mean $\frac{1}{2}N$ (as measured by the probability of having *at least* m positive values exceeding a significance level), then the graduation shows overall bias.

 ## 29.7. Example of χ^2 test and sign tests

Example 29.1. *Consider the example of graduation by the Gompertz curve:*
- *The z_x can computed for 80 values, and the χ^2 statistic is 245.*
- *For a confidence level of 95%, and $80 - 2 = 78$ degrees of freedom with $\chi^2_{0.95,78} = 58.7$, we reject the hypothesis that the z_x are normally distributed. Hence the graduation lacks fidelity.*
- *On the other hand, the sign test provides little evidence of this. The number of positive z_x is 40, out of the 80 observations (not surprisingly), so that the number of positive signs is not unusual.*

29.8. The cumulative test for goodness-of-fit

As a variant on the χ^2 test for goodness-of-fit, it is possible to test whether the graduated mortality rates explain the *total* number of deaths across all ages. That is, we consider the random variable

$$\Theta = \sum_{x} \theta_x.$$

If each $\theta_x \tilde{\;} N(E_x \overset{o}{q}_x, E_x \overset{o}{q}_x \overset{o}{p}_x)$ and are independent, we should have Θ normally distributed with mean:

$$E(\Theta) = \sum_{x} E_x \overset{o}{q}_x$$

and variance

$$\mathbf{var}(\Theta) = \sum_{x} E_x \overset{o}{q}_x \overset{o}{p}_x$$

and thus the following statistic can be examined for normality:

$$\frac{\Theta - \sum_x E_x \overset{o}{q}_x}{\sqrt{\sum_x E_x \overset{o}{q}_x \overset{o}{p}_x}} \sim N(0,1).$$

29.9. Tests based on ordering

All the tests considered so far do not take any account of the *order* in which the mortality differences occur. That is, only the distribution of the differences z_x matters. What happens when the z_x are positive at low ages x (say) and negative at high ages, but clustered around zero as a whole?

There are two tests that are designed to take account of the ordering by age of z_x:

- the grouped signs test
- the serial correlation test.

29.10. The grouped signs test

This is (like the signs test) a nonparametric test based on the number of clusters in z_x, which are positive or negative. Note that a cluster means a run in z_x values when they are ordered by age.

Suppose there are N values of z_x, and they can be divided into:

- n_1 positive values, and
- $n_2 = N - n_1$ negative values.

What is the probability of observing exactly t positive clusters? To answer this question, note that

- There are $\binom{N}{n_1}$ possible sequences of positive and negative values.
- n_1 positive values can be divided into t clusters in $\binom{n_1-1}{t-1}$ ways.
  - we have to insert $t-1$ dividers between the values $1, 2, \ldots n_1 - 1$
- n_2 negative values can be separated by t positive clusters in $\binom{n_2+1}{t}$ ways
  - we have to insert t dividers between the values $0, 1, 2, \ldots n_2$.

Hence the probability of observing exactly t positive clusters is

$$\pi_t = \frac{\binom{n_1-1}{t-1}\binom{n_2+1}{t}}{\binom{N}{n_1}}.$$

Hence we can calculate the probability of observing up to t positive clusters. If this exceeds our level of significance, we can reject the assumption that clustering is random. In practice the distribution of t can be approximated by a normal distribution (how?).

29.11. Example of the grouped signs test

Example 29.2. *Going back to our example of Gompertz graduation, it can be calculated that there are exactly $t = 18$ positive clusters, with $n_1 = n_2 = 40$.*
The distribution of t has a mean of

$$\frac{n_1 (n_2 + 1)}{n_1 + n_2} = 20.5$$

and a standard deviation of

$$\frac{n_1 n_2}{(n_1 + n_2)^{3/2}} = 2.2$$

so that the grouped sign test offers little evidence against the graduation.

29.12. The serial correlation test

However, in the previous example, the clusters occur mainly at older ages, so that another test might be applied. This leads us to a parametric test based on serial correlations. This last test takes account of the actual values of z_x, and thus is a parametric test. It can be implemented by taking the sequences for various $k > 0$:

- $A = \{z_1, z_2, \ldots z_{N-k}\}$
- $B = \{z_{k+1}, z_{k+2}, \ldots z_N\}$
- calculating the correlation coefficient ρ between A and B for different values of the lag k.

It is well known that has a mean of 0 and a variance of $\frac{1}{N}$, so that testing $\rho \sqrt{N}$ against a unit normal distribution can identify the presence of clustering in the z_x.

> CHAPTER THIRTY

Summary: estimation and graduation

We now consider the question: What is the connection between estimation of (crude) mortality rates and their graduation for constructing a life table? We consider the following data and variables at age x:

- exposures $N = E_x$
- deaths $\theta_1, \theta_2, \ldots \theta_N$
- total deaths $\Theta_x = \theta_1 + \theta_2 + \cdots + \theta_N$
- true mortality rate q_x
- estimated mortality rate $\hat{q}_x$ – modelling
- graduated mortality rate $\overset{\circ}{q}_x$ – graduation.

30.1. Modelling

Estimation is usually carried out by the method of maximum likelihood:

Model	Likelihood $\mathcal{L}$	Estimate
Binomial	$\prod_i q_x^{\theta_i} \left(1 - q_x\right)^{1-\theta_i}$	$\hat{q}_x = \frac{\Theta_x}{N}$
Poisson	$e^{-\mu_x N} \frac{(\mu_x N)^{\Theta_x}}{\Theta_x!}$	$\hat{\mu}_x = \frac{\Theta_x}{N}$
Binomial plus	$\prod_i {}_{b_i - a_i} q_{x+a_i}^{\theta_i} \left(1 - {}_{b_i - a_i} q_{x+a_i}\right)^{1-\theta_i}$	$\hat{q}_x = \dfrac{\Theta_x}{\sum\limits_{i=1}^{n}(1-a_i) - \sum\limits_{\theta_i=0}(1-b_i)}$
Kaplan Meier	$\prod_t [G(t-1) - G(t)]^{d_t} \cdot \prod_t G(t)^{c_t} =$ $\prod_t \lambda_t^{d_t} (1 - \lambda_t)^{n_{t-1} - d_t}$	$\hat{\lambda}_t = \frac{d_t}{n_{t-1}}$
Cox: risk factor weights $\boldsymbol{\beta}$	$\dfrac{e^{\boldsymbol{\beta}^T \mathbf{z}_{\theta_1}}}{\sum\limits_{i \in N} e^{\boldsymbol{\beta}^T \mathbf{z}_i}} \dfrac{e^{\boldsymbol{\beta}^T \mathbf{z}_{\theta_2}}}{\sum\limits_{i \in N \backslash \theta_1} e^{\boldsymbol{\beta}^T \mathbf{z}_i}} \cdots \dfrac{e^{\boldsymbol{\beta}^T \mathbf{z}_{\theta_m}}}{\sum\limits_{i \in N \backslash \theta_1 \backslash \cdots \backslash \theta_{m-1}} e^{\boldsymbol{\beta}^T \mathbf{z}_i}}$	$\hat{\boldsymbol{\beta}}$

30.2. Graduation

Many approaches may be used for graduation, as this can be a subjective affair.

Method	Basis	Procedure	Assessment of $\overset{\circ}{q}_x$
Graphical	$\hat{q}_x \pm 2\sqrt{\frac{\hat{q}_x}{E_x}}$		handfit $\overset{\circ}{q}_x$ within region
By mathematical formula	$\hat{q}_x = F(x)$	MLE $\mathcal{L} = \prod_x \binom{E_x}{\Theta_x} q_x^{\Theta_x} (1 - q_x)^{E_x - \Theta_x}$	$\overset{\circ}{q}_x$ comes from fitted parameters of $F(x)$
		OLS/WLS $SSE = \sum_x w_x [\hat{q}_x - F(x)]^2$	
		Chi-square $\chi^2 = \sum_x \frac{(\Theta_x - q_x E_x)^2}{q_x(1 - q_x)E_x}$	
By standard table	$\hat{q}_x = G\left(q_x^{ST}\right)$	OLS/WLS $SSE = \sum_x w_x [\hat{q}_x - G(q_x^{ST})]^2$	$\overset{\circ}{q}_x$ comes from fitted parameters of $G\left(q_x^{ST}\right)$
Splines and blending	not examinable		

30.2.1 Assessing smoothness

Consider nth order differences, $\Delta^n \overset{\circ}{q}_x$, for $n = 1, 2, 3$.

30.2.2 Assessing fidelity

Consider *standardised differences*

$$z_x = \frac{\Theta_x - \overset{\circ}{q}_x E_x}{\sqrt{\overset{\circ}{q}_x \left(1 - \overset{\circ}{q}_x\right) E_x}}.$$

Tests across the *whole of the age range* for:

- goodness-of-fit using the test for $\chi^2 = \sum_x z_x^2$
- normality using Pearson $\chi^2 = \sum_{bins} \frac{(Actual - Expected)^2}{Expected}$ with $Actual = $ observed number of values of z_x in each bin
- overall bias (low or high graduated rates) using the sign test for m positive values of z_x, with probability $\binom{N}{m} \left(\frac{1}{2}\right)^N$.

  Tests over age bands by analysing for:

- normality of *cumulative* standardised differences $\frac{\sum_x \Theta_x - E_x \overset{\circ}{q}_x}{\sqrt{\sum_x E_x \overset{\circ}{q}_x \overset{\circ}{p}_x}} N(0, 1)$

- runs of signs with n_1 positive values, n_2 negative values of z_x. If there are t positive clusters, this occurs with probability

$$\pi_t = \frac{\binom{n_1-1}{t-1}\binom{n_2+1}{t}}{\binom{n_1+n_2}{n_1}}.$$

  The statistic t has mean of $\frac{n_1(n_2+1)}{n_1+n_2}$ and a standard deviation of $\frac{n_1 n_2}{(n_1+n_2)^{3/2}}$
- serial correlation of z_x.

CHAPTER THIRTY-ONE

Experience rating and Markov processes

In Chapter 11, we considered transitions between states, such as health, illness or death. These are examples of Markov chains (or processes), where the probability of transition from one state to another depends only on the current state. This is part of a much deeper branch of statistics. However, it has many applications to actuarial science, besides financial contracts based on multiple states, or insurance underwriting.

In this chapter, we consider its application to no–claim–bonus (NCB) schemes, which are used commonly in motor or other types of general insurance to inform the riskiness of an insured based on their past claims history. As we shall see, the requirement of transition based only on a current state, rather than a history, can be easily overcome.

31.1. The risk premium

The *risk premium* is the pricing of the pure risks that underlie an insurance contract, ignoring for the moment practical issues such as:
- how much the insurer can earn on invested premiums
- whether the insurer's expenses are covered
- the insurer's profit margins.
  The main issues in establishing a risk premium for an insurer are:
- the distribution of claim frequencies per unit of 'exposure'
- the distribution of claim amounts per claim
- the 'exposure' resulting from a single insurance contract
- how exposures vary over time, for example with inflation.

31.2. Exposures

What is 'exposure'?
- It is a measure of the possible loss in a contract, for example the insured value of a vehicle.
- It clearly depends on the design of an insurance contract, for example limitations of cover.

- It may also depend on factors which are known to the insured but not to the insurer (e.g. number of kilometres driven in a year).

The analysis of claim frequencies and claim amounts for pricing is to be covered in later stages of this unit, and involves heavy use of statistical techniques.

31.3. Exposures and asymmetry in information

The dependence of exposures on factors that are unknown to the insurer is a nasty problem, for example the worst drivers seeking insurance. This is sometimes called 'adverse selection'.

There is a related problem, called 'moral hazard'. Here, insured drivers take more risks, confident in the knowledge they will not have to pay fully for them.

How do insurers deal with these problems?

31.4. Experience rating

Insurers can counter-react by using *experience rating*. Here, the premium for an insured depends on an insured's previous claims experience. The classic example of this is in no-claim bonus (NCB) schemes. These are commonly used in motor insurance, but also in health insurance.

31.5. NCB schemes

An NCB scheme consists of:
- a set of 'ratings' or categories that indicate how safe an insured driver is. Rating 1 is usually the safest, and there may be up to 5 rating levels.
- A discount from the normal premium for each rating level:

Rating	Bonus
1	50%
2	25%
3	0%

- rules for moving between rating levels, for example:
  - move down a rating if a claim is made in any year
  - move up a rating if no claims are made for 2 years
  - stay at rating 1 forever if at this level for 10 years
  - In the US, a 5-year claims history is often employed.

31.6. Modelling NCB schemes

An **NCB** scheme can be modelled as a Markov chain in which:
- Each rating level is a state of the chain.
- The probability of moving from one rating level to another depends only on the current rating level (and not past levels).
- The probability of moving from rating i to rating j is constant over time and denoted p_{ij}.
- $\mathbf{P} = [p_{ij}]$ is called the *transition matrix* of the scheme.

If for an insured $\boldsymbol{\pi}^t = [\pi_1^t, \pi_2^t, \dots \pi_n^t]$ is the probability of being states $i = 1, 2 \dots n$, then it is clear that

$$\pi_j^{t+1} = \sum_{i=1}^{n} \pi_i^t p_{ij}.$$

In matrix notation, this can be written simply as

$$\boldsymbol{\pi}^{t+1} = \boldsymbol{\pi}^t \mathbf{P}.$$

31.7. Equilibrium distribution

In theory, we can use the relationship $\boldsymbol{\pi}^{t+1} = \boldsymbol{\pi}^t \mathbf{P}$ to calculate how the probability distribution of rating levels changes over time.

Is there an *equilibrium* distribution, that is, one which becomes stable eventually?

The answer is provided by the theory of Markov chains:
- If it is always possible to move eventually from one rating level to any other.
- And there is a finite expectation of time to return to a rating level from a given rating level.
- Then there will be an equilibrium probability distribution of rating levels.
- This is given by the limit as $t \to \infty$ of $\boldsymbol{\pi}^t$, denoted simply by $\boldsymbol{\pi}$.
- Clearly, we have $\boldsymbol{\pi} = \boldsymbol{\pi} \mathbf{P}$, so that $\boldsymbol{\pi}$ is a (left) eigenvector of $\mathbf{P}$.

31.7.1 Equilibrium distribution

Here is an example.

Example 31.1. *Suppose there are three rating levels, with a transition matrix*

$$\mathbf{P} = \begin{bmatrix} 0.1 & 0.9 & 0 \\ 0.1 & 0 & 0.9 \\ 0 & 0.1 & 0.9 \end{bmatrix}$$

The equilibrium probability distribution $\boldsymbol{\pi} = [\pi_1, \pi_2, \pi_3]$ *thus satisfies the equations:*

$$0.1\pi_1 + 0.1\pi_2 = \pi_1$$
$$0.9\pi_1 + 0.1\pi_3 = \pi_2$$
$$0.9\pi_{21} + 0.1\pi_3 = \pi_3.$$

31.8. Equilibrium distribution

Example 31.2. *In addition, as* $\boldsymbol{\pi}$ *is a probability distribution:*

$$\pi_1 + \pi_2 + \pi_3 = 1.$$

This allows us to solve

$$\pi_1 = \frac{1}{91}, \pi_2 = \frac{9}{91}, \pi_3 = \frac{81}{91}.$$

An obvious objection to the example above is that it is only the *current* rating level that is relevant to pricing. *This objection can be circumvented by defining what is meant by a 'state'.* It may be defined as the current rating, along with, say, the last 5 years' ratings (or claims history). In the example above. This expands the number of 'states' from 3 to 15. This complicates the analysis, but the analysis is still tractable. Some simple examples follow.

31.9. Exercises

1. **An** *NCB* **scheme with multiple accidents**
    An insurer operates a No Claims Discount system with three levels of discount:

Level	Discount
1	50%
2	20%
3	0%

The **NCB** system operates in practice under the following procedure.
- The annual premium at level 3 (i.e. with no discount) is $1000.
- If a policyholder makes no claims in a policy year, they move to the next high discount level (or remain at level 1). In all other cases, they move to (or remain at) discount level 3.
- For a policyholder who has not yet had an accident in a policy year, the probability of an accident occurring is 0.1. The time at which an accident occurs in the policy year is denoted by T, where $0 \le T \le 1$ indicates the time at which an accident occurs during a policy. It is assumed that T has a uniform distribution.
- Given that a policyholder has had their first accident, the probability of them having a second accident in the same policy year is $0.4(1 - T)$.
- You may ignore the possibility that a policyholder will have more than two accidents in a policy year.
- The cost to the policyholder of each accident has an exponential distribution with mean $2000.
- After each accident, the policyholder decides whether or not to make a claim by comparing the increase in the premium they would have to pay in the next policy year with the claim size. In doing this, they assume that they will have no further accidents.

(i) Show that the probability distribution of the number of accidents K, that a policyholder has in a year, is

K	Probability
0	0.9
1	0.08
2	0.02

(ii) For each level of discount, calculate the probability that a policyholder makes n claims in a policy year, where $n = 0, 1, 2$.
(iii) Write down the transition matrix.
(iv) Derive the steady-state distribution.

Solution

The probability of no accidents in a year is clearly $1 - 0.1 = 0.9$.
The probability of at least accident in a year 0.1. This can occur at time T, which has a uniform distribution. The probability of no further accidents is $1 - 0.4(1 - T)$, so that the probability of exactly one

accident is

$$0.1 \int_0^1 \left[1 - 0.4 \left(1 - T \right) \, dT \right] = 0.1 \left[0.6 + \frac{1}{2} \times 0.4 \right] = 0.08.$$

The probability of two accidents is therefore $1 - 0.9 - 0.08 = 0.02$.
If a policyholder has no accidents, he will move to the next higher
NCB level if he is on rating 2 or 3, and stay at rating 1 if he is currently
at this level.

NCB level	Discount if claim	Discount if no claim	Claim threshold
1	0%	50%	500
2	0%	50%	500
3	0%	20%	200

And hence the probabilities of claim for one or two accidents is as
follows:

	Probability of exceeding claim threshold	
NCB level	1 accident	2 accidents
1	0.7788	0.9511
2	0.7788	0.9511
3	0.9048	0.9909

The probability of exceeding the claim threshold X for a single accident under the exponential distribution is $e^{-X/2000.}$ Where there are
two accidents, at least one claim will be made if the threshold is ex-
ceeded for either accident, so that the probability of at least one claim
is $1 - \left(1 - e^{-X/2000.} \right)^2$. This gives the following transition matrix:

NCB level	1	2	3
1	0.9187	0.0000	0.0813
2	0.9187	0.0000	0.0813
3	0.0000	0.9078	0.0922

In the above matrix, the probability of moving to level 3 is the same
as that of making at least one claim, weighted by the probabilities that
either one or two accidents occur.
The eigenvector associated with the stable distribution can be easily
computed as

[0.8431   0.0746   0.0822]

2. An *NCB* scheme with history

Another insurer operates a different **NCB** system, with deeper levels of discount than in question 2:

NCBLevel	Discount
1	70%
2	30%
3	0%

The rules of operation are that:

- A claim in any year will move the policyholder down to level 3, unless he has been at level 1 for 2 consecutive years, in which case he will move to level 2.
- A claim-free year will result in a move up one level, unless the policyholder is at level 2, in which case he must have 2 *consecutive* claim-free years.

The insurance has been targeted at young drivers, who may always be expected to claim if an accident occurs. The probability of an accident in any year is 0.3, but the probability of more than one accident in any year is negligible.

a. Show that the **NCB** scheme with the three **NCB** levels as states is *not* a Markov chain.

b. Define the states of a process as the current **NCB** level, paired with the previous year's **NCB** level. [For example, (2, 1) would represent a policyholder who is currently at level 1, having been at level 2 last year. Show that there are eight possible states are (1, 1), (1, 2), (2, 1), (2, 2), (2, 3), (3, 1), (3, 2), (3, 3), and that these states define a Markov chain.]

c. Find the transition matrix of the Markov process.

d. Find its stable distribution and the average level of discount offered by the scheme.

Solution

The three **NCB** levels do not provide a Markov chain, as the probability of moving to level 1 from level 2 depends also on the level in the previous year. Similarly for the movement from level 1 to level 2.

The following table shows that we can predict the state of a policy-holder given only his current state:

States	If claim	If no claim
11	21	11
12	31	11
21	32	22
22	32	12
23	32	12
31	33	23
32	33	23
33	33	23

The transition matrix is therefore:

States	11	12	21	22	23	31	32	33
11	0.7	0	0.3	0	0	0	0	0
12	0.7	0	0	0	0	0.3	0	0
21	0	0	0	0.7	0	0	0.3	0
22	0	0.7	0	0	0	0	0.3	0
23	0	0.7	0	0	0	0	0.3	0
31	0	0	0	0	0.7	0	0	0.3
32	0	0	0	0	0.7	0	0	0.3
33	0	0	0	0	0.7	0	0	0.3

which can be solved for the stable distribution:

[0.343   0.147   0.103   0.072   0.138   0.044   0.094   0.059]

Weighting this by the discount for each state, namely

Discount   70%   70%   30%   30%   30%   0%   0%   0%

we calculate an average discount of 24%.

International actuarial notation

Discrete time

Interest and life table functions

v	$= \frac{1}{1+i}$	discount factor for interest
d	$= \frac{i}{1+i}$	discounted interest
$a_{\overline{n}|}$	$= \frac{1-v^n}{i}$	value of an annuity certain
$Ia_{\overline{n}|}$	$= \frac{\ddot{a}_{\overline{n}|}-nv^n}{i}$	value of an increasing annuity certain
ℓ_x		number of people surviving to age x
${}_tp_x$	$= \frac{\ell_{x+t}}{\ell_x}$	probability of survival to age x
q_x	$= 1 - \frac{\ell_{x+1}}{\ell_x}$	probability of death between ages x and $x+1$
K_x	$\mathbf{prob}\,(K_x = t) = \frac{\ell_{x+t}-\ell_{x+t+1}}{\ell_x}$	curtate lifespan of a person aged x
e_x	$= \mathbf{E}\,(K_x)$	curtate expectation of life for a person aged x

Financial functions

A_x	$= \mathbf{E}\left(v^{K_x+1}\right)$	value of a lifetime insurance to a person aged x
a_x	$= \mathbf{E}\left(a_{\overline{K_x}|}\right)$	value of a lifetime annuity to a person aged x
$\ddot{a}_x$	$= a_x + 1 = \mathbf{E}\left(\ddot{a}_{\overline{K_x+1}|}\right)$	value of an immediate lifetime annuity
$A_{x:\overline{n}|}$	$= \mathbf{E}\left[v^{\min(K_x+1,n)}\right]$	value of a limited insurance to a person aged x
$\ddot{a}_{x:\overline{n}|}$	$= \mathbf{E}\left[\ddot{a}_{\overline{\min(K_x+1,n)}|}\right]$	value of a limited annuity
$A^1_{x:\overline{n}|}$	$= \mathbf{E}\left[v^{K_x+1}\chi_{n-K_x}\right]$	value of a limited temporary insurance
$A^{\;1}_{x:\overline{n}|}$	$= v^n\frac{\ell_{x+n}}{\ell_x}$	value of a pure endowment

Deferred, increasing or frequently payable functions

${}_{m|}a_x$	$= v^m\frac{\ell_{x+m}}{\ell_x}a_{x+m}$	a lifetime annuity deferred for m years
${}_{m|}A_x$	$= v^m\frac{\ell_{x+m}}{\ell_x}A_{x+m}$	a lifetime insurance deferred for m years
IA_x	$= \mathbf{E}\left[(1+K_x)\,v^{K_x+1}\right]$	value of an increasing insurance
$I\ddot{a}_x$	$= \mathbf{E}\left(I\ddot{a}_{\overline{K_x+1}|}\right)$	value of an increasing annuity
$\ddot{a}^{(m)}_x$	$= \ddot{a}_x - \frac{m-1}{2m}$	value of a lifetime annuity payable, frequency m
$\ddot{a}^{(m)}_{x:\overline{n}|}$	$= \ddot{a}_{x:\overline{n}|} - \frac{m-1}{2m}\left(1 - v^n\frac{\ell_{x+n}}{\ell_x}\right)$	value of a limited annuity payable, frequency m

Continuous time

Interest and life table functions

δ	$= \ln(1+i)$	force of interest
$\bar{a}_{\overline{n}\rvert}$	$= \frac{1-v^n}{\delta}$	value of an annuity certain
$I\bar{a}_{\overline{n}\rvert}$	$= \frac{\bar{a}_{\overline{n}\rvert}-nv^n}{\delta}$	value of an increasing annuity certain, starting at 0
μ_x	$= -\frac{1}{\ell(x)}\frac{d\ell(x)}{dx}$	instantaneous mortality at age x (or force of mortality)
T_x	$\mathbf{pdf}(T_x = t) = -\frac{1}{\ell(x)}\frac{d\ell(x+t)}{dt}$	complete lifespan of a person aged x
$\overset{o}{e}_x$	$= \mathbf{E}(T_x)$	complete expectation of life for a person aged x

Financial functions

$\overline{A}_x$	$= \mathbf{E}\left(v^{T_x}\right)$	value of a lifetime insurance to a person aged x
$\bar{a}_x$	$= \mathbf{E}\left(\bar{a}_{\overline{T_x}\rvert}\right)$	value of a continuous lifetime annuity to a person aged x
$\overline{A}_{x:\overline{n}\rvert}$	$= \mathbf{E}\left[v^{\min(T_x,n)}\right]$	value of a limited insurance to a person aged x
$\bar{a}_{x:\overline{n}\rvert}$	$= \mathbf{E}\left(\bar{a}_{\overline{\min(T_x,n)}\rvert}\right)$	value of a limited continuous annuity
$\overline{A}^{\,1}_{x:\overline{n}\rvert}$	$= \mathbf{E}\left[v^{T_x}\chi_{n-T_x}\right]$	value of a limited temporary insurance

Deferred, increasing or frequently payable functions

$_{m\rvert}\bar{a}_x$	$= v^m \frac{\ell_{x+m}}{\ell_x}\bar{a}_{x+m}$	a continuous lifetime annuity deferred for m years
$_{m\rvert}\overline{A}_x$	$= v^m \frac{\ell_{x+m}}{\ell_x}\overline{A}_{x+m}$	a continuous lifetime insurance deferred for m years
$I\overline{A}_x$	$= \mathbf{E}\left[T_x v^{T_x}\right]$	value of an increasing continuous insurance
$I\bar{a}_x$	$= \mathbf{E}\left(I\bar{a}_{\overline{T_x}\rvert}\right)$	value of an increasing continuous annuity

AMC00 – life table and benefit values

Age x	$\ell_{[x]}$	$\ell_{[x-1]+1}$	ℓ_x	$\ddot{a}_x$	$I\ddot{a}_x$
20	9,983,699	9,985,487	9,986,216	28.303	635.448
21	9,979,057	9,980,844	9,981,583	28.135	625.649
22	9,974,367	9,976,183	9,976,921	27.963	615.727
23	9,969,649	9,971,474	9,972,222	27.785	605.682
24	9,964,883	9,966,728	9,967,485	27.601	595.518
25	9,960,070	9,961,934	9,962,701	27.412	585.235
26	9,955,200	9,957,092	9,957,869	27.218	574.836
27	9,950,262	9,952,183	9,952,970	27.018	564.324
28	9,945,247	9,947,197	9,947,993	26.812	553.702
29	9,940,185	9,942,134	9,942,940	26.600	542.973
30	9,935,066	9,936,994	9,937,779	26.381	532.141
31	9,929,879	9,931,767	9,932,502	26.157	521.209
32	9,924,577	9,926,424	9,927,089	25.925	510.182
33	9,919,118	9,920,934	9,921,520	25.688	499.065
34	9,913,484	9,915,260	9,915,776	25.443	487.861
35	9,907,615	9,909,380	9,909,816	25.191	476.577
36	9,901,492	9,903,246	9,903,613	24.933	465.218
37	9,895,076	9,896,839	9,897,136	24.667	453.791
38	9,888,327	9,890,109	9,890,336	24.394	442.301
39	9,881,188	9,882,998	9,883,156	24.113	430.758
40	9,873,589	9,875,457	9,875,556	23.825	419.166
41	9,865,453	9,867,408	9,867,458	23.529	407.536
42	9,856,722	9,858,774	9,858,794	23.225	395.875
43	9,847,309	9,849,488	9,849,488	22.913	384.192
44	9,837,117	9,839,431	9,839,431	22.594	372.498
45	9,826,050	9,828,529	9,828,529	22.266	360.801
46	9,813,973	9,816,656	9,816,656	21.931	349.112
47	9,800,744	9,803,679	9,803,679	21.587	337.443
48	9,786,209	9,789,444	9,789,444	21.236	325.805
49	9,770,189	9,773,771	9,773,771	20.876	314.209
50	9,752,455	9,756,471	9,756,471	20.509	302.669
51	9,732,803	9,737,319	9,737,319	20.134	291.196
52	9,710,923	9,716,063	9,716,063	19.751	279.805
53	9,686,508	9,692,414	9,692,433	19.360	268.509
54	9,659,210	9,666,021	9,666,118	18.963	257.322

continued on next page

Age x	$\ell_{[x]}$	$\ell_{[x-1]+1}$	ℓ_x	$\ddot{a}_x$	$I\ddot{a}_x$
55	9,628,617	9,636,521	9,636,772	18.558	246.258
56	9,594,355	9,603,496	9,604,007	18.146	235.331
57	9,555,955	9,566,532	9,567,396	17.728	224.557
58	9,512,928	9,525,156	9,526,477	17.304	213.949
59	9,464,710	9,478,853	9,480,731	16.874	203.521
60	9,410,685	9,427,021	9,429,582	16.439	193.289
61	9,350,180	9,369,014	9,372,401	15.999	183.267
62	9,282,487	9,304,159	9,308,519	15.555	173.468
63	9,206,832	9,231,703	9,237,197	15.108	163.906
64	9,122,396	9,150,836	9,157,637	14.657	154.594
65	9,028,326	9,060,710	9,069,000	14.204	145.543
66	8,923,713	8,960,433	8,970,375	13.750	136.766
67	8,807,636	8,849,057	8,860,811	13.295	128.274
68	8,679,154	8,725,611	8,739,311	12.840	120.075
69	8,537,336	8,589,125	8,604,857	12.386	112.178
70	8,381,265	8,438,602	8,456,406	11.933	104.590

Useful mathematical techniques

The following mathematical results are useful for analysis of benefits in continuous time in this unit.

1. Definition of derivative as a limit

$$\frac{df}{dt} = \lim_{dt \to 0} \frac{f(t+dt) - f(t)}{dt}.$$

2. Chain rule (function-of-a-function rule):

$$\frac{d}{dt}[f(g(t))] = \frac{df}{dg} \cdot \frac{dg}{dt}.$$

3. Taylor expansion:

$$f(t+h) = f(t) + hf'(t) + \frac{1}{2}h^2 f''(t) + \ldots + \frac{h^n}{n!} f^{(n)}(t) + \ldots.$$

4. Product rule:

$$\frac{d}{dt}(uv) = v\frac{du}{dt} + u\frac{dv}{dt}$$

and integrating in (a, b) we get rule for integration by parts

$$\int_a^b \frac{d}{dt}(uv)\,dt = [uv]_a^b$$

$$= \int_a^b v\frac{du}{dt}\,dt + \int_a^b u\frac{dv}{dt}\,dt.$$

A useful application of this is to find the mean under an exponential distribution $\mu \int_0^\infty t e^{-t/\mu}\,dt$, by putting $u = t$ and $v = e^{-t/\mu}$.

5. Integrating factors for solving a first-order homogeneous differential equations of the form

$$\frac{df}{dt} + \alpha(t)f(t) = \beta(t).$$

Multiply by a function $M(t)$ so that

$$M(t)\frac{df}{dt} + \alpha(t)f(t)M(t) = \frac{d}{dt}(Mf)$$

and this works when

$$\frac{1}{M}\frac{dM}{dt} = \frac{d\ln M}{dt} = \alpha(t)$$

or

$$M = e^{\int \alpha(t)dt}.$$

The differential equation now may be solved from

$$\frac{d}{dt}(Mf) = \beta(t).$$

6. Differentiating an integral:

$$\frac{d}{dt}\int_{a(t)}^{b(t)} f(s,t)\,ds = b'(t)f[b(t),t] - a'(t)f[a(t),t] \text{ — use chain rule}$$

$$+ \int_{a(t)}^{b(t)} \frac{\partial}{\partial t}f(s,t)\,ds.$$

7. More matrix algebra.

B.1. Eigenvalues and eigenvectors

An $n \times n$ square matrix $\mathbf{A}$ has an eigenvalue λ if there exists an $n \times 1$ vector $\mathbf{x}$ such that

$$\mathbf{Ax} = \lambda\mathbf{x}.$$

We know that every such matrix has n eigenvalues (counted with multiplicity), since they are roots of the nth degree polynomial equation:

$$\det(\mathbf{A} - \lambda\mathbf{I}) = 0.$$

However, some of the eigenvalues may be complex numbers (i.e. involve $i = \sqrt{-1}$).

B.2. Diagonalisation

Consider all the eigenvectors $\{\mathbf{x}_1, \mathbf{x}_2, \ldots \mathbf{x}_n\}$ corresponding to the eigenvalues $\{\lambda_1, \lambda_2, \ldots \lambda_n\}$.

If $\{\mathbf{x}_1, \mathbf{x}_2, \ldots \mathbf{x}_n\}$ are linearly independent (i.e. no nontrivial linear combination of them will equal 0), then the matrix of column vectors

$$\mathbf{X} = [\mathbf{x}_1, \mathbf{x}_2, \ldots \mathbf{x}_n]$$

has *full rank*, and is therefore invertible. That is $\mathbf{X}^{-1}$ exists. In this case, the matrix $\mathbf{A}$ is said to be *diagonisable*, and

$$\mathbf{AX} = [\mathbf{Ax}_1, \mathbf{Ax}_2, \ldots \mathbf{Ax}_n]$$
$$= [\lambda_1 \mathbf{x}_1, \lambda_2 \mathbf{x}_2, \ldots \lambda_n \mathbf{x}_n]$$
$$= \mathbf{X}\Lambda$$

where

$$\Lambda = \begin{bmatrix} \lambda_1 & 0 & 0 & 0 \\ 0 & \lambda_2 & 0 & 0 \\ 0 & 0 & \ddots & 0 \\ 0 & 0 & 0 & \lambda_n \end{bmatrix}$$

is a diagonal matrix of eigenvalues. This can be written simply as

$$\mathbf{A} = \mathbf{X}\Lambda\mathbf{X}^{-1}.$$

B.3. The benefits of diagonalisation

Almost all square matrices are *diagonisable*—in particular all symmetric matrices (which arise as covariances). Once a matrix is diagonalised, it is easy to calculate its powers, for example:

$$\mathbf{A}^m = \underbrace{\mathbf{X}\Lambda\mathbf{X}^{-1} \cdot \mathbf{X}\Lambda\mathbf{X}^{-1} \cdot \ldots \cdot \mathbf{X}\Lambda\mathbf{X}^{-1}}_{m \text{ times}}$$
$$= \mathbf{X}\Lambda^m \mathbf{X}^{-1}.$$

It is even possible to calculate its exponential:

$$e^{\mathbf{A}} = \mathbf{I} + \mathbf{A} + \frac{1}{2!}\mathbf{A}^2 + \cdots + \frac{1}{m!}\mathbf{A}^m + \cdots$$
$$= \mathbf{I} + \mathbf{X}\Lambda\mathbf{X}^{-1} + \frac{1}{2!}\mathbf{X}\Lambda^2\mathbf{X}^{-1} + \cdots \frac{1}{m!}\mathbf{X}\Lambda^m\mathbf{X}^{-1} + \cdots$$
$$= \mathbf{X}e^{\Lambda}\mathbf{X}^{-1}$$

and its square root, if all eigenvalues are nonnegative:

$$\mathbf{C} = \sqrt{\mathbf{A}} = \mathbf{X}\sqrt{\Lambda}\mathbf{X}^{-1}.$$

This last function is an example of a (symmetric) Cholesky decomposition, as $\mathbf{A} = \mathbf{C}^2$, which can be used to simulate a normal distribution with covariance matrix $\mathbf{A}$.

B.4. Nondiagonisable matrices

All is not lost when a (nonsymmetric) matrix cannot be diagonalised. In this case, the eigenvectors $\{\mathbf{x}_1, \mathbf{x}_2, \ldots \mathbf{x}_n\}$ are not linearly independent. However, the *Jordan canonical form* may be used to generate *generalised* eigenvectors of the form

$$(\mathbf{A} - \lambda \mathbf{I})^m \mathbf{x} = 0$$

and $\mathbf{A} = \mathbf{X}\Lambda\mathbf{X}^{-1}$ still holds with

$$\Lambda = \begin{bmatrix} J_1 & 0 & 0 & 0 \\ 0 & J_2 & 0 & 0 \\ 0 & 0 & \ddots & 0 \\ 0 & 0 & 0 & J_p \end{bmatrix}$$

with each matrix J_m being a sub-diagonal matrix:

$$J_m = \begin{bmatrix} \lambda & 0 & 0 & 0 \\ 1 & \lambda & 0 & 0 \\ 0 & 1 & \ddots & 0 \\ 0 & 0 & 1 & \lambda \end{bmatrix}$$

and the sizes of J_m summing to n. Where $\mathbf{A}$ is *diagonisable*, the size of each J_m is 1. Thus to solve the equation

$$\frac{\partial \mathbf{Q}}{\partial t} = \Lambda \mathbf{Q}$$

we need to solve in general equations for each block J_m of the form

$$\frac{\partial \mathbf{q}}{\partial t} = J_m \mathbf{q} = \begin{bmatrix} \lambda & 0 & 0 & 0 \\ 1 & \lambda & 0 & 0 \\ 0 & 1 & \ddots & 0 \\ 0 & 0 & 1 & \lambda \end{bmatrix} \begin{bmatrix} q_1 \\ q_2 \\ \vdots \\ q_m \end{bmatrix}$$

or

$$\frac{\partial q_1}{\partial t} = \lambda q_1$$

$$\frac{\partial q_2}{\partial t} = q_1 + \lambda q_2$$

$$\vdots$$

$$\frac{\partial q_m}{\partial t} = q_{m-1} + \lambda q_m$$

and so, allowing for the restriction $\mathbf{q} = 1$ at $t = 0$:

$$q_1(t) = e^{\lambda t}$$

$$q_2(t) = e^{\lambda t} \int e^{-\lambda s} q_1(s)\, ds = 1 + t e^{\lambda t}$$

$$\vdots$$

$$q_m(t) = e^{\lambda t} \int e^{-\lambda s} q_{m-1}(s)\, ds.$$

APPENDIX C

Exercises for Section 1.9 – defined benefits

C.1. Assignment

You are the appointed actuary to the Pembroke City Council super-annuation fund, and are responsible for assessing the financial position of the fund as of 1 January 2009. The fund has $33 million in assets as of that date.

The benefits provided by the fund are the same as those discussed in the second example in lectures, that is,

Cause of exit	Benefits
retirement r	15% of FAS for each year of service at exit
resignation w	Accumulation of past contributions of 10% of salary
death d	15% of FAS for each *potential* year of service at age 60
disability i	A lifetime pension of 60% of FAS, payable weekly

FAS means the average of the salaries payable in the 3 years prior to exit from service.

You have been provided with the membership of the fund as of 1 January 2009; see the 'membership' tab of the spreadsheet Assignment 1.

This comprises the following information for each member:
- date of birth
- date of service
- current rate of salary
- accumulated contributions of 10% of salary.

Your assessment of the fund's position is to be based on the following assumptions:
- a fund earnings (i.e. discount) rate of 6% pa
- salary growth of 3% pa, together with promotional increases related to age
- growth of disability pensions with price inflation, assumed to be 2% pa
- dependent decrement rates aq_x^r, aq_x^w, aq_x^d, aq_x^i related to age x
- a life table for the mortality of disability pensioners q_x.

193

Details are contained in the 'decrement' tab of the spreadsheet.

1. In terms of the assumptions provided in this tab, explain how:

    a. The combined effect of inflationary and promotional salary increases can be modelled by the salary scales s_x and z_x as shown.

    b. The annuity factors $\bar{a}_x$, as shown for disability pensioners, can be derived from the disability pensioner mortality q_x.

    Your method of valuing benefits is to project benefits forward for each member individually. This is achieved under the 'projection' tab as follows:

    -   A member ID can be entered in the pink cell as indicated.
    -   This will pull in from the 'membership' tab the details for the relevant member.
    -   The relevant years of age and service (the grey panel) are then set up for the member, as well as the corresponding decrement rates (the blue panel).

2. Provide formulas for the projection of future benefits (for both past and future service – the olive panels), as well as future salary (the pink panel). An example for retirement benefits is given. (In answering this question you may either submit your own version of the spreadsheet or provide an example of formulas for each type of benefit.)

    Once you are satisfied with your benefit projections, you can run them for the entire membership. This can be done by executing the VBA macro named 'value', or simply by clicking the large blue circle on the 'projection' tab.

3. The valuations of each member's benefits will be summarised in the 'results' tab. Use these results to:

    a. assess the funding position of the fund as of 1 January 2009 (the coverage of past service liabilities by fund assets)

    b. recommend a contribution rate to support future service benefits.

C.2. Assignment

You are the appointed actuary to the St. Regius private hospital superannuation fund, and are responsible for assessing the financial position of the fund as of 1 January 2010. The fund has $75 million in assets as of that date.

The benefits provided by the fund are as follows:

Cause of exit	Benefits
retirement r	20% of FS for each year of service at exit
resignation w	A percentage of FS for each year of service at exit
	The percentage starts at 12% and increases by 1% for each whole year of service until it reaches 20%
death d	20% of FS for each *potential* year of service at age 60
disability i	A lifetime pension of 75% of FS, payable weekly

FS means the final rate of salary payable at the date of exit from service.

Members are required to contribute 3% of their salary. The balance of contributions needed to finance benefits is met by the employer.

You have been provided with the membership of the fund as of 1 January 2010; see the 'membership' tab of the Assignment 2. This comprises the following information for each member:

- date of birth
- date of service
- current rate of salary.

Your assessment of the fund's position is to be based on the following assumptions:

- a fund earnings (i.e. discount) rate of 6% pa
- salary growth of 3% pa, together with promotional increases related to age as shown in the 'decrements' tab
- growth of disability pensions with price inflation, assumed to be 2% pa
- *independent* decrement rates q_x^r, q_x^w, q_x^d, q_x^i related to age x as shown in the 'decrements' tab
- a life table for the mortality of disability pensioners q_x as shown in the 'decrements' tab.

Questions

In terms of the assumptions provided, explain how:

1. Dependent decrement rates can be derived.
2. The annuity factors $\bar{a}_x$, can be derived from the disability pensioner mortality q_x.
3. The funding position of the fund as of 1 January 2010 (the coverage of past service liabilities by fund assets) can be assessed.
4. You would recommend a contribution rate to support future service benefits.

C.3. Assignment

You are the appointed actuary to the Victorian Parliamentary Contributory Superannuation Fund, and are responsible for assessing the financial position of the fund as of 1 July 2011. The fund has $38 million in assets as of that date.

The benefits provided by the fund are generally as follows are lifetime pensions, with reversion to the member's spouse, as follows:

Cause of exit	Annual pension
retirement or resignation r, subject to the rules described below	$A \times R \times B$
otherwise:	A lump sum equal to the accumulated member contributions of 11.5% of salary
death d, whether in service or during retirement or disability, payable to the spouse of the member	2/3 of the retirement pension, subject to a minimum of $40\% \times B$
disability i	The same as the retirement pension

Members are required to contribute 11.5% of their salary. The balance of contributions needed to finance benefits is met by the government.

With these benefits, the parameters are determined as follows:

- PS means service as a member, or 20.5 years, whichever is the lesser, at the date of exit.
- A member of former member is entitled to an annual lifetime pension on retirement or resignation if:
  - $PS > 12$, or
  - $PS > 6$ and is over aged 60.
- R is the total salary of the member, divided by the total basic salary whilst in Parliament, at the date of exit (i.e. an adjustment to B for responsibility in parliament).
- The parliamentary base salary B is the same as that for members of Federal Parliament, currently, $140910 pa,
- The factor A is determined as follows:

PS	A
$PS \geq 20.5$	75%
$8 \leq PS \leq 20.5$	$50\% + 2\%(PS - 8)$
$PS \leq 8$	50%

You have been provided with the membership of the fund as of 1 July 2011; see the 'members' tab of the spreadsheet Assignment 3. This comprises the following information for each member:

- name
- electorate
- house (i.e. House of Assembly MLA or Legislative Council MLC)
- date of birth
- date of election
- gender
- current value of R (expressed as an addition, e.g. a value of 8 means $R = 1.08$).

Assumptions

Your assessment of the Fund's position is to be based on the following assumptions:

- Elections are held every 4 years, and all retirements take place at these times.
- A fund earnings (i.e. discount) rate of 6% pa
- Basic salary growth of 4% pa
- Indexation of pensions with price inflation, assumed to be 3% pa
- *Independent* decrement rates q_x^r, q_x^d, q_x^i related to age x as shown in the 'decrements' tab, according to either house or gender. (This is because the Legislative Council is elected on a different timetable to the House of Assembly.)
- A life table for the mortality of retirement or disability pensioners q_x as shown in the 'decrements' tab, according to gender.
- A male member has a spouse 3 years younger.
- A female member has a spouse 3 years older.
- R remains constant over the career of a member (as all senior positions must be filled by one or another member).

Questions

In terms of the assumptions provided, assess and explain:
1. *dependent* decrement rates
2. The benefit liability as of 1 July 2011 attributable to completed service.
3. The government contribution rate (as a % of salary) to support future service benefits.
4. How the assumptions for retirement rates can be justified, and how they may be improved. (A history of membership since 1900 is included.)

C.4. Assignment

ImagineLawyers is a legal firm with headquarters in Australia specialising in intellectual property law. The firm has 250 employees working in several countries. You are the appointed actuary to the ImagineLawyers superannuation fund, and are responsible for assessing the financial position of the fund as of 1 January 2012. The fund has $45 million in assets as of that date.

The benefits provided by the fund are as follows:

Cause of exit	Benefits
retirement r	20% of FS for each year of service at exit
resignation w	A percentage of FS for each year of service at exit
	The percentage starts at 9%, and increases by 2% for each whole year of service until it reaches 20%
death d	20% of FS for each *potential* year of service at age 60
disability i	A lifetime nonreversionary pension of 75% of FS, payable weekly

FS means the salary paid in the 12 months *before the date of exit* from service.

All contributions needed to finance benefits are met by the employer.

You have been provided with the membership of the fund as of 1 January 2012; see the 'membership' tab of the accompanying spreadsheet Assignment 4. This comprises the following information for each member:
- date of birth
- date of service
- current annual rate of salary.

Your assessment of the fund's position is to be based on the following assumptions:
- a fund earnings (i.e. discount) rate of 6% pa
- salary growth of 3% pa, together with promotional salary increases related to age as shown in the 'decrements' tab
- growth of disability pensions with price inflation, assumed to be 2% pa
- *independent* decrement rates q_x^r, q_x^w, q_x^d, q_x^i related to age x as shown in the 'decrements' tab
- all employees retire on their 60th birthday or in the year following
- a life table for the mortality of disability pensioners q_x as shown in the 'decrements' tab.

Questions

In your report, explain how:

1. *Dependent* decrement rates can be derived.
2. The annuity factors $\bar{a}_x$ can be derived from the disability pensioner mortality q_x.
3. The funding position of the fund as of 1 January 2012 (the coverage of past service liabilities by fund assets) can be assessed.
4. Vested benefits are those that would be payable if all employees left service *voluntarily* as of the valuation date, 1 January 2012. Assess these benefits and discuss how they relate to the past service liabilities in (3).
5. You would recommend a contribution rate to support future service benefits, and deal with the funding surplus or deficiency in (3).

C.5. Supplementary material

Supplementary material related to this chapter can be found online at https://doi.org/10.1016/B978-0-32-390172-7.00038-5.

Sample exams

D.1. Sample Exam 1

Unless otherwise indicated, the *standard basis* for all numerical calculations involving life tables and benefits in this examination is AMC00 *Ultimate* at 3% pa interest, values of which are also set out in Appendix A.

1. 'Selection' refers to the process by which the mortality characteristics of a group of people are determined.

   Define four types of selection, and illustrate each type by reference to one or more of the following groups:
   - people accepted for permanent insurance by medical underwriting
   - retirees who elect a pension benefit rather than a lump sum
   - academic staff at universities
   - immigrants
   - war veterans.

Solution

The four types of selection are:
- temporary initial selection, which occurs when people are screened before entry into a group. This can occur by medical underwriting or by the process of granting entry to immigrants.
- class selection, which refers to permanent characteristics that are risk factors for mortality. Academic staff may be expected to have higher levels of education and lifestyles, and hence lower mortality than other occupations.
- time selection, which refers to temporal factors that affect mortality. The occurrence of conflicts might cause stress related conditions with war veterans.
- adverse selection, which is based on the ability to exploit an organisation's lack of complete information of a member. Retirement pensioners are an example—retirees in ill health will prefer a lump sum.

---

2. Calculate:

- the probability that a life aged 40 will die within the next 20 years
- the probability that two brothers aged 20 and 25 will both reach their 50th birthday
- the probability that one of a triplet, all aged 30, will die before his brothers

$1 - \frac{\ell_{60}}{\ell_{40}} = 1 - \frac{9429582}{9875556} = 4.516\%$

$\frac{\ell_{50}}{\ell_{20}} \frac{\ell_{50}}{\ell_{25}} = \frac{9{,}756{,}471}{9{,}986{,}216} \frac{9{,}756{,}471}{9{,}962{,}701} = 95.677\%.$

Solution

There are six ways for the order of the deaths of the triplets to occur, and in two of these a given triplet will die first. Hence by symmetry the probability is 1/3.

In extending a life table from discrete time to continuous time, various assumptions can be made about the mortality at nonintegral ages. For a given integral age x and a given probability of death q_x, these assumptions can be expressed in terms of the life table $\ell(x + t)$ for $0 \le t \le 1$ as follows:

Description	Assumption	$_tp_x = \frac{\ell(x+t)}{\ell(x)}$
uniform distribution of deaths	$\ell(x + t)$ is linear in t	$1 - t \cdot q_x$
constant force of mortality	$\mu(x + t) = -\frac{1}{\ell(x+t)} \frac{\partial \ell(x+t)}{\partial t}$ is constant	$[q_x]^t$
the Balducci assumption	$1 - \frac{\ell(x+1)}{\ell(x+t)}$ is proportional to $(1 - t)$	$\frac{1-q_x}{1-(1-t)q_x}$

Show that the survival probabilities $_tp_x$ for $0 \le t \le 1$ in the table above are consistent with the assumptions made.

—decreasing functions of t, so that they are potentially survival probabilities.

Solution

It is easily verified that each of the functions $_tp_x$ has value 1 at $t = 0$, and value $1 - q_x$ at $t = 1$. In addition, they are all To show they have the properties claimed:

$1 - t \cdot q_x$ is clearly linear in t, and also linearly related to $\ell(x + t)$.

If $\frac{\ell(x+t)}{\ell(x)} = \left[q_x\right]^t$, then $-\frac{1}{\ell(x+t)}\frac{\partial\ell(x+t)}{\partial t} = -\frac{1}{\left[q_x\right]^t}\left[q_x\right]^t \ln\left(q_x\right) = -\ln\left(q_x\right)$,
which is constant over the year of age.
If $\frac{\ell(x+t)}{\ell(x)} = \frac{1-q_x}{1-(1-t)q_x}$, then $\ell(x+1) = \ell(x)\left(1-q_x\right)$ and $\ell(x+t) = \ell(x)\frac{1-q_x}{1-(1-t)q_x}$, so that

$$1 - \frac{\ell(x+1)}{\ell(x+t)} = 1 - \frac{1-q_x}{1-q_x}\left[1-(1-t)q_x\right]$$

$$= (1-t)q_x$$

which is proportional to $(1-t)$.

3. Show that the following recurrence relations hold:

$$\ddot{a}_x = 1 + vp_x \cdot \ddot{a}_{x+1}$$

and

$$I\ddot{a}_x = \ddot{a}_x + vp_x \cdot I\ddot{a}_{x+1}.$$

Demonstrate these relations for $x = 50$ under the standard basis.

Solution

The definition of $\ddot{a}_x$ is

$$\ddot{a}_x = \sum_{t=0}^{\infty} v^t \cdot {}_t p_x$$

$$= \sum_{t=0}^{\infty} v^t \cdot {}_{t-1}p_{x+1} \cdot p_x$$

$$= 1 + vp_x \sum_{t=1}^{\infty} v^{t-1} \cdot {}_{t-1}p_{x+1}$$

$$= 1 + vp_x \cdot \ddot{a}_{x+1}$$

and similarly,

$$I\ddot{a}_x = \sum_{t=0}^{\infty} (t+1) v^t \cdot {}_t p_x$$

$$= \ddot{a}_x + \sum_{t=0}^{\infty} tv^t \cdot {}_{t-1}p_{x+1} \cdot p_x$$

$$= \ddot{a}_x + vp_x \sum_{t=1}^{\infty} tv^{t-1} \cdot {}_{t-1}p_{x+1}$$

$$= \ddot{a}_x + vp_x \cdot I\ddot{a}_{x+1}.$$

We have

$$1 + vp_{50} \cdot \ddot{a}_{51} = 1 + \frac{1}{1.03} \frac{9,737,319}{9,756,471} 20.509$$
$$= 20.509$$
$$= \ddot{a}_{50}$$

and

$$\ddot{a}_{50} + vp_{50} \cdot I\ddot{a}_{51} = 20.509 + \frac{1}{1.03} \frac{9,737,319}{9,756,471} 291.196$$
$$= 302.669$$
$$= I\ddot{a}_{50}.$$

4. For a life aged 40, calculate under the standard basis:
   - A_{40}
   - $A_{40:\overline{20}|}$
   - $\ddot{a}_{[40]}$ — evaluated at select mortality
   - $\ddot{a}^{(4)}_{40:\overline{20}|}$.

Solution

We have from the life table functions provided

$$A_{40} = 1 - d\ddot{a}_{40}$$
$$= 1 - \frac{0.03}{1.03} 23.825$$
$$= 0.306,$$

$$A_{40:\overline{20}|} = 1 = d\ddot{a}_{40:\overline{20}|}$$
$$= 1 - d\left[\ddot{a}_{40} - v^{20} \cdot {}_{20}p_{40}\ddot{a}_{60}\right]$$

$$= 1 - \frac{0.03}{1.03}\left[23.825 - 1.03^{-20}\frac{9,429,582}{9,875,556}16.439\right]$$

$$= 0.559,$$

$$\ddot{a}_{[40]} = 1 + vp_{[40]} + v^2 \cdot p_{[40]} \cdot p_{[40]+1} \cdot \ddot{a}_{42}$$

$$= 1 + \frac{1}{1.03}\frac{9,867,408}{9,873,589} + \frac{1}{1.03^2}\frac{9,858,794}{9,873,589}23.225$$

$$= 24.394,$$

$$\ddot{a}^{(4)}_{40:\overline{20}|} = \ddot{a}^{(4)}_{40} - v^{20} \cdot {}_{20}p_{40}\ddot{a}^{(4)}_{60}$$

$$= 23.825 - \frac{3}{8} - 1.03^{-20}\frac{9,429,582}{9,875,556}\left(16.439 - \frac{3}{8}\right)$$

$$= 14.957.$$

5. In personal injury cases involving loss of income to an employee, the value of the employee's future income has to be estimated. It is not uncommon for a court of law to approximate $\bar{a}_x$ by the value of $1 pa. in future salary, *payable with certainty* for the complete expectation of life $\overset{o}{e}_x$, that is,

$$\bar{a}_x \simeq \bar{a}_{\overline{e}|}.$$

Show from the definition of $\overset{o}{e}_x = \mathbf{E}(T_x)$ that

$$\overset{o}{e}_x = \int {}_tp_x \, dt.$$

For a given level of $\overset{o}{e}_x = w$, say, show that the survival rates ${}_tp_x$ which maximise $\bar{a}_x$ are those corresponding to zero mortality for w years. Hence show that

$$\bar{a}_x < \bar{a}_{\overline{\overset{o}{e}_x}|}.$$

Solution

The definition of $\overset{o}{e}_x$ is

$$\overset{o}{e}_x = \mathbf{E}(T_x)$$

$$= -\int t \cdot \frac{1}{\ell(x)} \frac{d\ell(x+t)}{dt} dt$$

$$= -t\ell(x+t)|_0^\infty + \int \frac{\ell(x+t)}{\ell(x)} dt$$

$$= \int {}_t p_x \, dt$$

where integration by parts is used in the third line. We also have

$$\bar{a}_x = \int e^{-\delta t} \, {}_t p_x \, dt.$$

Thus, for a given value of $\overset{o}{e}_x = w$, the value $\bar{a}_x$ is maximised when ${}_t p_x$ is as large as possible for as long as possible.

The maximum value of ${}_t p_x$ is 1, and this can hold until $t = w$, from which point ${}_t p_x = 0$. Hence the maximum value of $\bar{a}_x$ is

$$\bar{a}_x = \int_0^w e^{-\delta t} \, dt = \bar{a}_{\overline{\overset{o}{e}_x}|}.$$

6. A life insurer has introduced a 10-year endowment assurance contract with the following features:
   - premiums payable annually
   - a simple reversionary bonus of 2% pa (declared after the end of each year)
   - expenses of 5% of the first year's premium
   - expenses of 2% pa of the premiums in the 2nd and subsequent years.

   Provide a formula for the premium *rate* $\overline{P}$ for an initial unit sum assured for a life aged 30.

   Basis: AMC00 *Select*, 3% pa interest

   If, in addition, a fixed administrative cost of $500 is incurred initially per policy, how would you adjust the first year's premium?

Solution

The value of the benefit is

$$98000 \cdot A_{[30]:\overline{10}|} + 2000 \cdot IA_{[30]:\overline{10}|}$$

whereas the value of premiums is

$$\overline{P}\ddot{a}_{[30]:\overline{10}|}.$$

Hence the equation of value is

$$0.98\overline{P}\ddot{a}_{[30]:\overline{10}|} + 0.03\overline{P} = 98000 \cdot A_{[30]:\overline{10}|} + 2000 \cdot IA_{[30]:\overline{10}|}$$

and

$$\overline{P} = \frac{98000 \cdot A_{[30]:\overline{10}|} + 2000 \cdot IA_{[30]:\overline{10}|}}{0.98\ddot{a}_{[30]:\overline{10}|} + 0.03}.$$

If a fixed initial cost of $500 applies, it is most equitable to add this as a policy fee to the first year's premium (obtained by multiplying the initial sum assured by the premium rate).

7. Show that the insurer's surplus in question (6) is a random variable U, where

$$U = 0.98\overline{P}\ddot{a}_{\overline{\min(K_{30}+1,\,10)}|} - [0.98 + 0.02\min(K_{30}+1,\,10)]\, v^{\min(K_{30}+1,10)}$$
$$- 0.03\overline{P}.$$

Hence show that

$$\mathbf{var}\,(U) = \alpha^2 \cdot A^*_{30:\overline{10}|} + 2\alpha\beta \cdot IA^*_{30\overline{10}|} + \beta^2 \cdot IIA^*_{30:\overline{10}|}$$
$$- \left[\alpha \cdot A_{30:\overline{10}|} + \beta \cdot IA_{30:\overline{10}|}\right]^2$$

where
$\alpha = 0.98\left(\frac{\overline{P}}{d}+1\right)$
$\beta = 0.02$
$IIA^*_{x:\overline{n}|} == \mathbf{E}\left[[\min(K_{30}+1,\,10)]^2\, v^{\min(K_{30}+1,10)}\right]$
and functions with * are evaluated at an interest rate $i^2 + 2i$.

Solution

If the curtate lifetime of the insured is K_{30}, then the value of future premiums, net of expenses, is

$$0.98\overline{P}\ddot{a}_{\overline{\min(K_{30}+1,\,10)}|} - 0.03\overline{P}$$

and the value of future benefits is

$$[0.98 + 0.02 \min (K_{30} + 1, 10)] \, v^{\min(K_{30}+1,10)}$$

as the benefit starts as an amount of 1 in the first year for $K_{30} = 0$, and increasing by 0.02 each year.

The difference between these values gives the surplus U as a function of the random variable K_{30}. This can also be written as

$$U = 0.98\overline{P}\frac{1 - v^{\min(K_{30}+1,10)}}{d}$$
$$- [0.98 + 0.02 \min (K_{30} + 1, 10)] \, v^{\min(K_{30}+1,10)} - 0.03\overline{P}$$
$$= \overline{P}\left(\frac{0.98}{d} - 0.03\right) - 0.98 v^{\min(K_{30}+1,10)}\left[\frac{\overline{P}}{d} + 1\right]$$
$$- 0.02 \min (K_{30} + 1, 10) \, v^{\min(K_{30}+1,10)}.$$

As the first term is constant, it can be ignored in evaluating $\mathbf{var}\,(U)$. The rest of the terms are

$$-\alpha v^{\min(K_{30}+1,10)} - \beta \min (K_{30} + 1, 10) \, v^{\min(K_{30}+1,10)}.$$

Thus

$$\mathbf{var}\,(U) = \mathbf{E}\left[\begin{array}{c} \alpha^2 v^{2\min(K_{30}+1,10)} + 2\alpha\beta \min (K_{30} + 1, 10) \, v^{2\min(K_{30}+1,10)} \\ + \beta^2 \, [\min (K_{30} + 1, 10)]^2 \, v^{2\min(K_{30}+1,10)} \end{array}\right]$$
$$- \mathbf{E}\left[\alpha v^{\min(K_{30}+1,10)} + \beta \min (K_{30} + 1, 10) \, v^{\min(K_{30}+1,10)}\right]^2$$
$$= \alpha^2 \cdot A^*_{30:\overline{10}|} + 2\alpha\beta \cdot IA^*_{30:\overline{10}|} + \beta^2 \cdot IIA^*_{30:\overline{10}|}$$
$$- \left[\alpha \cdot A_{30:\overline{10}|} + \beta \cdot IA_{30:\overline{10}|}\right]^2$$

8. A life office issues a 4-year nonprofit endowment assurance policy to a male life aged 61 exact for a sum assured of $100,000 payable on survival to the end of the term or at the end of the year of death if earlier. Premiums are payable annually in advance throughout the term of the policy.

   There is a surrender benefit payable equal to a return of premiums paid, with no interest. This benefit is payable at the end of the year of surrender.

   The life office uses the following bases relating to this contract:

Basis:	Pricing	Reserving	Profit testing
Mortality	AMC00 *Select*	AMC00 *Ultimate*	AMC00 *Select*
Surrenders	None	None	5% of policies in first 3 years.
Interest	4% pa.	4% pa.	5% pa.
Initial expenses	$500	None	$500
Renewal expenses	$50 pa plus 2% of premium	None	$50 pa plus 2% of premium

Provide formulas for:

the annual premium payable under the contract

the net premium reserves required per policy over its term

the profits expected on the policy over its term

Hence provide a formula for the expected profit margin on this contract, assuming a risk discount rate of 8% pa.

Solution

The gross annual premium is given by

$$\overline{P} = \frac{100000 \cdot A_{[61]:\overline{4}|} + 500}{0.98 \ddot{a}_{[61]:\overline{4}|}} + 50$$

where functions are evaluated at 4% pa

The net premium is given by

$$P = 100000 \frac{A_{61:\overline{4}|}}{\ddot{a}_{61:\overline{4}|}}$$

$$= 100000 \frac{1 - d\ddot{a}_{61:\overline{4}|}}{\ddot{a}_{61:\overline{4}|}}$$

$$= 100000 \left(\frac{1}{\ddot{a}_{61:\overline{4}|}} - d \right)$$

so that reserves at duration t are

$$_tV = 100000 A_{61+t:\overline{4-t}|} - P\ddot{a}_{61+t:\overline{4-t}|}$$

$$= 100000\left[1 - d\ddot{a}_{61+t:\overline{4-t}} - \left(\frac{1}{\ddot{a}_{61:\overline{4}}} - d\right)\ddot{a}_{61+t:\overline{4-t}}\right]$$

$$= 100000\left[1 - \frac{\ddot{a}_{61+t:\overline{4-t}}}{\ddot{a}_{61:\overline{4}}}\right].$$

Let $a\ell_x$ be the multiple decrement table derived from the independent mortality rates $q_{[61]}, q_{[61]+1}, q_{63}, q_{63}$ and the independent withdrawal rates $q^w = 0.05$, that is,

$$aq_{61}^d = q_{[61]}\left[1 - \frac{1}{2} \times 0.05\right]$$

$$aq_{61}^w = 0.05\left[1 - \frac{1}{2}q_{[61]}\right]$$

and so on.

Then profit testing can be undertaken for each policy as follows:

Year:	1	2	3	4
Transfer in	0	$_1V$	$_2V$	$_3V$
Premium	$\overline{P}$	$\overline{P}$	$\overline{P}$	$\overline{P}$
Expenses	$-550 - 0.02\overline{P}$	$-50 - 0.02\overline{P}$	$-50 - 0.02\overline{P}$	$-50 - 0.02\overline{P}$
Withdrawal	$-aq_{61}^w\overline{P}$	$-aq_{62}^w(2\overline{P})$	$-aq_{63}^w(3\overline{P})$	$-aq_{64}^w(4\overline{P})$
Death	$-100000aq_{61}^d$	$-100000aq_{62}^d$	$-100000aq_{63}^d$	$-100000aq_{64}^d$
Interest	$.05[0.98\overline{P} - 550]$	$.05[_1V + 0.98\overline{P} - 50]$	$.05[_2V + 0.98\overline{P} - 50]$	$.05[_3V + 0.98\overline{P} - 50]$
Transfer out	$-\frac{a\ell_{62}}{a\ell_{61}} \cdot {_1V}$	$-\frac{a\ell_{63}}{a\ell_{62}} \cdot {_2V_x}$	$-\frac{a\ell_{64}}{a\ell_{63}} \cdot {_3V_x}$	$-\frac{a\ell_{65}}{a\ell_{64}} \cdot {_4V_x}$
Profit	sum of above	sum of above	sum of above	sum of above
survival factor to year start	1	$\frac{a\ell_{62}}{a\ell_{61}}$	$\frac{a\ell_{63}}{a\ell_{61}}$	$\frac{a\ell_{64}}{a\ell_{61}}$

The sum of the product of *profit* × *survival* factors gives the profit signature. The net present value at 8% interest of the profit signature, divided by the NPV of the *premium* × *survival* factor, gives the expected profit margin.

9. Let x be the age at commencement of an assurance for a variable sum assured $S(t)$ at time t in continuous time. If $V(t)$ denotes the reserve and P the annualised premium, show from first principles that Thiele's equation holds in continuous time:

$$\frac{\partial V}{\partial t} = \mu_{x+t}[V(t) - S(t)] + \delta V(t) + P.$$

Consider the case where $S(t) = V(t) + B$, that is the reserve is payable on death, together with a fixed amount B. Show that the reserve is then

$$V(t) = e^{\delta t} \int_0^t e^{-\delta s} [-\mu_{x+s} B + P] \, ds.$$

Hence show that if the term of the assurance is n years, then the premium is

$$P = B \frac{\int_0^n e^{-\delta t} \mu_{x+t} dt}{\bar{a}_{\overline{n}|}}.$$

How is this premium different from that for an assurance for a constant sum assured B?

Solution

In a small time interval $[t, t + dt]$ the following transactions may be observed:

- a reserve of $V(t)$ is available at the start of the period
- this is accumulated with interest $\delta V(t) \cdot dt$ to the end of the period
- a premium of amount $P \cdot dt$ is paid
- claims of amount $\mu_{x+t} S(t) \cdot dt$ are paid
- the survivors at the end of the period are $1 - \mu_{x+t} \cdot dt$

Hence the reserve at the end of the period *per survivor* is $V(t + dt)$, where

$$V(t + dt) \left(1 - \mu_{x+t} \cdot dt\right) = V(t) + \delta V(t) \cdot dt + P \cdot dt - \mu_{x+t} S(t) \cdot dt.$$

This can be written

$$\frac{V(t + dt) - V(t)}{dt} = \mu_{x+t} \left[V(t + dt) - S(t)\right] + \delta V(t) + P.$$

In the limit as $dt \to 0$, we get Thiele's equation.

If the sum assured is equal to the reserve plus a fixed amount B, the equation becomes

$$\frac{\partial V}{\partial t} = -\mu_{x+t} B + \delta V(t) + P.$$

This is a differential equation with an integrating factor $e^{-\delta t}$:

$$\frac{\partial}{\partial t} \left(e^{-\delta t} V\right) = e^{-\delta t} [-\mu_{x+t} B + P]$$

and integrating between time 0 and t:

$$e^{-\delta t} V = \int_0^t e^{-\delta s} [-\mu_{x+s} B + P] \, ds$$

as $V(0) = 0$. If the term of the policy is $t = n$, then $V(n) = 0$, and so

$$P \int_0^n e^{-\delta s} \, ds = B \int_0^n e^{-\delta s} \mu_{x+s} \, ds$$

from which the result follows.

If the sum assured was simply B, then the premium would be

$$P = B \frac{\int_0^n e^{-\delta t} \cdot {}_t p_x \cdot \mu_{x+t} \, dt}{\bar{a}_{x:\overline{n}|}}.$$

Thus the probability of survival has been eliminated when the reserve is payable as an additional benefit on death.

10. An insurer is introducing a trauma insurance contract (sometimes called 'critical illness' insurance). Under this contract, benefits are payable on the occurrence of serious medical conditions (i.e. traumas, such as cancer), which are expensive to treat.

Benefits are payable on up to two traumas. In addition, a death benefit is payable whenever the insured dies within the term of the policy. However, the total benefit that can be paid is restricted to $1 million, as is shown below:

*Let i or j denote any of the four possible states $\{A, B, C, D\}$, where:
- A is the active or healthy state
- B is the state after the first trauma
- C is the state after the second trauma
- D is death.

An annual premium is payable only while the insured is in state A. Then denote as follows:

$$\mu^{ij}(x) = \text{transition intensity from state } i \text{ to state } j \text{ at age } x$$

$$p^{ij}(x, t) = \text{probability of transition from state } i \text{ at age } x \text{ to state } j$$
$$\text{at age } x + t.$$

Derive a formula for the annual premium for a policy of term n year using the above probabilities and a force of interest δ.

Solution

The value of the first trauma benefit is

$$VB = 400000 \int_0^n e^{-\delta t} p^{AA}(x, t)\, \mu^{AB}(x+t)\, dt$$

that is, it is based on the probability of remaining active to time t, followed by a trauma at that time.

Similarly, the value of the second trauma benefit is

$$VD = 400000 \int_0^n e^{-\delta t} p^{AB}(x, t)\, \mu^{AC}(x+t)\, dt$$

that is, it is based on the probability of having a trauma before time t, followed by another trauma at that time.

The value of death benefits is

$$VD = 1000000 \int_0^n e^{-\delta t} p^{AA}(x, t)\, \mu^{AD}(x+t)\, dt$$
$$+ 600000 \int_0^n e^{-\delta t} p^{AB}(x, t)\, \mu^{BD}(x+t)\, dt$$
$$+ 200000 \int_0^n e^{-\delta t} p^{AC}(x, t)\, \mu^{CD}(x+t)\, dt$$

whilst the value of premiums is

$$P \int_0^n e^{-\delta t} p^{AA}(x, t)\, dt.$$

Hence

$$P = \frac{VB + VC + VD}{\int_0^n e^{-\delta t} p^{AA}(x, t)\, dt}.$$

11. The symbol A^3_{xyz} is used to denote the value of a unit assurance payable at the end of the year of death of x provided it occurs after that of y and z.

Assuming a uniform distribution of deaths within integral years, derive an expression for evaluating A^3_{xyz} in terms of standard life table functions.

What is the longest period over which the benefit A^3_{xyz} can reasonably be funded by premiums?

Show, by general reasoning or otherwise, that:

- $A^3_{\substack{xyz \\ 1}} + A^3_{\substack{xyz \\ 1}} = A^3_{xyz}$
- $A^1_{xyz} + A^1_{\substack{xyz}} + A^1_{\substack{xyz}} = A_{xyz}$
- $A^1_{xyz} + A^2_{xyz} + A^3_{xyz} = A_x.$

Solution

Let K_x, K_y, K_z denote the curtate lifetimes of x, y, z, respectively. Then a benefit B is payable at time $K_x + 1$ as follows:

- $B = 1$ if $K_y \leq K_z < K_x$
- $B = 1$ if $K_z \leq K_y < K_x$
- $B = \frac{1}{2}$ if $K_y < K_z = K_x$
- $B = \frac{1}{2}$ if $K_z < K_y = K_x$
- $B = \frac{1}{3}$ if $K_z = K_y = K_x$
- $B = 0$ otherwise.

The last four benefits follow from the uniform distribution of deaths, which implies that the time of death, where two or more lives die in the same year, is uniformly distributed. Hence

$$A^3_{xyz} = \sum_{K_x} v^{K_x+1} prob\,(K_x) \cdot prob\,(K_y < K_x) \cdot prob\,(K_z < K_x)$$

$$+ \frac{1}{2} \sum_{K_x} v^{K_x+1} prob\,(K_x) \cdot prob\,(K_y = K_x) \cdot prob\,(K_z < K_x)$$

$$+ \frac{1}{2} \sum_{K_,} v^{K_x+1} prob\,(K_x) \cdot prob\,(K_z = K_x) \cdot prob\,(K_y < K_x)$$

$$+ \frac{1}{3} \sum_{K_x} v^{K_x+1} prob\,(K_x) \cdot prob\,(K_z = K_x) \cdot prob\,(K_y = K_x).$$

The longest period for premiums is during the lifetime of x. It cannot reasonably be longer than this, as then premiums might have to be recouped after the benefit has been paid. If y or z dies before x, there is still an incentive (in fact a greater incentive) for the premiums to be paid.

The benefit in $A^3_{\substack{xyz \\ 1}} + A^3_{\substack{xyz \\ 1}}$ is payable whether y dies first or z dies first. Hence it is payable whenever x dies last, and so is equal to A^3_{xyz}.

The benefit in $A^1_{xyz} + A^1_{xyz} + A^1_{xyz}$ is payable on the first death of any of x, y, z. Hence it is equal to the assurance on the joint life status. The benefit in $A^1_{xyz} + A^2_{xyz} + A^3_{xyz}$ is payable on the death of x, whether it is first, second or last. Hence it is equal to A_x.

D.2. Sample Exam 2

1. In a particular country, employers provide retirement benefits for their employees. Employers may:
    *   provide a retirement pension directly for an employee, or
    *   purchase a lifetime annuity of similar amount from a life insurer in favour of the employee, or
    *   offer terms to an employee to elect to convert their pension to a lump sum.

    It is observed that the mortality of insured annuitants is generally lighter than that of pensioners who are funded directly by an employer.
    a. Suggest reasons why this may be so.
    b. Describe the types of selection that may be operating under these circumstances.

Solution

An employer who is obliged to provide a retirement pension for a healthy employee has two options: to insure the pension with a life insurer, or to offer commutation terms to the employee (i.e. have the employee bear the risk of retirement income). Thus employers may be expected to insure only healthy lives, leading to the lighter mortality experience for insurers. In addition, insurers may price their products to be attractive only to healthy individuals.

The issue is of adverse selection on the part of employers. There is also adverse selection on the part of employees—only the higher mortality risks would accept commutation terms.

Lastly, there is temporal selection as the health of employees us improved with advancing medical technology. These risks may be passed to an insurer or to employees under the employer's options.

2. Calculate $_{0.7}p_{30.5}$ and $_{0.7}p_{[30.5]}$ under the assumption of:
    a. a uniform distribution of deaths between integral ages of life

b. a constant force of mortality between integral ages of life

---

Solution

Under the UDD assumption, we have $\ell_{x+t} = t\ell_{x+1} + (1-t)\ell_x$ for $0 \leq t \leq 1$. Hence

$$
\begin{aligned}
{}_{0.7}p_{30.5} &= \frac{\ell_{31.2}}{\ell_{30.5}} = \frac{0.8\ell_{31} + 0.2\ell_{32}}{0.5\ell_{30} + 0.5\ell_{31}} \\
&= \frac{0.8 \times 9932502 + 0.2 \times 9927089}{0.5 \times 9937779 + 0.5 \times 9932502} \\
&= 0.99963
\end{aligned}
$$

and

$$
\begin{aligned}
{}_{0.7}p_{[30.5]} &= \frac{\ell_{[31]|+1.2}}{\ell_{[30]+0.5}} = \frac{0.8\ell_{[30]+1} + 0.2\ell_{32}}{0.5\ell_{[30]} + 0.5\ell_{[30]+1}} \\
&= \frac{0.8 \times 9931767 + 0.2 \times 9927089}{0.5 \times 9935066 + 0.5 \times 9931767} \\
&= 0.99974.
\end{aligned}
$$

If the force of mortality is constant between integral ages, then $\ell_{x+t} = \ell_x \left(\frac{\ell_{x+1}}{\ell_x} \right)^t$. Hence

$$
\begin{aligned}
{}_{0.7}p_{30.5} &= \frac{\ell_{31.2}}{\ell_{30.5}} = \frac{\ell_{31} \left(\frac{\ell_{32}}{\ell_{31}} \right)^{0.2}}{\ell_{30} \left(\frac{\ell_{31}}{\ell_{30}} \right)^{0.5}} \\
&= \frac{\ell_{32}^{0.2} \ell_{31}^{0.3}}{\ell_{30}^{0.5}} \\
&= \frac{9927089^{0.2} 9932502^{0.3}}{9937779^{0.5}} \\
&= 0.99963
\end{aligned}
$$

and

$$
{}_{0.7}p_{[30.5]} = \frac{\ell_{[31]|+1.2}}{\ell_{[30]+0.5}} = \frac{\ell_{[30]+1} \left(\frac{\ell_{32}}{\ell_{[30]+1}} \right)^{0.2}}{\ell_{[30]} \left(\frac{\ell_{[30]+1}}{\ell_{[30]}} \right)^{0.5}}
$$

$$
= \frac{\ell_{32}^{0.2} \ell_{[30]+1}^{0.3}}{\ell_{[30]}^{0.5}}
$$

$$
= \frac{9927089^{0.2} 9931767^{0.3}}{9935066^{0.5}}
$$

$$
= 0.99974.
$$

3. For a life aged 30 exact calculate, under the standard basis for ultimate mortality, the value of the following benefits:
   a. an endowment assurance of $1 for a term of 20 years
   b. an annuity of $1 pa, payable yearly with certainty for 20 years. The annuity commences immediately on the death of the insured.
   c. a lifetime annuity of $1 pa, payable quarterly but deferred for 20 years
   d. a benefit payable at the end of the year of death. The initial benefit is $1000 but reduces by $100 for each year since commencement, until the benefit reaches zero.

Solution

$$
A_{30:\overline{20}|} = 1 - d\ddot{a}_{30:\overline{20}|} = 1 - d\left(\ddot{a}_{30} - v^{20}\frac{\ell_{50}}{\ell_{30}}\ddot{a}_{50}\right)
$$

$$
= 1 - \frac{0.03}{1.03}\left(26.381 - 1.03^{-20}\frac{9756471}{9937779}20.509\right)
$$

$$
= 0.55633
$$

$$
\overline{A}_{30} \cdot \ddot{a}_{\overline{20}|} = \left(1 - d\ddot{a}_{30} + \frac{1}{2}\right)\frac{1 - v^{20}}{d}
$$

$$
= \left(1 - \frac{0.03}{1.03}26.381 + 0.5\right)\frac{1 - 1.03^{-20}}{0.03}1.03
$$

$$
= 11.211
$$

$$
_{20|}\ddot{a}_{30}^{(4)} = v^{20}\frac{\ell_{50}}{\ell_{30}}\left(\ddot{a}_{50} - \frac{3}{8}\right)
$$

$$
= 1.03^{-20}\frac{9756471}{9937779}\left(20.509 - \frac{3}{8}\right)
$$

$$
= 10.944
$$

$$1100 \cdot A_{30:\overline{11}|} - 100 \cdot IA_{30:\overline{11}|}$$

$$= 1100 \left[1 - d\ddot{a}_{30:\overline{11}|} \right] - 100 \left[\ddot{a}_{30:\overline{11}|} - d \cdot I\ddot{a}_{30:\overline{11}|} \right]$$

$$= 1100 - \left(1100d + 100 \right) \left(\ddot{a}_{30} - v^{11} \frac{\ell_{41}}{\ell_{30}} \ddot{a}_{41} \right)$$

$$\quad + 100d \left[I\ddot{a}_{30} - v^{11} \frac{\ell_{41}}{\ell_{30}} \left(I\ddot{a}_{41} + 11\ddot{a}_{41} \right) \right]$$

$$= 1100 - \left(1100 \frac{0.03}{1.03} + 100 \right)$$

$$\quad \times \left(26.381 - 1.03^{-11} \times \frac{9867458}{9937779} 23.529 \right)$$

$$\quad + 100 \frac{0.03}{1.03} \left(532.141 - 1.03^{-11} \right.$$

$$\quad \left. \times \frac{9867458}{9937779} \left(419.166 + 10 \times 23.529 \right) \right)$$

$$= 27.781.$$

4. A life insurer issues a deferred annuity to a male life aged 40 exact. The annuity is for a nominal amount of $100 pa, payable monthly, but commences only at age 60. During the deferment period, the annuity increases with annual reversionary bonuses. After commencement, the annuity is indexed to CPI on an annual basis.

The insurer prices the contract on the following basis:

Basis	During deferment	After commencement
Interest	6% pa	6% pa
Mortality	AMC00 select	PNML00
Annuity increases	3% pa	2% pa
Initial commission	87.5% of the total annual premium	
Initial expenses	$350 paid at policy commencement date	
Renewal commission	2.5% of each monthly premium from the start of the	
Renewal expenses	$120 at the start of the second and subsequent policy years	
Annuity expense		1% of each annuity payment

Provide formulas to assess the monthly premium payable in advance during the period of deferment.

> **Solution**
>
> Using the principle of equivalence for the annualised premium P:
>
> $$(0.975P - 120)\,\ddot{a}^{(12)}_{[40]:\overline{20}|} = 230 + 85\%P$$
>
> $$+ 100 \times 1.01 \times 1.03^{20} 1.06^{-20} \frac{\ell_{60}}{\ell_{[40]}} \ddot{a}^{(12)}_{60}$$
>
> where
> - $\ddot{a}^{(12)}_{[40]:\overline{20}|}$ is evaluated at 6% interest, AMC00 select mortality and
> - $\ddot{a}^{(12)}_{60}$ is evaluated at an interest rate of $\frac{1.06}{1.02} - 1 = 3.92\%$, PNML00 mortality.

5. An insurer provides lifetime assurances to married couples, aged x and y on a *joint life* basis (i.e. at the end of year of the *first* death). A benefit of S is payable in the first year, and this increases by a fixed amount of Q for each subsequent year.
   Annual premiums of amount P are payable only whilst *both* lives survive.
   a. Why must the premium payments be restricted to the period whilst both lives survive?
   b. Formulate the insurer's liability at time t in terms of the curtate joint lifespan K_{xy}.
   c. Show that the *expected value* of the insurer's liability at time t is the reserve:

   $$_tV_{xy} = [S + (t-1)\,Q] \cdot A_{x+t,y+t} + Q \cdot IA_{x+t,y+t} - P \cdot \ddot{a}_{x+t,y+t}.$$

   d. Formulate an expression for the *variance* of the insurer's liability at time t in terms of standard IAA notation.

> **Solution**
>
> If the premium were payable after the first death, then there is no incentive for the insured to pay, as the benefit has been paid.
> At time t, the variable $K_{x+t,y+t}$ denotes the time to the end of year of the first death. Given its value $u = K_{x+t,y+t}$, the insurer's liability is
>
> $$L = (S + tQ + Qu) \cdot v^{u+1} - P \cdot \ddot{a}_{\overline{u+1}|}.$$

This has expected value

$$E(L) =_t V_{xy} = [S + (t-1)\,Q] \cdot A_{x+t,y+t} + Q \cdot IA_{x+t,y+t} - P \cdot \ddot{a}_{x+t,y+t}.$$

Its variance is

$$\mathbf{var}\,(L) = \mathbf{var}\left[(S + tQ + Qu) \cdot v^{u+1} - P \cdot \frac{1 - v^{u+1}}{d}\right]$$

$$= \mathbf{var}\left[v^{u+1}\left(S + (t-1)\,Q + Q(u+1) + \frac{P}{d}\right)\right] \cdot$$

$$= \left(S + (t-1)\,Q + \frac{P}{d}\right)^2 \mathbf{var}\,(v^{u+1}) + Q^2 \mathbf{var}\left[(u+1)\,v^{u+1}\right]$$

$$+ 2Q\left(S + (t-1)\,Q + \frac{P}{d}\right) cov\left[v^{u+1}, (u+1)\,v^{u+1}\right]$$

$$= \left[S + (t-1)\,Q + \frac{P}{d}\right]^2 \left[A'_{x+t,y+t} - A^2_{x+t,y+t}\right]$$

$$+ Q^2 \left\{E\left[(u+1)^2\,v^{2(u+1)}\right] - IA_{x+t,y+t}\right\}$$

$$+ 2Q\left(S + (t-1)\,Q + \frac{P}{d}\right)\left[IA'_{x+t,y+t} - A_{x+t,y+t} \cdot IA_{x+t,y+t}\right].$$

Functions with $'$ are evaluated at an interest rate j such that $1 + j = (1+i)^2$. This is all expressed in standard notation except for $E\left[(u+1)^2\,v^{2(u+1)}\right]$, which has to be evaluated separately.

6. Another insurer provides lifetime assurances to married couples, aged x and y on a *last survivor* basis (i.e. a fixed benefit of S is payable at the end of year of the *last* death). Annual premiums of amount P are payable whilst *one or both* lives survive.

   a. Give a formula for the premium P in terms of standard IAA notation. You may ignore expenses.

   b. The reserve held for such a contract at time t depends on who is alive at that time:
      - if both x and y are alive at time t, the reserve held is denoted $_tV_{\overline{xy}}$
      - if only x is alive at time t, the reserve held is denoted $_tV_x$
      - if only y is alive at time t, the reserve held is denoted $_tV_y$

      Show, by general reasoning or otherwise, that the equations of value for reserves at time t are as follows:

$$(1+i)\,(_tV_x + P) =_{t+1} V_x \cdot p_{x+t} + q_{x+t}S$$

$$(1+i)\left({}_{t}V_{x}+P\right)={}_{t+1}V_{y}\cdot p_{y+t}+q_{y+t}S$$
$$(1+i)\left({}_{t}V_{\overline{xy}}+P\right)={}_{t+1}V_{\overline{xy}}p_{x+t}p_{y+t}$$
$$+\,q_{x+t}p_{y+t}\cdot{}_{t+1}V_{y}$$
$$+\,q_{y+t}p_{x+t}\cdot{}_{t+1}V_{x}$$
$$+\,q_{x+t}q_{y+t}S.$$

c.   Suppose for a particular contract both x and y are alive at the start of year t, but that x dies during the year whilst y survives. What is the insurer's profit/loss for the year?

Solution

The premium must satisfy the principle of equivalence:

$$Pa_{\overline{xy}}=SA_{\overline{xy}}.$$

If only x is alive at time t, then the reserve at that time, together with the premium P and interest, must be sufficient to provide for expected benefits to x plus the reserve at time $t+1$, that is,

$$(1+i)\left({}_{t}V_{x}+P\right)={}_{t+1}V_{x}\cdot p_{x+t}+q_{x+t}S.$$

Similarly, if only y is alive at time t.
If both x and y are alive at time t, then there are four possibilities during year t:
- both x and y survive with probability $p_{x+t}p_{y+t}$, in which case a reserve of ${}_{t+1}V_{\overline{xy}}$ is required
- x dies and y survives, with probability $q_{x+t}p_{y+t}$, in which case a reserve of ${}_{t+1}V_{y}$ is required
- y dies and x survives, with probability $q_{y+t}p_{x+t}$, in which case a reserve of ${}_{t+1}V_{x}$ is required
- both x and y die with probability $q_{x+t}q_{y+t}$, in which case a benefit of S is payable

This leads to the equation of balance:

$$(1+i)\left({}_{t}V_{\overline{xy}}+P\right)={}_{t+1}V_{\overline{xy}}p_{x+t}p_{y+t}$$
$$+\,q_{x+t}p_{y+t}\cdot{}_{t+1}V_{y}$$

$$+ q_{y+t}p_{x+t} \cdot_{t+1} V_x$$
$$+ q_{x+t}q_{y+t}S.$$

If both x and y are alive at time t, and only y survives the year, the reserve required at time t is $_{t+1}V_y$ but the assets available are $(1+i)\left(_tV_{\overline{xy}} + P\right)$. Hence the loss is

$$_{t+1}V_y - (1+i)\left(_tV_{\overline{xy}} + P\right).$$

7. A friendly society provides income replacement and disability benefits for employees. The contract is structured as follows:

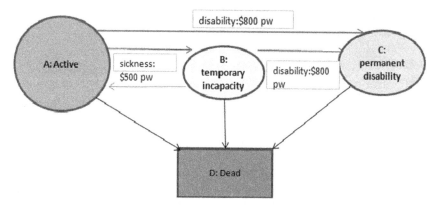

Under this contract, weekly benefits are payable:

- at a basic level of $500 pw to replace income whilst an employee is temporarily prevented from working by sickness or injury. In this case, the benefits commence only after 6 months of ceasing work, and are limited to a 2-year period.
- at a higher level of $800 pw to provide income and medical treatments for permanent disabilities. These benefits commence immediately and cease only on death.

Let i or j denote any of the four possible states $\{A, B, C, D\}$, where:

- A is the active or healthy state
- B is the state of temporary incapacity
- C is the state of permanent disability
- D is death.

Employees can return to health from state B, but not from the other states.

A weekly premium is payable only while the insured is in state A.

Then denote as follows:

$\mu^{ij}(x) =$ transition intensity from state i to state j at age x

$p^{ij}(x, t) =$ probability of transition from state i at age x to state j

at age $x + t$

$p^{\overline{ii}}(x, t) =$ probability of remaining continuously in state i

at age x to age $x + t$.

Derive a formula for the weekly premium for a policy of term n years using the above probabilities and a force of interest δ.

Solution

The value of the temporary incapacity benefit is

$$VB = 500 \times 52 \int_0^n e^{-\delta t} p^{AA}(x, t)\, \mu^{AB}(x + t)$$

$$\times \left[\int_{0.5}^2 e^{-\delta s} p^{\overline{BB}}(x + t, x + t + s)\ ds \right] dt$$

that is, it is based on the probability of remaining active to time t, suffering temporary incapacity at that time, then waiting for 0.5 year before commencement of benefit given by the inner integral. This also allows for a limit of 2 years on payment of the benefit. Note that this benefit can be paid more than once during the contract, if the insured recovers from an earlier incapacity.

Similarly, the value of the permanent incapacity benefit is

$$VC = 800 \times 52 \int_0^n e^{-\delta t} p^{AC}(x, t)\, dt$$

that is, it is based on the probability of having a trauma before time t, followed by another trauma at that time.

The value of annual premiums P is

$$VP = P \int_0^n e^{-\delta t} p^{AA}(x, t)\, dt.$$

Hence

$$P = \frac{VB + VC}{VP}.$$

8. A life insurer issues a 3-year unit-linked endowment assurance contract to a male life aged 40 exact. This type of contract operates under two funds, a unit fund for investing premiums, and a cash fund for providing death benefits, as illustrated below.

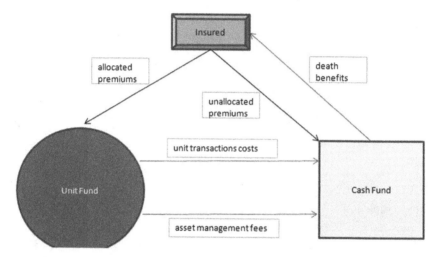

Details of the operation of the contract are as follows:

- Level premiums of $4000 per annum are payable yearly in advance throughout the term of the policy or until earlier death.
- 95% of the premium is allocated to units in the first policy year, 100% in the second and 105% in the third.
- A policy fee of $50 is deducted from the bid value of units at the start of each year.
- The units are subject to a bid-offer spread of 5% on purchase.
- An annual management charge of 2% of the bid value of units is deducted at the end of each policy year.
- Management charges are deducted from the unit fund before death, surrender and maturity benefits are paid.
- If the policyholder dies during the term of the policy, the death benefit of 125% of the bid value of the units is payable at the end of the policy year of death.
- On maturity, 100% of the bid value of the units is payable.

- The policyholder may surrender the policy only at the end of the first and second policy years. On surrender, the bid value of the units less a surrender penalty is payable at the end of the policy year of exit. The surrender penalty is $1000 at the end of the first policy year and $500 at the end of the second policy year.

The insurer uses the following assumptions in carrying out profit tests of this contract:

Basis	Year 1	Year 2	Year 3
Unit fund asset return	5.5%	5.25%	5.0%
Cash fund return	4%	4%	4%
Expense	$200	$50	$50
Commission, % of premium	15%	2%	2%
Surrenders, % of policies	15%	10%	–
Risk discount rate	9%	9%	9%

a. Describe the methodology that you would use to project the profit *vector* emerging under the contract.

b. How would you assess the profit *signature* from (a)?

c. How would the information in (a) or (b) be useful to the insurer? Describe at least three applications.

Solution

Let $a\ell_x$ be the multiple decrement table, starting with $a\ell_{40} = 1$, derived from the independent mortality rates q_{40}, q_{41}, q_{42} and the independent withdrawal rates $q_{40}^w = 0.15$, $q_{41}^w = 0.1$, that is,

$$aq_{40}^d = q_{40}\left[1 - \frac{1}{2} \times 0.15\right]$$

$$aq_{40}^w = 0.15\left[1 - \frac{1}{2}q_{40}\right]$$

$$a\ell_{41} = \left(1 - aq_{40}^d - aq_{40}^w\right)a\ell_{40}$$

and so on. Then the unit fund can be projected for each contract surviving at the start of each year as follows (in terms of units, not $):

Year:	1	2	3
Bid price, soy	$u_0 = 1$	u_1	u_2
Ask price, soy	$u_0 \times 1.05$	$u_1 \times 1.05$	$u_2 \times 1.05$
Bid price, eoy	$u_1 = u_0 \times 1.055$	$u_2 = u_1 \times 1.0525$	$u_3 = u_2 \times 1.05$
Balance brought forward, per surviving contract	0	U_1	U_2
Allocated premium, less commission	$0.85 \frac{0.95 \times 4000}{1.05 u_0}$	$0.98 \frac{1.00 \times 4000}{1.05 u_1}$	$0.98 \frac{1.05 \times 4000}{1.05 u_2}$
Policy fee	$-\frac{250}{u_0}$	$-\frac{50}{u_1}$	$-\frac{50}{u_2}$
Management fees	$-0.02 \times$ sum of above	$-0.02 \times$ sum of above	$-0.02 \times$ sum of above
Balance per contract, after management fees	$U_1 = 0.98 \times$	$U_2 = 0.98 \times$ sum of above	$U_3 = 0.98 \times$ sum of above

Then profit testing can be undertaken in the cash fund for each policy as follows:

Year:	1	2	3
Balance at soy	0	Balance at eoy c/f	Balance at eoy c/f
Unallocated Premium	0.05×4000	0	-0.05×4000
Acquisition costs	$0.15 \frac{0.95 \times 4000}{1.05 u_0}$	$0.02 \frac{1.00 \times 4000}{1.05 u_1}$	$0.02 \frac{1.05 \times 4000}{1.05 u_2}$
Interest	$0.04 \times$ sum of above	$0.04 \times$ sum of above	$0.04 \times$ sum of above
Management fees	− as in unit fund	− as in unit fund	− as in unit fund
Surrender penalty	$1000 a q_{40}^w$	$500 a q_{41}^w$	$500 a q_{42}^w$
Death benefits	$-0.25 a q_{40}^d U_1$	$-0.25 a q_{41}^d U_2$	$-0.25 a q_{42}^d U_3$
Balance at eoy	sum of above	sum of above	sum of above
Profit	Balance at eoy −balance at soy	Balance at eoy balance at soy	Balance at eoy −balance at soy
Survival factor to year start	1	$\frac{a\ell_{41}}{a\ell_{40}}$	$\frac{a\ell_{42}}{a\ell_{40}}$

soy

The sum of the product of profit × survival factors gives the profit signature. The net present value at 9% interest of the profit signature, divided by the NPV of the premium × survival factor, gives the expected profit margin.

These results may be useful in assessing

- the profitability of the contract against other business of the insurer;
- the appropriate reserving requirements;
- the growth rate of writing the contract on a self-sustainable basis.

D.3. Sample Exam 3

1. Explain why different life tables may be used to model the mortality of:
   - the general population
   - people who are insured for permanent insurances (e.g. lifetime or endowment assurances)
   - people who are insured for temporary insurances (i.e. assurances of restricted term)
   - annuitants
   - retired pensioners
   - disability pensioners.

Solution

The different groups of people have been 'selected' by different means:

- The mortality of the general population is driven by the customs, institutions and government policies, particularly in health care.
- The motivation of people who are permanently insured is not just for death cover, but also for a means of saving. Given the underwriting process involved, their mortality should be lower than the general population.
- The motivation of people who are insured under temporary insurance is just for death cover. Given that underwriting is also usually required, the mortality of this group should be higher than those covered by permanent insurance.
- Annuitants are insuring themselves against income not being available over a long lifespan, and hence should be expected to have the lightest mortality of all.
- Retirement pensioners (for those fortunate to access a pension rather than a lump sum benefit) have survived a long career.

2. In a geographic mortality investigation, you have observed that the aggregate mortality of residents in neighbouring suburbs may be very

different. Suburbs with very high-*wealth* residents (e.g. Toorak) may exhibit higher aggregate mortality than suburbs with high-*income* residents (e.g. South Yarra).

a. Explain how this may be so.

b. Explain briefly how you would construct an overall mortality statistic to avoid this problem.

Solution

The phenomenon may arise because suburbs with high-wealth residents may be generally older than those with high-income residents. The effect of age may be removed by using a standardised mortality statistic:

$$\overline{m} = \frac{\sum_x m_x \overline{E}_x}{\sum_x \overline{E}_x}$$

where $\overline{E}_x$ is the exposure from a standard life table, and m_x is the age-specific central mortality rate for age x for the population. By applying standard exposures, the effect of the population's age structure is removed.

---

12 In terms of the standard basis, calculate:

a. $_{20|}a_{20:\overline{20|}}$

b. $A^1_{20:\overline{20|}}$

c. $I\ddot{a}^{(2)}_{[20]:\overline{2|}}$.

Solution

a.

$$_{20|}a_{20:\overline{20|}} = v^{20}\frac{\ell_{40}}{\ell_{20}}a_{40:\overline{20|}}$$

$$= 1.03^{-20}\frac{9875556}{9986216}$$

$$\times \left[23.825 - 1 - 1.03^{-20}\frac{9429582}{9875556}(16.439 - 1)\right]$$

$$= 0.547\,54 \times 14.66$$

$$= 8.026\,9.$$

b.

$$A^1_{20:\overline{20}|} = 1 - d\ddot{a}_{20:\overline{2}|} - v^{20}\frac{\ell_{40}}{\ell_{20}}$$

$$= 1 - \frac{0.03}{1.03}\left(28.303 - 1.03^{-20}\frac{9875556}{9986216}23.825\right)$$

$$- 1.03^{-20}\frac{9875556}{9986216}$$

$$= 0.008\,056\,2.$$

c. We have

$$I\ddot{a}^{(2)}_{[20]:\overline{2}|} = \frac{1}{2}\left(1 + \frac{1.03^{-0.5}}{2}\frac{\ell_{[20]} + \ell_{[20]+1}}{\ell_{[20]}}\right.$$

$$+2 \times 1.03^{-1}\frac{\ell_{[20]+1}}{\ell_{[20]}} + 1.03^{-1.5}\frac{\ell_{[20]+1} + \ell_{22}}{\ell_{[20]}}\right)$$

$$= \frac{1}{2}\left(1 + 1.03^{-0.5}\frac{9983699 + 9980844}{2 \times 9983699}\right.$$

$$+\frac{2}{1.03}\frac{9980844}{9983699} + 1.03^{-1.5}\frac{9980844 + 9976921}{9983699}\right)$$

$$= 2.919\,4.$$

3. A benefit is described by a random variable B for a person aged exactly x:

$$B = \begin{cases} a_{\overline{n-K_x}|} & \text{for } K_x < n \\ 0 & \text{otherwise} \end{cases}$$

Formulate the value of this benefit in terms of conventional actuarial notation.

Solution

The benefit is an annuity payable on death for the remainder of the term to time n. It is the same as an annuity certain for a term of n, less a lifetime annuity restricted to this term. Hence

$$\mathbf{E}(B) = a_{\overline{n}|} - a_{x:\overline{n}|}.$$

---

4. **a.** Derive an expression, in terms of $_tp_x$ only, for the curtate expectation of life e_x at exact age x.

b. In a certain population the mortality rate q_x is constant at 0.02 for all ages x. For a life aged exactly 25, calculate the curtate expectation of life.

c. Assess and explain an approximation for the complete expectation of life $\overset{o}{e}_{25}$.

Solution

The curtate expectation of life e_x is the expected value of K_x. Hence

$$e_x = \sum_{t=0}^{\infty} t \cdot \frac{\ell_{x+t} - \ell_{x+t+1}}{\ell_x}$$

$$= \sum_{t=0}^{\infty} t \cdot {}_t p_x - \sum_{t=0}^{\infty} t \cdot {}_{t+1} p_x$$

$$= \sum_{t=1}^{\infty} {}_t p_x.$$

If $q_x = 0.02$ for all ages x, then ${}_t p_x = 0.98^t$. Hence

$$e_x = \sum_{t=1}^{\infty} {}_t p_x$$

$$= \sum_{t=1}^{\infty} 0.98^t$$

$$= \frac{0.98}{1 - 0.98} = 49.$$

If a death occurs, it is likely to be at the midpoint of a year of age on average. Hence $\overset{o}{e}_x \simeq e_x + \frac{1}{2}$.

---

5. Let u be a status involving one or more lives or terms, and K_u the start of the year in which that status fails.
   a. Describe how u may be formulated for:
   (i) an endowment assurance to a person aged x for a term of n years
   (ii) a joint life assurance to a married couple aged x and y
   (iii) an assurance payable when:
   - x dies within n years, or
   - y dies within m years,

- at time n where $n > m$

whichever is the earliest.

b. Using the relationship $d\ddot{a}_{\overline{z}|} + v^{z+1} = 1$ or otherwise, show that in these cases:

$$A_u = 1 - d\ddot{a}_u$$

c. Show that

$$\mathbf{var}\left[a_{\overline{K_u}|}\right] = \frac{1}{d^2}\left[{}^2A_u - (A_u)^2\right]$$

and explain the meaning of ${}^2A_u$.

Solution

  (i) $u = 20 : \overline{m}|$

  (ii) $u = xy$

 (iii) $u = x : [y : \overline{m}|] : \overline{m}|$

The relationship $d\ddot{a}_{\overline{z}|} + v^{z+1} = 1$ holds for any z. Putting $z = K_u$, and taking expectations, we have

$$A_u = 1 - d\ddot{a}_u.$$

We also have

$$\ddot{a}_{\overline{z}|} = \frac{1 - v^{z+1}}{d}$$

so that

$$\mathbf{var}\left[\ddot{a}_{\overline{z}|}\right] = \frac{1}{d^2}E\left[\left(v^{z+1}\right)^2\right] - \frac{1}{d^2}E\left(v^{z+1}\right)^2$$

$$= \frac{1}{d^2}\left[{}^2A_u - (A_u)^2\right].$$

The symbol ${}^2A_u$ is the value of an assurance at an interest rate j such that $(1+j)^2 = 1 + i$.

---

6. In a certain country, people finance their retirement by purchasing combined deferred annuity and pure endowment benefits. Under a recent law in this country, these contracts must be purchased on a person's birthday nearest age z years, where z is the age at which the person's complete expectation of life is equal to their current age: $\overset{o}{e}_z = x$.

Each contract is funded by a single premium paid by the person on the birthday nearest age z.

A person aged exactly x wishes to purchase one of each of these policies. Each contract provides:

- a weekly annuity payable of $\$10,000$ per year from the 65th birthday to the birthday nearest exact age $2z$ or until death (if earlier).
- a pure endowment lump sum of $\$100,000$ on survival to the birthday nearest exact age $2z$.

a. Give a formula for the single premium in terms of x and z. You may disregard expenses and profit loadings.

b. Discuss the factors that should be taken into account in pricing the contracts.

Solution

By the principle of equivalence, the premium is the sum of the value of a deferred annuity from age 65 and a pure endowment payable at age $2z$, valued at age z:

$$P = 10,000v^{65-z}\frac{\ell_{65}}{\ell_z}\bar{a}_{65:\overline{85-2z}|} + 100,000v^z\frac{\ell_{2z}}{\ell_z}.$$

This assumes that $z < 65$, which may not hold if mortality is light! Thus mortality improvements, and factors affecting mortality (e.g. lifestyle, geography), should be allowed for.

---

8 In managing its operations, a life insurer may use several bases for different aspects of its business. For example, a different basis may be used for pricing, reserving and profit testing as follows:

Basis:	Pricing	Reserving	Profit testing
Mortality	AMC00 *Select*	AMC00 *Ultimate*	AMC00 *Select*
Interest	6% pa.	4% pa.	7% pa.
Bonus	simple reversionary bonus at 4% pa	same	same
Initial expenses	60% of the 1st premium	None	60% of the 1st premium
Renewal expenses	5% of premiums after the 1st	None	5% of premiums after the 1st

a. Explain how different bases may be justified.

b. A discount rate of, say, 12% pa, different from all the interest rates above, might be applied to value the profit signature arising from profit testing. How could this be justified?

Solution

Different bases may be used because:

- pricing is about being competitive whilst maintaining solvency. Therefore realistic levels of expenses are needed, as well as of mortality in accordance with the insurer's underwriting procedures.
- Reserving is a usually a statutory task and, therefore, is usually conservative. As expenses may vary significantly over time, a net premium basis is appropriate.
- Profit testing needs to be conducted on the most realistic basis possible and, therefore, needs to allow for the gross premium as well as the best estimates of expenses.

Profits may be discounted at the shareholders' required rate of return on capital, which may exceed the interest rate bases of all the above. This capital is needed to underwrite growth of the business.

---

7. A wealthy farmer has died, leaving a farm of value F, which generates continuous income at a rate of δ pa.

He is survived by a family comprising:

- his present spouse, aged y
- a son of his former marriage, aged b
- a grandson from his son, aged z
- a younger daughter of his present marriage, aged g.

His will provides as follows:

- His younger child g will receive $\frac{1}{3}$ of the income of the farm until she turns 18.
- His spouse y will receive the balance of the income of the farm during her lifetime.
- Upon the death of his spouse, his son b will receive the income during his lifetime.
- Upon the death of his son, his daughter g will receive the income during her lifetime.
- After the death of all the above, the grandson z (if alive) will inherit the farm.

The farmer's family are perplexed by his will, and have agreed to sell the farm immediately, dividing the proceeds between them.

a. Show that the sum of all interests of the spouse, son, daughter and grandson is equal to the value of the farm F. You may assume that the farm does not appreciate in value and that the interest is valued at a discount rate of δ pa., the same as the rate of income from the farm.

b. Assess the value of the interests of the spouse, son, daughter and grandson in terms of conventional actuarial notation, using a discount rate δ pa.

Solution

The total income at rate δF, when valued at the same rate in perpetuity, must equal the initial value of the estate $F = \frac{\delta}{\delta} F$.

The various interests may be valued as a proportion of the farm's value F as follows:

Interest	Amount
His daughter g	$\frac{\delta}{3}\bar{a}_{g:\overline{18-g}\rceil}$
His spouse y	$\delta\bar{a}_y - \frac{\delta}{3}\bar{a}_{g:\overline{18-g}\rceil}$
His son b	$\delta\left(\bar{a}_b - \bar{a}_{by}\right)$
His daughter g	$\delta\left(\bar{a}_g - \bar{a}_{g:\overline{by}}\right)$
His grandson z	$\delta\left(\bar{a}_z - \bar{a}_{z:\overline{byg}}\right)$

This will not necessarily sum to 1, as the grandson may die before the last of the others. To allow for this, each interest in the above should be expressed as a fraction of their sum.

---

8. A health insurer offers contracts for medical treatment on a single-year basis. The amount of benefit payable depends on the medical condition of the insured, and is payable on a daily basis for the duration of the year. The premium must be paid at the start of each year. If the insured wishes to extend the insurance to the following year, then the premium payable will depend on the condition of the insured at that time.

A variety of medical conditions are admitted, for example:

- health
- pregnancy
- pregnancy with complications
- injury without hospitalisation
- injury with hospitalisation

- rehabilitation
- skin cancer
- death

All benefits cease on death or at the conclusion of the contract.

Let i or j denote any of the medical conditions, and let B_i be the daily benefit for condition i.

Also denote:

$\mu^{ij}(x)$ = transition intensity from condition i to condition j at age x

$p^{ij}(x, t)$ = probability of transition from condition i at age x

to condition j at age $x + t$

$p^{\overline{ii}}(x, t)$ = probability of remaining continuously in condition i

at age x to age $x + t$.

a. Suggest why the insurance is advantageous to the insurer on a single-year basis.
b. If ω denotes death, what is $p^{\omega, j}(x, t)$?
c. For a person aged x with medical condition i, formulate the single premium payable P^i_x in terms of the symbols defined above, and a force of interest δ.
d. What further considerations could the insurer take into account in pricing the contract, apart from age and the medical condition of the insured?

Solution

The advantage of the contract design is that the insurer's risk is limited to 1 year. If the health of the insured deteriorates, this is reflected in the premium charged for the following year.

As death is a terminal state, $p^{\omega, j}(x, t) = 0$.

An insured in state i may transition to any other state j. From the information provided, $B_\omega = 0$, and if h denotes health, $B_h = 0$. The premium that should be charged according to the principle of equivalence is the total value of the benefits possible:

$$P^i_x = 365 \sum_j \int_0^1 e^{-\delta t} p^{ij}(x, t) B_j dt$$

Transition intensities μ^{ij} do not appear, as there is no benefit payable upon a transition (but only during a certain state).

Other factors that may be taken into account in pricing are, for example:

- the duration of the existing condition
- mitigating or aggravating factors for that condition (e.g. body mass index)
- occupation
- gender.

D.4. Sample Exam 4

1. Explain why different life tables apply to:
    a. the general population
    b. individual applicants for insurance
    c. individual applicants for annuities from insurers
    d. employees insured for death benefits through their employer's super fund.

Solution
• Life tables for the general population are based on censuses, and capture all factors affecting the population. These include social, medical and technological factors.   • Applicants for insurance need to undergo an underwriting process, and thus would be more likely to be healthier than the general population.   • Annuitants would expect higher longevity risk.   • Employees insured through their employer are not usually underwritten. The risk is specific to the employer's industry and employment policies.

2. Express in standard notation and evaluate:
    a. An ordinary annuity payable quarterly for a person aged 50 for 20 years.
    b. A 3-year joint life assurance to brothers aged 30 and 33, with *select mortality* for both.

Solution

a.

$$a^{(4)}_{50:\overline{20}|} = a^{(4)}_{50} - v^{20}\frac{\ell_{70}}{\ell_{50}}a^{(4)}_{70}$$

$$= \left(20.509 - 1 + \frac{3}{8}\right)$$

$$- \frac{1}{1.03^{20}}\frac{8456406}{9756471}\left(11.933 - 1 + \frac{3}{8}\right) = 14.457$$

b.

$$A_{[30][33]:\overline{3}|} = \frac{1}{\ell_{[30][33]}}\left[\begin{array}{c} v\left(\ell_{[30][33]} - \ell_{[30]+1,[33]+1}\right) \\ +v^2\left(\ell_{[30]+1,[33]+1} - \ell_{32,35}\right) \\ +v^3\left(\ell_{32,35} - \ell_{33,36}\right)\end{array}\right]$$

$$= \frac{1}{9935066 \times 9919118}$$

$$\times\left[\begin{array}{c}\frac{9935066\times9919118-9931767\times9915260}{1.03}\\ +\frac{9931767\times9915260-9927089\times9909816}{1.03^2}\\ +\frac{9927089\times9909816-9921520\times9903613}{1.03^3}\end{array}\right]$$

$$= 6.9988 \times 10^{-4} + 9.6057 \times 10^{-4} + 1.084 \times 10^{-3}$$

$$= 2.7445 \times 10^{-3}.$$

---

3. Consider a contract which provides a decreasing assurance over n years. The benefit commences at amount n, and reduces by 1 for each year until it reaches 0 at time n.

   a. Show that its value is

   $$(n+1)\cdot A_{x:\overline{n}|} - IA_{x:\overline{n}|} - A^{\,1}_{x:\overline{n}|}$$

   b. Suppose a premium of P_t is payable at the start of year t. Show that the reserve $_tV$ at time t, just before the payment of premium, satisfies the relationship

   $$_{t+1}V \cdot p_{x+t} + (n-t)\,q_{x+t} = (1+i)\,(_tV + P_t)$$

   c. Suppose that P_t is constant over the n years, sufficient to give $_nV = 0$. Explain the defects of this contract design.

d. Over what period should a constant premium be determined to finance this benefit?

Solution

a. $(n+1) \cdot A_x$ provides a benefit of $n+1$ in year t, whilst IA_x provides a benefit of $t+1$ for $t = 0, 1 \ldots n-1$. Thus in the first year the benefit is n; in year t the benefit is $n-t$, and in the final year 1. The endowment assurance provides a terminal benefit of $n+1$ whilst the increasing assurance provides n. Hence a benefit of 1 must be excluded on termination.

b. The reserve at the start of year t, plus the premium P_t payable, accumulated with interest, must provide death benefits of $n-t$ for deaths during the year, as well as the reserve for survivors at year end.

c. As the benefit at commencement of the contract is n, and the premium is fixed, the reserves are likely to be negative during the early years of the contract. This would be compensated over the final years, but also means an insured can surrender the policy in the early years without fully meeting the cost of benefits.

d. The premium and the term over which it is payable should be set to avoid negative reserves. This must be analysed using the equation of equilibrium in (b).

---

4. Consider an immediate lifetime annuity issued by an insurer to a person aged x by a single premium.
   a. Show that the reserve at time t is $_tV_x = \ddot{a}_{x+t}$.
   b. In year t, show that the insurer's profit is:
   - if the annuitant dies during the year, the profit is

   $$(1+i)\, a_{x+t}.$$

   - if the annuitant survives the year, the loss is

   $$(1+i)\, a_{x+t} - \ddot{a}_{x+t+1}.$$

   c. If the annuitants during the year die with probability q_{x+t} as expected, show that the insurer's profit is zero.
   d. If the annuitants during the year actually die at a rate $\bar{q}_{x+t}$, show that the insurer's profit is

   $$\left(\bar{q}_{x+t} - q_{x+t}\right) \ddot{a}_{x+t+1}.$$

e. If the actual return on assets is $\bar{i}$, what is the insurer's interest profit/loss during the year?

Solution

For an expected mortality rate of q_{x+t}, the overall profit is

$$q_{x+t}(1+i)a_{x+t} + p_{x+t}\left[(1+i)a_{x+t} - \ddot{a}_{x+t+1}\right]$$
$$= (1+i)a_{x+t} - p_{x+t}\ddot{a}_{x+t+1}$$
$$= 0.$$

For an actual mortality rate of $\bar{q}_{x+t}$, the overall profit is

$$\bar{q}_{x+t}\left[(1+i)a_{x+t}\right] + \bar{p}_{x+t}\left[(1+i)a_{x+t} - \ddot{a}_{x+t+1}\right]$$
$$= (1+i)a_{x+t} - \bar{p}_{x+t}\ddot{a}_{x+t+1}$$
$$= \left(\bar{q}_{x+t} - q_{x+t}\right)\ddot{a}_{x+t+1}.$$

If the actual interest rate is $\bar{i}$, then the overall profit is

$$\bar{q}_{x+t}\left(1+\bar{i}\right)a_{x+t} + \bar{p}_{x+t}\left[\left(1+\bar{i}\right)a_{x+t} - \ddot{a}_{x+t+1}\right]$$
$$= \left(1+\bar{i}\right)a_{x+t} - \bar{p}_{x+t}\ddot{a}_{x+t+1}$$
$$= \left(\bar{q}_{x+t} - q_{x+t}\right)\ddot{a}_{x+t+1} + \left(\bar{i} - i\right)a_{x+t}$$

so that the interest profit is $\left(\bar{i} - i\right)a_{x+t}$.

---

5. A family has pension entitlements, payable continuously as follows:
    a. A young father aged x is entitled to a pension of $1 pa for life after retiring from military service.
    b. His spouse aged y is entitled to a reversionary pension, of 60% of her husband's pension on his death.
    c. Their son aged z is entitled to 10% of his father's pension upon the death of his parents until reaching age 18.
        Evaluate each of these entitlements in standard notation.
    d. Suppose that the family may bear more children in the future, in year t with probability $\beta(t)$. Further children are entitled to the same pension as in (c).
        Evaluate these potential entitlements.

Solution

a. $\bar{a}_x$

b. The spouse receives a 60% pension, but not while their spouse survives. Hence $0.6 \left(\bar{a}_y - \bar{a}_{xy} \right)$

c. The son receives a 10% pension, but only after both his parents have died. Hence $0.1 \left(\bar{a}_{z:\overline{18-z}|} - \bar{a}_{\overline{xy}:\overline{18-z}|} \right)$

d. In future year t, the probability of another birth is $\beta(t)$, but both parents must survive to this time with probability ${}_t p_{xy}$. Hence the value is

$$\sum_{t=0}^{\infty} v^t \beta(t) \cdot {}_t p_{xy} \cdot \left(\bar{a}_{0:\overline{18-z}|} - \bar{a}_{\overline{x+t,y+t:18-z}|} \right)$$

The possibility of multiple births in a single year is discounted.

---

6. A major employer provides maternity benefits for its staff, at the rate of 18 weeks of paid leave. Only the first pregnancy is compensated, and you may assume it lasts for 9 months.

This is a cost to the employer, as it has to employ replacement staff during this time. A benefit of S is also provided if a pregnant staff member dies during childbirth.

The states for the maternity scheme are as follows:

State	Symbol
active work	a
pregnancy	m
death	d
resignation	r

These are depicted in the diagram below.
Also denote:

$$\mu^{ij}(x) = \text{transition intensity from state } i \text{ to state } j \text{ at age } x$$

$$p^{ij}(x,t) = \text{probability of transition from state } i \text{ at age } x \text{ to state}$$
$$j \text{ at age } x+t$$

$$p^{\overline{ii}}(x,t) = \text{probability of remaining continuously in state } i \text{ at age } x$$
$$\text{to age } x+t.$$

a. Explain why $p^{ma}(x,t) = 0$ for $t \leq \frac{9}{12}$.

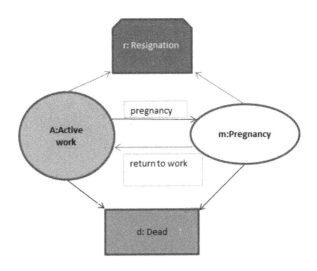

b. Explain why $p^{mr}(x, t) = 0$ for $t \le \frac{18}{52}$.

c. For a given female staff member currently aged x with salary W, assess the present value of these entitlements in terms of the probabilities set out above.

Solution

a. The employee will not return to work whilst pregnant.

b. The employee is unlikely to resign whilst on maternity benefits.

c. For pregnancy to occur at time t, the employee must be actively employed with probability $p^{\overline{aa}}(x, t)$ and then become pregnant with probability $\mu^{am}(x + t)\, dt$. She would then receive a benefit of 18 weeks of salary provided she does not die, which has value at time t:

$$W \int_0^{18/52} v^u p^{\overline{mm}}(x, u)\, du$$

If she dies during pregnancy, then the value of the death benefit at time t is

$$S \int_0^{9/12} v^u p^{\overline{mm}}(x, u)\, \mu^{md}(x)\, du$$

Thus the cost of the maternity scheme for the employee is

$$\int_0^\infty v^t p^{\overline{aa}}(x, t) \mu^{am}(x+t) \times$$

$$\left[W \int_0^{18/52} v^u p^{\overline{mm}}(x, u)\, du + S \int_0^{18/52} v^u p^{\overline{mm}}(x, u)\, \mu^{md}(x)\, du \right] dt$$

Note: If the question had allowed more than one pregnancy, then multiple active states would be required, e.g. employment with $0, 1, 2$· pregnancies, including the possibility of resignation and re-employment.

7. A bank provides a combined insurance and investment contract as follows.

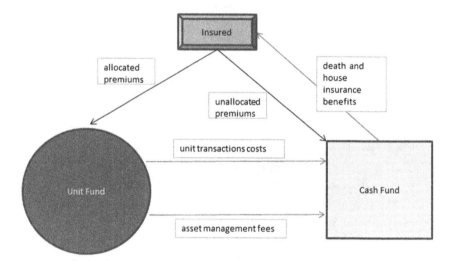

Details of the operation of the contract are as follows:
- Level premiums of P per annum are payable yearly in advance throughout the term of the policy or until earlier death.
- α_t of the premium is allocated to investment units in year t.
- A policy fee of e deducted from the bid value of units at the start of each year.
- The units are subject to a bid-offer spread of $b\%$ on purchase.
- An annual management charge of $f\%$ of the bid value of units is deducted at the end of each policy year.
- Management charges are deducted from the unit fund before death, surrender and maturity benefits are paid.

- If the policyholder dies during the term of the policy, a death benefit of S, less the bid value of the units, is payable at the end of the policy year of death.
- The policy also provides house and contents insurance at an expected yearly cost of H_t in year t.
- On surrender or maturity in year t, 100% of the bid value of the units U_t is payable. The unit values vary according to the fund earning rate r_t.

a. Explain how U_t moves from year to year.

b. Then describe the methodology that you would use to project the profit *vector* emerging under the contract in year t.

c. How would you assess the profit *signature* from (b)?

d. Describe briefly, in words, the major risks faced by the insurer with this contract design.

Solution

a. The unit value increases (or decreases) at rate r_t or with the addition of new units through allocated premiums or deduction of expenses:

Year	t
Unit value soy	U_t
Allocated premiums	$\alpha_t \overline{P}$
Transaction costs	$-b\alpha_t \overline{P}$
Unit value eoy, before fees	$(1 + r_t) \times$ sum of above
Management fees	$(-f_t) \times$ sum of above
Unit value eoy, after fees	U_{t+1}

b. Then profit testing during year t can be undertaken as follows:

Year:	t
Unallocated premium	$(1 - \alpha_t)\overline{P}$
Transaction costs	$b\alpha_t \overline{P}$
Asset based fees	$\frac{fU_{t+1}}{1-f}$
Expense	$-e$
Death	$-aq_x^d \max(S - U_{t+1}, 0)$
Household insurance	$-H_t$
Interest	$i\left[(1 - \alpha_t)P + b\alpha_t \overline{P} - e\right]$
Profit	sum of above

c. The profit signature may be derived from the profit vector by allowing for the probability of survival to the start of any year.

d. The main risks are in decreasing order:
  • investment, which determines the value of units U_t through the investment earning rate r_t
  • household insurance claims H_t
  • mortality

8. The profit signature PS_t for a 5-year policy under question (7) is

$$PS_t = [-200, -50, 50, -50, 300]$$

The shareholders' required return on capital is r:

a. Provide an expression for the present value of profits to shareholders.

b. Provide a conservative value of the capital needed to support this contract, given that a policyholder can surrender at any time.

Solution

a. Denote $x = \frac{1}{1+r}$. The present value of profit is

$$\sum_{t=1}^{5} x^t \cdot PS_t$$

b. The contract can be progressively zeroised as follows whilst maintaining the value of the profit signature at rate r.

Year	1	2	3
1	-200	$-200 - 50x$	$-200 - 50x$
2	-50	-50	0
3	70	$70 - 50x$	$70 - 50x$
4	-50	0	0
5	300	300	300

The capital required is thus $200 + 50x$.

Bibliography

Dickson, D. C. M., Hardy, M. R., & Waters, H. R. (2009). *Actuarial mathematics for life contingent risks*. Cambridge University Press.

O'Neill, A. (1977). *Life contingencies*. Heinemann.

Promislow, S. D. (2015). *Fundamentals of actuarial mathematics*. Wiley Desktop Editions.

Vajda, S. (1984). *Mathematical methods in economics*. John Wiley and Sons. Chapter 18.

Index

A

Accident mortality, 157
Accrued
  benefits, 69, 71, 73
  benefits payable, 70
  benefits value, 71, 73
  death value, 70
  defined benefits, 69, 70
  resignation benefit, 73
  retirement value, 70
Adverse selection, 29, 105, 112, 176
Allocated premiums, 79
Annual premium, 41, 42, 56–58, 82, 179
Annual premium gross, 58
Annuity
  deferred, 22
  functions, 11
  payable, 18, 21, 26, 34, 40
  payable frequently, 18
Asset value, 71

B

Balducci
  assumption, 125
  estimator, 126, 127
Barnett's formula, 156
Benefits
  accrued, 69
  defined, 68
  rules, 68
Body Mass Index (BMI), 146, 147
Bonus loadings, 57
Breslow's approximation, 144, 145

C

Cash fund, 78–80
Censoring, 115, 116, 131, 136, 138
  examples, 115
  informative, 116
  noninformative, 116
Child mortality, 157

C (continued)

Class selection, 29, 105
Complete lifespan, 23–25
Contingent
  annuities, 98
  insurances, 95–98
Continuous
  insurances, 25
  time, 1, 24, 49–51, 62, 85, 95, 98, 99, 115, 130, 131
Cox model, 141–143, 145, 146
Crude mortality rate, 110
Crude population mortality rate, 109
Cumulative standardised differences normality, 165, 172
Curtate
  joint lifespan, 33
  lifespan, 5, 6, 9, 11–13, 16, 17, 33, 37, 58

D

Death
  benefit, 41, 73, 79, 101
  benefit payments, 80
  in continuous time, 166
  member, 125
  probability, 23, 27, 49, 125, 132, 134, 138, 143
  rate, 62
  strain at risk, 49, 50
Decrement
  disability, 72
  independent rates, 61
  operating, 61
  rates, 85, 86, 149, 150
Deferral
  period, 15
  procedure, 15
Deferred
  annuity, 22
  benefit, 14, 15
  benefit value, 14
  period, 14, 101
Defined benefits, 68

Disability
    benefits, 70, 71
    decrement, 72
    pension value, 73
    pensioners, 7, 105, 107
    temporary, 67
Discounted value, 9, 24
Discrete ages, 23

E

Endowment insurance, 12–14, 16, 43
Equation of equilibrium, 46–48
Equilibrium distribution, 177, 178
Expenses
    loadings, 56, 57
    loadings amount inclusive, 56
    payment, 75
    recovery, 56
Exponentially increasing annuity, 17

G

Gompertz
    curve, 154, 155, 168
    graduation, 170
Graduated mortality rates, 168, 171
Graduated rates, 155, 156, 165, 166
Graduation process, 150
Gross
    annual premium, 58
    premium, 56, 58, 59, 75, 83
    premium paid, 75
    premium with-profit, 57
    premiums payable value, 58
Grouped signs test, 169, 170

H

Heterogeneous
    population, 149
    risks, 141
Homogeneous population, 141

I

Increasing annuity certain, 17
Independent decrements, 64, 92
Indirect standardisation, 110

Instantaneous
    decrement rate, 86
    mortality rate, 23
Insurance
    company, 55, 138
    contract, 44, 56, 57, 75, 175
    cover, 79
    operation, 55
    sickness, 4, 88
    temporary, 41, 79
    underwriting, 175
    variances, 16
Insured
    lives for endowment insurances, 7, 107
    lives for temporary insurances, 107
    persons, 31
Interest
    earnings, 54
    rate, 3, 11, 16, 17, 41, 57, 72
Interval censoring, 116
Invested premiums, 175
Investment return, 78

J

Joint
    life table, 33
    probability density function, 118
    status, 34, 37, 95

K

Kaplan–Meier estimator, 134, 137
Kolmogorov forward equations, 86

L

Lapse rates, 112
Level premium, 65, 93
Life table, 3, 5, 7, 10, 11, 18, 21, 23, 25,
        26, 29, 30, 33, 103
    construction, 107
    joint, 33
Lifetime
    annuity, 10, 11, 13, 18, 25
    annuity joint, 34
    annuity payable, 40
    distribution, 115
    insurance, 9, 12, 24, 34, 43, 45, 49, 57
    insurance contract, 75

insurance joint, 34
insurance payable, 95
insurance single, 34
Likelihood function, 119, 125, 131, 133,
    138, 159
Local population, 113
Log likelihood, 119, 134, 146, 147
Lump sum, 101

M

Mathematical graduation, 153, 154, 161
Medical
    exam, 30
    examination, 29
    screening, 30, 105, 111
Minimum chi-square method (MCSM),
    161
Monthly
    payments, 18, 22
    premium, 101
Mortality
    accident, 157
    characteristics, 111
    comparisons, 109
    constant force, 27, 28, 53
    estimate, 125
    experience, 29, 105, 111, 113
    factors, 29, 103, 105
    independent rates, 64, 92
    investigation, 111, 112, 115, 125, 131,
        138, 150
    law, 24, 125
    modelling, 3, 5
    models, 24, 115
    profit/loss, 47
    rates, 5, 6, 16, 24, 30, 53, 102, 104,
        107–113, 115, 123, 125, 130, 141,
        149–151, 153, 171
    risks, 123, 141
    statistics raw, 155
    status, 131
Multiple
    deaths, 130, 144
    deaths likelihood, 144
    decrement, 68, 85
    decrement models, 67
    decrement table, 61, 62, 65, 69, 70

N

Nelson–Aalen estimator, 137
Net premium reserves, 83
No-claim bonus (NCB) schemes, 175–179
Nonunit reserves, 82
Normality tests, 167

P

Partial likelihood, 142–145
Partial likelihood estimator, 145
Payment
    deferral, 12
    expenses, 75
    premium, 101
    single, 40
Perk's curve, 156
Permanent disability, 67
Poisson
    model, 129, 130
    model properties, 129
    multiple deaths, 130
    parameter, 129
Policyholder, 56, 111, 112, 179–181
Population
    exposures, 109
    members, 151
Population life table, 3, 5
Premium
    assessment, 56
    basis, 83
    gross, 56, 58, 59, 75, 83
    inclusive, 57
    paid return, 64, 92
    payment, 101
    risk, 175
    single, 54
    value, 101
Pricing, 3, 43, 55–57, 61, 75, 77, 149, 175,
    176, 178
Probability
    death, 23, 27, 49, 125, 132, 134, 138,
        143
    density, 23, 24
    distribution, 97, 178, 179
Profit
    loadings, 43
    margin, 81, 82, 84
    signature, 76, 77, 80–82

testing, 75, 79, 80
vector, 75
Proportional hazards, 141, 146
Prospective reserves, 45, 47, 58, 59
Pure endowment, 14

R

Random variable, 5, 6, 9, 15, 16, 23, 33,
    44, 53, 58, 117, 118, 168
Rating level, 176–178
Rating level probability distribution, 177
Renewal expenses, 75, 83
Reserving, 43, 44, 55, 61, 75, 77
Resignation benefit, 69–73
Resignation benefit accrued, 73
Retired pensioners, 7, 105, 107
Retirement
    benefits, 67, 70
    effect, 151
Retrospective reserves, 45–49, 59
Return on transfers, 77
Reversionary annuity, 39
Revised profit, 82
Risk
    factors, 7, 29, 104, 105, 107, 112, 130,
        141, 142, 147
    premium, 175

S

Selection, 104, 105
    adverse, 29, 105, 112, 176
    class, 29, 105
    spurious, 29, 105
    time, 29, 105, 111
Senescent mortality, 157
Sickness
    benefit, 90
    example, 88, 89
    insurance, 4, 88
Single
    lifetime insurance, 34
    payment, 40
    premium, 54
    premium payable, 54

Spurious selection, 29, 105
Standardised
    differences, 165, 172
    mortality differences, 166
    mortality rate, 110
Standardised Mortality Ratio (SMR), 113
Surrender value, 61
Survival
    function, 131, 135–138, 149
    probability, 5, 6, 10, 15, 23, 27, 41, 131,
        137, 138

T

Temporary
    disability, 67
    initial selection, 29, 104, 111, 112
    insurance, 41, 79
Testing
    for fidelity, 165
    for smoothness, 165
The method of MLE, 117, 124, 129, 134,
    138, 142, 145, 159
Thiele's equation, 49
Time selection, 29, 105, 111
Truncation, 116

U

Ultimate mortality, 30, 83
Unallocated premiums, 79
Underwriting process, 29, 30, 104, 105
Unit linked insurances, 78, 80
Upfront expenses, 80

V

Value premium, 101

W

With-profit gross premium, 57
Withdrawal
    experience, 112
    rate, 62

Z

Zeroisation, 80